It's a girl thing

It's a girl thing

Understanding the neuroscience behind educating and raising girls

Dr Michael C. Nagel

Copyright © Michael C. Nagel 2021

All rights reserved. No part of this book may be reproduced or transmitted in any form or by any means, electronic or mechanical, including photocopying, recording or by any information storage and retrieval system, without prior permission in writing from the publisher.

First published as *It's A Girl Thing* in 2008 by Hawker Brownlow Education. This revised and updated edition published by Amba Press in 2021.

Amba Press
Melbourne, Australia
www.ambapress.com.au

Editor – Natasha Harris
Cover designer – Alissa Dinallo
Printed by IngramSpark

ISBN: 9781922607089 (pbk)
ISBN: 9781922607096 (ebk)

A catalogue record for this book is available from the National Library of Australia.

This book is dedicated to my daughter, Maddie. When Maddie first arrived in the world I was immediately smitten with being a father and raising a daughter. Precocious and opinionated from the youngest of ages Maddie presented such strength in conviction and determination with each passing year and as evident in all of her successes thus far. She has grown into a beautiful young woman with the world at her feet and I am so very proud of her.

Contents

List of illustrations	viii
Acknowledgements	ix
Introduction: Sugar and spice and all things gender specific!	1
Chapter 1: Sex and gender	7
Chapter 2: The developing brain	16
Chapter 3: Boys and girls *are* different	36
Chapter 4: The developing brain and growing up female	60
Chapter 5: 'I love you': emotions and the female brain	73
Chapter 6: 'I hate you': relationships and the female brain	81
Chapter 7: 'It's a girl thing'	92
Chapter 8: Experiences matter!	104
Epilogue: Pink and blue in perspective	127
Notes	130
Bibliography	144
Index	175

Illustrations

Figures

2.1 Brain development in utero	18
2.2 Synaptic transmissions between neurons	20
2.3 Learning windows: Key periods of neural connectivity	23
2.4 Myelin wrapped around an axon	24
2.5 Structures of the brain	27
2.6 The brain's lobes and functions	32
3.1 Corpus callosum	46

Tables

3.1 The sexually dimorphic brain	52
4.1 A summary of neurological changes	70

Acknowledgements

Writing a book is full of highs and lows ... a labour of love if you will. Having the faith and support of others as they travel with you along that journey is invaluable. I feel fortunate and blessed to be able to acknowledge those who have helped me ride the highs of writing with joy, and combat the lows with conviction.

First and foremost, nothing I do is without the support and inspiration of my partner and best friend. Dr Laura Scholes is not only a brilliant researcher and scholar in her own right but she unknowingly inspires me to be better at all that I do and all that I am each day. She helps to shape my thoughts, mind, heart and soul and as such has helped shape much of the work you are about to read.

Second, many of us can be inspired by what happens to others and how they handle the challenges life throws their way. A friendship that was forged in high school has blessed me as an adult when I saw the perseverance and tenacity of my friend, Reiney Walter. Not long ago, Reiney experienced what can best be described as a traumatic brain illness that saw him undergo more than one surgery resulting in various challenges including measures of vision impairment. Seemingly unperturbed by it all, or at least showing an unwillingness to let his predicament slow him down, Reiney got on with things and continued being a loving father, husband and good friend to all who know him. I have always marvelled at his courage and tenacity which also provides me with a constant reminder to never sweat the little things and always be thankful for what I am, what I have and what I do!

Third, putting words to paper is one thing, drawing it all together as a book is something quite different. To that end I want to acknowledge the fantastic work of Natasha Harris for helping shaping the language around my thoughts. And, if not for Alicia Cohen and Amba Press you may not be holding this book in your hands. It is still a bit hard for me to conceive that for some, writing a book about girls, is either controversial, brave, or both; for Alicia, writing about girls was neither. Instead a book about girls was an imperative and she supported my convictions and ideas. For her trust in my judgement and work I am grateful and I look forward to a lengthy partnership in this and other projects.

Introduction

Boys and girls are both having problems, but they're having different problems.[1]

— Dr Leonard Sax

Sugar and spice and all things gender specific

There's a boy crisis! This may seem like an odd start to an exploration of the female brain and neurological development in girls, but hear me out. You see, during the 1980s and 1990s it appeared that schools were in the midst of a girl crisis. This crisis was brought to our attention through the work of scholars and educators who informed the wider public about the great degree of inequity in the practice of schooling girls. In an effort to redress this situation, a great deal of time, money and effort was used to enhance educational outcomes and opportunities for girls. This long overdue focus on girls' education brought about a welcome process of introspection that allowed all those concerned with the educational outcomes of girls to effect institutional change. One of the collateral effects of such work is a contribution to the apparent crisis that exists for boys in schools in the twenty-first century. Advocates for boys' educational outcomes often described the attention given to girls as a contributing factor to the boy crisis. Consider the following quote published in 2002 by the Australian government in a report targeting the enhancement of educational outcomes for boys:

Girls' education strategies and programs have, as a by-product of their original purpose, assisted girls through the social and

> *economic changes of the last 20 years. In comparison, over this period, little has been done to help boys understand and negotiate the same changes.*[2]

While the above comment is obviously diplomatically expressed, reading between the lines, the report suggested that too much attention on girls resulted in too little attention on boys which in turn constituted a boy crisis. Given such history it is not too much of a stretch to then assume then that spending an inordinate amount of time on boys will ultimately result in a girl crisis and the pendulum will continue to swing. In the end, focusing on one gender at the expense of another does neither any long-term good. What if, however, we decided to look at how both boys and girls succeed and fail rather than assuming one is always doing better than the other? Yes, by some measures there does appear to be a boy crisis, but let us not forget that for many girls there are problems and challenges in how they experience life and school, how they negotiate relationships, how they view themselves and most importantly how they develop into healthy and happy human beings.

This book seeks to explore the types of challenges noted above through the prism of neuroscience. By uncovering the intricacies and idiosyncrasies of the female brain, I want to explore its impact on how a girl engages with the world around her and the crucial and often gender-specific role it plays in how she also behaves and learns. Too often we wrongfully assume that girls are learning and behaving well given the dynamics and expectations of a classroom. This view is premised on girls' overt behaviour which, generally speaking, meshes nicely with the expectations of most school environments. And while girls tend to perform better academically by many measures, there is evidence to suggest that many girls are disadvantaged in other ways, both within educational contexts and beyond the confines of a school. Consequently, we can't assume that all girls are succeeding when the reality is that many aspects of life and school can be problematic for girls. Much of this may be due to a lack of understanding of female neurological development and how a girl's brain operates, matures and grows. This book explores this development with a view to providing ideas and strategies for girls at home and in school, while also providing insights into various challenges and issues linked to growing up female.

Before looking at female neural development and how to support that development, it is important to acknowledge the specifics of my background and expertise. First, while I am not able to offer a first-hand account of what it means to be female, my experiences as an educator and researcher do allow me a degree of authority in merging neuroscience with the day-to-day existence of growing up female. The perspectives presented are drawn from professional experience as a social scientist, research, scholar and author in conjunction with a careful analysis and synthesis of the relevant research related to the topics discussed throughout this book. I offer a certain perspective and can only hope that as the reader progresses through each page they bear in mind that the ideas presented are a genuine attempt to link what neuroscience is telling us about how the brain develops, the differences between the male and female brain and how we might look to enhance the lives of girls in social and educational contexts. This is not to say that all girls are the same, but rather to bring to light a myriad of ideas that will prove useful in any agenda for educating and raising girls.

In developing this perspective, I have also drawn on the work of many authors and experts across a range of disciplines to help facilitate a better understanding of the world that girls experience each and every day. Furthermore, the contributions of experts are coupled with the views of many girls as provided through my own research work in this area. Hopefully, I am able to do all of these individuals justice in meshing their life experiences with the important work done by neuroscientists.

It is also significant to note that males and females share more similarities than differences. Equally significant is the reality that no two girls are identical and the environment each and every girl grows up in will shape not only their neurological architecture but also their life chances. Race, class and culture, among many other factors, will impact upon the life chances and success of girls. That being said, it is beyond the scope of this work to map out the complex interplay that occurs at the nexus of race, geography, culture, ethnicity and socio-demographics. There are books available to those who wish to explore the sociological parameters of growing up female. This is not to say that society and culture are not important. Instead, this book recognises that within the field of neuroscience a nature (biology and genetics) versus nurture (society and culture) dichotomy is a moot point: the brain influences how we experience the world and the world around us influences how our brain is shaped and develops.[3] In simpler terms, the human brain is a product of innate biological characteristics that impact on how we engage with the environment around us while that same environment can shape aspects of our brain and behaviour. This book focuses on how the female brain develops and how certain experiences can influence that development and be created to foster healthy development.

Given the role of the environment, one might ask why it is significant to look at neuroscience and how the brain develops. After all, we can have some measure of influence on the environment, but we can't really change a brain, can we? It turns out that while there are some things we can't change, neuroscientific and psychological research does offer us insights into how we might positively affect many aspects of development and enhance an individual girl's potential. However, we must always bear in mind that when we look closely at the earliest stages of brain development, much of the brain's architecture and physiology is in place long before it interacts with the world around it. Hardwiring of the female brain occurs in utero and as such a blueprint for behaviour and learning is set out very early in the lives of the girls and young women around us.

To that end, the first chapter of this book looks at the differences between the terms sex and gender and what that means in terms of working with girls. Indeed, our understanding around the complexities associated with the term 'gender' alone have grown in magnitude over the last few decades requiring us to have, at the very least, a cursory understanding of that term and how its links to the term 'sex'. This is followed by a chapter focusing on how the brain develops over time. I have presented some of the information in chapters 1 and 2 in my other works focused on boys, so those who have read those volumes may be inclined to skim through the initial few pages or use them as a review of their neuroscientific literacy.[4] That being said, the emphasis of this work looks at the developing female brain so reviewing previous information in a new context may prove helpful.

After looking at the developing brain, Chapter 3 then explores the nature of sex differences in the brain and how some of those differences influence behaviour and learning. Chapter 4 seeks to map out links between the developing brain and 'growing up female'. From infancy to adolescence, the lives of girls are deeply intertwined with the realities of the world around them and the physiological and neurological implications of maturation. Historically, however, much of our understanding of child development and the challenges and issues associated with girls was not as well informed by current understandings of how the brain changes, how the female brain differs from the male brain and how all of this can impact on behaviour, learning and overall growth and development.

The final sections of this book take all of the information in the earlier chapters and focus it on three particular areas. Chapter 5 focuses on emotional development and how the emotional part of the brain influences behaviour and thinking in ways that are unique to girls. Chapter 6 moves the discussion on emotions further by linking it with the importance of relationships for girls and how relationships differ between the sexes. Chapter 7, in turn, explores challenges for girls related to adolescence and contemporary issues associated with mental health and wellbeing. You may note that I make no specific mention of cognition and only a tacit reference to thinking. This is not to say that these areas are not important, but rather that the research available suggests that the greatest predictors of success and happiness for girls in schools, and life in general, have direct links to the emotional and language centres of the brain and how girls negotiate relationships. Evidence of this is presented in chapters 5 through 7 and some discussion of cognition does occur in the last chapter, but this is not core to the issues presented. Again, I am not suggesting that all girls are the same, but a close inspection of the volumes of work available related to girls generally brings to the surface a common focus on emotion and relationships.

The final chapter of this book then turns to the importance of experiences with a view to further developing a framework for fostering familial, social and learning environments that provide positive experiences related to the intricacies of the developing female brain. Such a look also reminds us that if we are truly serious about enhancing the lives of girls, we must take into account the differences that exist between boys and girls. Perhaps this is the best way to stop the pendulum of crisis from swinging from one gender to another.

In its totality, this volume of work expands on previous work by this author and others within a framework of neuroscientific and psychological research. The overall aim is to provide teachers and parents with insights and evidence that suggest there are some important biological and physiological differences between boys and girls which impact on most aspects of behaviour and learning and many of these can be found within the brain. This is a very significant consideration given that the brain is the foundation for all that we think, feel and do. Importantly, this is not to suggest that one gender may be more superior than the other based on neurological differences; arguing that the brain of one sex is better than the other is as silly as arguing which sex has better genitalia. Or perhaps as the esteemed psychologist Steven Pinker notes:

> *…just because many sex differences are rooted in biology does not mean that one sex is superior, that the differences will emerge for all people in all circumstances, that discrimination against a person based on sex is justified, or that people should be coerced into doing things typical of their sex. But neither are the differences without consequences.*[5]

Indeed, the differences can be very consequential. This book is an exploration of both the differences, and some of the consequences, associated with a female brain to help teachers and parents to build a supportive and proactive environment for educating and raising girls.

1 Sex and gender

Most people you have met have a relatively unremarkable experience of being born male or female, identifying as a man or a woman, and feeling masculine or feminine within the cultural context in which they are raised.[1]

— *Professor Mark A Yarhouse*

Sex and gender are not the same thing but I will use those words interchangeably ... confused? Allow me to explain! Many individuals use the terms 'sex' and 'gender' synonymously while others insist that the two are different aspects of something similar. Because of such perceptions, there is often a great deal of confusion about the terms themselves and how they are used. This chapter begins by unpacking what the words 'sex' and 'gender' technically mean and how they have been used, before outlining how the terms are used in this book and my reasons for such an approach. To begin, then, a discussion of these terms and how they are often differentiated from one another.

Are sex and gender different?

This can be a confusing question for people, and the answer really depends on who you ask. If you searched Google for a definitive answer to whether sex and gender are the same thing you are likely to get millions, if not tens of millions, of potential results. Perhaps the abundance of results can be attributed to the fact that over the last few decades the terms 'sex' and 'gender' have become highly political in many contexts, and as such increasingly nuanced meanings have proliferated across these different contexts. However, the understanding of sex and gender of this book is deeply rooted in biology, and allows that sex and gender are indeed two sides of the same coin that have become blurred over time.

Again, it is important to emphasise that this book is underpinned by biological, psychological and neuroscientific research and evidence. Therefore, and in its simplest sense, sex refers to the biological differences of anatomy and physiology that distinguish a person as male or female. Gender, while being more difficult to define, typically embraces the labels 'masculine' and 'feminine' to describe the role of males and females in society or an individual's conceptual framework of themselves.[2] For most people, the words 'sex' and 'gender' are used synonymously to identify whether an individual is male or female, boy or girl, man or woman. For many researchers in the area of gender studies, however, gender is a social and cultural construction which can shape an individual's subjective sense of self and the culturally accepted notions of masculinity and femininity. And while this book adopts the synonymous use of sex and gender as a biological reality, it is important to describe why such an approach is deemed most suitable for educating and raising girls.

The biology of sex

It is well established in the scientific literature that 99.98 per cent of human beings are biologically male or female: being male or female is based on having an XX (female) or XY (male) chromosomal make-up and being able to produce the reproductive cells (ovum or eggs and sperm) of that sex.[3] This objective biological fact is a truism regardless of sexual orientation or notions of identity (which is explored later in this chapter). There are very rare circumstances where an individual has both XX and XY cells which can result in having components of both male and female genitalia and is referred to as being 'intersex'.[4] This condition is extremely rare – the best estimates suggest that intersex births account for approximately two out of every 10 000 births. A teacher would need to work with 100 different students a year over 35 years to have a better than a 50 per cent chance of encountering one intersex child.[5] The rarity of this condition is compounded by the fact that the vast majority of intersex individuals do not publicly present as male *and* female. Instead, intersex individuals adopt the gender that is most pronounced biologically and/

or physically. The intricacies of intersex are highly complex and beyond the scope of this book, but it is important to reiterate that the chances of a teacher encountering a student who is chromosomally intersex is exceedingly rare. Moreover, it isn't necessary to eliminate the categories of 'male' or 'female' or redefine sex in order to foster the acceptance of those who are different.[6] Parents of intersex children, however, will need to seek the appropriate professional advice to support their child given that disorders of sexual development are so rare and complex.

Although the chromosomal make-up related to sex is incontrovertible, there are some who suggest that gender is a social construct and as such can be 'fluid' or 'non-binary'. Such descriptors are premised more on subjective ideological interpretations of the influence of the environment on child development than on the substantive amount of scientific literature related to sex differences. In other words, there isn't any empirical proof that the social environment after birth alters a person's biological make-up or sexual orientation:[7] sex is a biological fact of our species and the misappropriation of that term to suggest that gender is 'fluid' or on a 'spectrum' is very contentious and scientifically incorrect. As noted above, 99.98 per cent of humans are either XX or XY, with all of the physical and physiological attributes associated with being female and male and will identify as being either male or female.[8] This is not to suggest that there aren't differences *among* males and *among* females, but even infants are able to distinguish the sex of other infants and demonstrate typical male and female behaviours long before any measure of culture or society can exact any influence.[9] Gender cannot be separated from biology, it is not alien to human nature, nor is it accidental or an arbitrary invention of society, but rather, it is at the core of human identity.[10] And while I recognise and acknowledge that the social and cultural environment does indeed play a part in shaping the minds of girls, this does not mean that notions around how some might construct ideas around gender aren't worthy of scrutiny.

The social construction of gender

Simone de Beauvoir, a French writer, philosopher, political activist, feminist and social theorist, once asserted that a woman is not born but made, suggesting that gender is a social construction.[11] While many things may be lost in translation, to read de Beauvoir's work is an interesting journey into the emergence of gender studies as a sociological discipline. In itself, her work could be characterised as somewhat 'anti-male' and perhaps that is to be expected – when she began to construct her sociological analysis of sex and gender in 1946, times were very different for both men and women. And while this chapter is not designed to offer a protracted defence or critique of de Beauvoir's work, it is important to note that her writing, along with those of other gender theorists, was instrumental in aspects of social change and the emergence of gender theory and gender studies as academic disciplines.

Gender theory, in itself, is likely where a degree of confusion about what it means to be male and female begins. Since the 1960s, gender theory has grown into an expansive and arguably ambiguous construction of a variety of subsets of topics under the term 'gender studies'. Universities teach courses ranging from 'gender schema theory' to 'gender prediction theory' to 'gendering theory' and numerous others which share the core idea that gender is fluid and a social construct, so that being a man or a woman is not linked to biology or being born male or female.[12] Such perspectives often result in calls for social change that can range on a wide continuum of overall intent and potential dangers. This is not to say that studies of gender cannot be helpful in some sense and, like many other types of social research, provide important narratives of human experience. However, these are 'theoretical' courses and fields of study – rich in philosophical and theoretical propositions but not supported by extensive scientific data and/or empirical evidence. Coupled with the current political climate around gender identity and gendered roles, such courses further muddy the waters of the imprecise sociological description of 'gender'.

This book is not concerned with sociological interpretations of gender, but the biology and neurobiology of sex and gender. Biological sex is either male or female, and as noted earlier, in conjunction with chromosomal makeup, is best defined by the types of reproductive cells (gametes) a person produces: males produce sperm and females produce eggs. From a biological perspective, sex is indeed binary.[13] In this book, therefore, sex and gender are used interchangeably and mean the same thing: being male or female is not something that is 'assigned' at birth, but, barring the rare occurrence of being intersex, is something 'recognised' at birth. This is not to say that there aren't degrees of variation within each gender, but by and large there are substantive reasons why girls might behave and engage with the world in different ways than boys and these result from the interplay of genetics and biology in the environment. Understanding and adopting such a position allows us to explore ideas and strategies that will assist parents and educators in providing girls with the tools they need to move forward in society. Nonetheless, it is also important to give some attention to notions of gender identity, given the increased recognition of transgender individuals and various agendas for supporting such individuals.

Sex and gender at the margins

As noted earlier in the chapter, most individuals have a relatively unremarkable experience of being born male or female. Men and women, boys and girls, almost always identify as male or female and feel masculine or feminine within the cultural context in which they are educated and raised.[14] However, there are degrees of masculinity and femininity resulting from experience, and individuals may even discuss what it means to be a man or woman during particular social and cultural contexts. Such considerations typically fall under notions of 'gender identity' and 'gender roles', concepts which are challenged and examined through the recognition of LGBTIQ identities and experiences. And while that particular label might suggest some measure of collective unity, each letter in itself represents something very different from each other letter.

The 'I' in refers to those individuals who are intersex and as noted earlier are representative of very rare circumstances. The L, G and B are indicative of sexual orientation: lesbian, gay and bisexual respectively. Interestingly, these categories appear reasonably stable across a population: approximately three per cent of men and one per cent of women identify as homosexual, 0.5 per cent of men and one per cent of women as bisexual and the remainder of a general population identifies as heterosexual.[15] It is important to note that sexual orientation is not the same as gender: those who identify as being gay or bisexual still acknowledge their respective biological sex as being male or female. Recent surveys conducted in times of increased societal acceptance of homosexuality and bisexuality have not shown a higher incidence of either sexual orientation.[16] In other words, whether an individual is heterosexual, homosexual or bisexual, biological sex is not a point of speculation, contention or subjective interpretation. This, however, is not the case when discussing the remaining letters, T and Q.

Q, within the LGBTIQ acronym, stands for 'queer'. The term itself is derived from postmodern and Marxist theory, and became prominent through gay liberation movements in the 1990s which saw the emergence of queer theory as a political and academic discourse and mechanism for dismantling homophobia.[17] The essence of queer theory is in the word queer, which signifies a sense of difference or strangeness, and is adopted by those individuals who desire to be seen as anything other than the 'norm'.[18] Today, to be queer can mean many things and it is often used as an umbrella term for all those in the LGBTIQ community and/or as a label to identify as anything other than heterosexual or biologically male or female. As such, it is difficult to define, and is open to a variety of definitions and interpretations even in the queer community itself. However, being queer does not negate the fact that unless a person also identifies as intersex, their sex/gender/biological identity will still consist of a chromosomal make up that is either XX (female) or XY (male). This is also true of transgender individuals – the T in LGBTIQ.

'Transgender' is an umbrella term that generally refers to individuals who experience or express their gender identity as incongruent to their biological sex.[19] For example, transgender individuals who are biologically female may express that they feel or identify as being male. Being transgender is a complex phenomenon and can also include individuals who identify as being not exclusively masculine or feminine ('non-binary', 'bigender', 'pangender', 'gender fluid' or 'agender') and the opposite of 'cisgender' (those whose gender identity and expression match their biological sex).[20] Currently, issues and challenges associated with being transgender appear highly politicised and as yet are not well understood by the scientific community. Historically, transgenderism fell under the label of 'gender identity disorder', suggesting that individuals who felt like they were trapped inside the wrong body were dealing with a psychological condition.[21] However, there is growing evidence that being transgender might actually be linked to biology itself.

As noted above, there are an increasing number of studies suggesting that transgendered individuals neurologically relate to the sex they identify with rather than their biological sex.[22] In other words, a scientific definition of what it means to be transgender recognises that while the sex of the body is unambiguous, the sex of the brain is decisive in determining one's sexual identity; a male brain in a female body will result in a person who feels like a man in a woman's body.[23] Such studies further affirm the notion that human brains, in themselves, can be male or female, which in turn helps build a case for different approaches to educating and raising boys and girls. This is covered in greater detail in Chapter 3, but the significance of these findings also plays a role in aspects of mental health and wellbeing. The biology of the brain clearly has profound implications for a person's sense of identity and for transgender individuals this can lead to a great degree of distress or what is referred to in the psychiatric literature as 'gender dysphoria'.[24]

It is difficult to even begin to imagine what it would be like to feel that your 'gendered' sense of self does not align with your biological self, especially when social biases may prevent such individuals from living satisfying lives. However, for teachers and parents it is important to remember that encountering young people who present themselves as transgender is rare. One notable exception is an apparent rise in adolescent girls identifying as non-binary or transgender, which may be linked to social media[25] (this is covered in much greater detail in chapters 7 and 8). Nonetheless, it is very difficult to determine what percentage of the Australian population may be transgender given the potential unwillingness by some to self-report and by the conflation of statistics that occurs when combining all individuals within the LGBTIQ community. For example, while the Australian Human Rights Commission suggested in 2014 that approximately 11 per cent of the Australian population had a diverse sexual orientation and fell under the parameter of LGBTIQ, there wasn't any breakdown as to the representation of each category within that group. Such statistics are undermined by other more recent studies estimating that 3.2 per cent of Australian adults identify as 'non-heterosexual'.[26] For those researchers the term 'non-heterosexual' was used to include all who identified as gay, homosexual, lesbian or those who construct their sexuality in other ways using non-heterosexual terminologies (e.g. queer).

A further difficulty in attempting to determine what proportion of a population identify as transgender may lie in how being transgender is defined. For example, if you define transgender to strictly mean those who wish to transition to the opposite sex, the best estimate of prevalence is nine per 100 000 or approximately 0.009 per cent.[27] However, if being transgender refers to individuals who 'feel' they are the opposite sex but do not wish to transition then the prevalence rises to 871 in 100 000 or about 0.871 per cent.[28] This suggests that perhaps such individuals may not actually be gender dysphoric but instead are struggling with a range of identity and psychological issues which in themselves are fluid and prone to change. Again, this is covered in greater detail in Chapter 7, but may be related to the behaviours of young children.

Teachers and parents alike must always remember that quite often children will playfully, and with degree of childhood curiosity, pretend to be the opposite sex.[29] Such explorations are not a sign of being transgender or of a child refuting their biological sex, but rather the normal experimentations children may embark on as they grow and mature. Consider also that up until roughly age seven or eight children have only a superficial understanding of sex and gender and are unlikely to maintain a coherent concept of gender identity where their identities link to their biology.[30] However, it is not uncommon for children to express that they are the opposite sex. For them, this is more an act of utility: if a young boy wants to play with dolls it is just easier for him to proclaim he is a girl so he can do so.[31] Moreover, such behaviours are as common as parents who worry about those behaviours, but these types of behaviour, play and exploration are a healthy sign of development whereby children are exploring the world through playful behaviour where gender is of little significance given their age. Remember that children will also pretend to be superheroes, monsters and puppies but that does not mean they intend to save or terrorise the planet or spend their lives fetching sticks. Moreover, and regardless of the gender 'play' noted above, the biological make-up of children manifested as being male or female will impact on many aspects of behaviour and learning.

Finally, while it is important to recognise that there are those who, for whatever reason, do not identify with their biological sex or position themselves as 'non-binary' or 'gender fluid', it is equally important to bear in mind that with the exception of about 0.02 per cent of the human population who are intersex, all other individuals, including those noted, are biologically male or female; gender identity and biological sex are not mutually exclusive. Additionally, and as alluded to in the discussion of transgender individuals above, there is substantive evidence that is provided throughout this book recognising the sexually dimorphic nature of the brain or what the layperson might refer to as the existence of a 'male' and 'female' brain. It is the 'female' brain and the biological sex differences in the brain that shape the foundation of this book. These sex differences are explored in greater detail in Chapter 4, but prior to unpacking the complexities of a female brain, the next chapter provides an overview of how the brain develops in utero and through adolescence.

Summary

The complexities surrounding the terms 'sex' and 'gender' can be very confusing for some. Today those complexities are exacerbated within a myriad of social, cultural and political agendas. In this book sex and gender are used interchangeably as the book is based on a biological framework. However, in many instances the term gender is used because we generally ascertain whether an individual is male or female based on presentable characteristics and not on ascertaining chromosomal makeup. It is therefore important to emphasise that the following chapters are premised on the biological reality that a female possesses an X and X chromosomal makeup and produces eggs, and as such will, on average, display certain behaviours and traits resulting from their biology. For parents and teachers who find themselves working through issues of identity with any young person, such matters often require assistance from professionals in mental health and wellbeing which is discussed in greater detail in Chapter 8.

The developing brain

... each brain is unique, ever-changing and exquisitely sensitive to its environment ... the whole is bound together in a dynamic system of systems that does millions of different things in parallel. It is probably so complex that it will never succeed in comprehending itself. Yet it never ceases to try.[1]

— *Rita Carter*

Imagining the unimaginable

Thirty years ago, President George HW Bush signed Proclamation 6158 declaring the 1990s the 'Decade of the Brain'. This important presidential statement was not only a worldwide catalyst for the contribution of greater research dollars to neuroscience but also helped expand research between neuroscience and other discipline fields. Moreover, not unlike the first half of the twentieth century being heralded as the age of physics, the beginning of the twenty-first century became the age of brain-mind science.[2] Psychologists, educators, doctors, therapists and others with professional interests in how the mind works started to delve into a reinvigorated and growing body of research focused on the brain. Questions surrounding mental illness, thinking and learning, memory, behaviour, emotions and general wellbeing could be teased out and re-examined due to advancements in technology. Functional brain scanning started to unlock mysteries of the brain and present them to the public in many forms. Indeed, if you look at the number of books and articles produced over the last three decades you would notice that this growth in reader-friendly explorations into the human mind has arguably surpassed any other era of brain-related work. Yet even after so much writing and research, it is revealing that there is so much more to know. As neuroscientist and author Joseph LeDoux has suggested, imagining the sophisticated nature of the grey matter between our ears is perhaps entirely unimaginable.[3] However, I think we should at least try!

What is it that makes the brain such a marvel of, and about, humanity? In order to better comprehend some of the amazing aspects of the brain, we can turn to what we have learned from neuroscience. With the incredible advances in research and technology, what once existed in theory is now supported by hard evidence. For example, neuroscientists had long suspected that different regions of the brain perform different primary functions, and now they can actually watch the brain at work and link brain structures and activity with human tasks and actions.

The ability to watch the brain at work has truly been one of the most fundamental advancements in the field of neuroscience. It has opened a whole new world of understanding about what some have described as the 'three-pound universe' that sits between our ears.[4] Some of the most fascinating discoveries have been made at the cellular level and have changed much of what we used to believe about how the brain grows and matures.

Brain development: a cellular journey

Not all that long ago, very little was known about early brain development. How a complex jungle of interconnected cellular pathways originated from a few initial cells in the early stages of embryonic development was a bit of a mystery. In fact, in the 1970s our collective naivety about the brain was clear in psychologists' assertions that newborn babies could not think and were little more than tiny beings capable of only simple automatic responses – in essence, carrots that could cry.[5] Today, we know that a great deal of neural activity occurs long before a child's first birthday.

Just seventeen days after conception, the brain begins to produce billions of neurons, or nerve cells. These neurons differ from other cells in a number of ways, perhaps the most significant being their structure and ability to transmit information to one another. Primarily composed of a nucleus, axons and dendrites, neurons have been identified as the foundation of human behaviour and learning.[6]

18 The developing brain

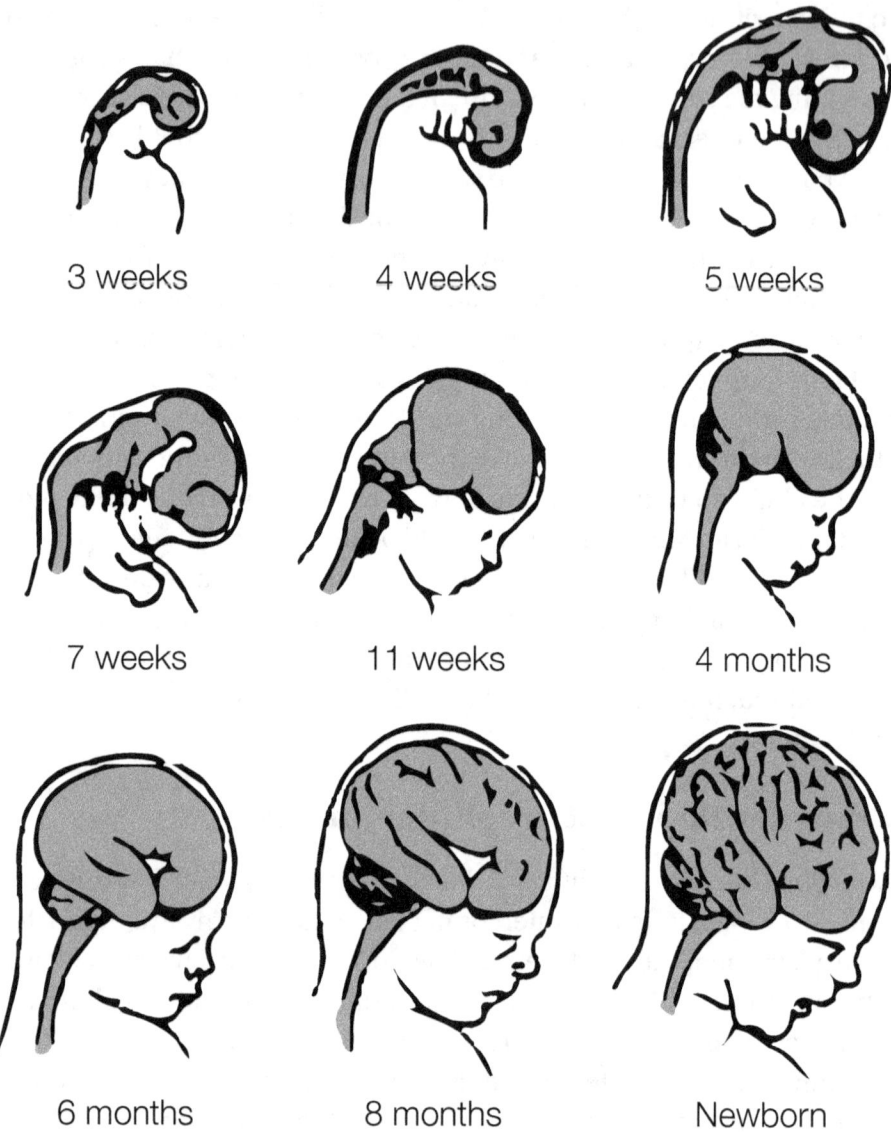

Figure 2.1 Brain development in utero[7]

By the seventeenth week of pregnancy the fetus will have approximately a billion brain cells. The proliferation of brain cells occurs at a rate of about 50,000 per second, and most of a human's brain cells are produced between the fourth and seventh months of gestation.[8] In fact, the brain of the fetus will produce roughly twice as many neurons as necessary to ensure the best possible chance of having a healthy brain and will later prune back unused cells.[9]

Interestingly, the brain cells don't begin in the precise location of their future roles and activity. Thus, the early stages of this important time period (about four and a half months into gestation) also sees neurons migrating to different regions of the brain to form connections (synapses) with other neurons.[10] This migration is facilitated by glial cells, which act as a type of supportive and protective tissue for neurons. By the time a newborn arrives, the distinct regions of the brain are all in place, though much more growth is still to occur.

With all of this activity happening at such an early stage, our understanding of a healthy pregnancy has undergone revision. For most women, the discovery of pregnancy prompts a change in various lifestyle behaviours including diet, smoking, alcohol consumption and the use of medications and other drugs. Given how early the production of neurons (neurogenesis) and synapses (synaptogenesis) occurs in utero, would-be parents need to consider these lifestyle changes much earlier, while trying to become pregnant. A great deal of neural development occurs before an expecting mother even realises she is pregnant, and what a mother consumes will impact the fetal environment and the developing fetal brain long before the end of the first trimester.[11]

On the day a child arrives it already has billions of neurons actively engaging with one another through electro-chemical impulses to form quadrillions of connections to ensure optimal neural connectivity. In response to new stimuli from the environment, the dendrites of neurons will continue to grow and multiply. If adequately and repeatedly stimulated, information will pass from one neuron to another like 'elegantly complex electro-chemical computers'.[12]

The process of learning depends on these connections between neurons. Neurons 'communicate' with one another through electro-chemical signals that occurs in response to environmental stimuli. A chemical messenger, known as a neurotransmitter, is passed across the small gap between neurons known as a synapse.[13]

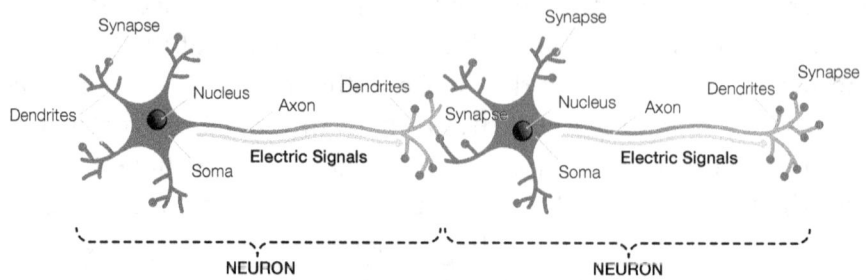

Figure 2.2 Synaptic transmissions between neurons[14]

Synaptic transmission of information is the primary catalyst for developing long term hard-wired neural circuits and could be considered as an act of learning. As our brains respond to the environment, they lay down neural connections that, over time and through repetition, become 'hardwired' pathways to behaving in a certain way. Connections that are not used repeatedly appear to be discarded or 'pruned' away at different stages throughout our lives.[15] The process of hardwiring neural connections demonstrates that brain development is actually a 'use it or lose it' process whereby practice makes permanent.

In the early stages of development, neural connections seem to proliferate most rapidly during the first three years of life and activity then plateaus until adolescence. The brain is the only organ in the body incomplete at birth and it will continue to grow for a number of years and change throughout our lifetimes,[16] however, the principal foundation of our neural anatomy is built early in our lives. By the age of two, the brains of toddlers are as active as those of adults and at age three a child's brain is two and a half times more active than adults' brains.[17] This level of activity remains high throughout the first decade of life and suggests that children, especially infants and toddlers, seem biologically geared for learning.[18]

Neurotransmitters, learning and experience

As already mentioned, neural development, or learning, involves not just neurons but the connections between them, facilitated by neurotransmitters. The presence, or absence, of particular neurotransmitters influences all levels of brain activity from actions of impulsivity and restfulness to thinking and attention to anger and ecstasy.[19] For example, melatonin helps to activate sleep and serotonin acts as a calming mechanism while dopamine wears numerous hats from serving as the basis of various curiosity-type behaviours, motivation and reward seeking to switching our levels and duration of attention.[20] In simpler terms, neurotransmitters are the primary mechanism for relaying information between neurons which in turn shapes how we feel and act in any moment.

Another important factor in this dance of brain chemistry refers to something known as the 'action potential' of neural firing, which helps to explain our individual differences. In neurochemistry, action potential refers to the individual thresholds we all possess when responding to certain environmental stimuli. For example, each of us will have a different threshold for various facets of taste. For some the threshold for tasting food that is very spicy is quite low while for others, mountains of chilli peppers have little effect. If a particular stimulus is too weak, neurons won't fire and react to that stimulus, crossing what is referred to as the 'response threshold', and consequently the action potential (or potential for neural action) is insignificant.[21] In other words, each individual will respond to environmental stimulation in ways that can be common amongst others or conversely unique to oneself. Thus, an individual's behaviour and learning is the result of a complex interplay between the varying stimuli that surround us as we grow and learn and the inherited genetic predispositions of our biochemistry.

In order for any measure of 'learning' to occur, the brain requires various forms and degrees of stimulation. Indeed, the lack of environmental stimuli early in life can have life-long effects. Nobel Prize-winning research examining the effects on vision of children born with congenital cataracts has offered perhaps the most compelling evidence of the importance of early stimulation on neural development. Generally speaking, this work showed that adults who develop cataracts and then have them removed experience a return to normal vision while children afflicted with congenital cataracts do not experience the same results. The researchers concluded that regions of the infant brain linked to the optic nerve did not receive adequate stimulation during a crucial developmental period, and consequently the neural connections necessary for normal sight were also hindered.[22] This research helped demonstrate that early neurological development maintains particular periods of maturation within specific regions and functions of the brain.

These periods of maturation were once labelled 'critical' periods but are now more commonly referred to as 'sensitive periods' of development.[23] Regardless of labels, these periods also provide a good example of 'experience expectant stimulation' in contrast to 'experience dependent growth'.

Experience expectant stimulation relates to those ordinary, day-to-day experiences the brain requires for particular hardwiring to occur while experience dependent stimulation refers to adaptive processes arising out of the specific contexts or unique features of a particular environment.[24] To put it another way, the brain expects certain types of stimulation for hardwiring to occur (nature) and depends on other types of stimulation or learning via engagement in the environment (nurture). For example, the brain expects to see things to hardwire for sight, while it depends on other types of stimulation to learn how to do things such as tie one's shoes. Furthermore, barring any physical impairments or significant deprivation of stimulation, the senses develop unencumbered, and it appears that children enter the world prewired for certain abilities that unfold as long as the brain receives the stimulation it expects.[25] Such findings have also provided the foundation for the types of insights noted below with regards to brain maturation, development and learning.

Around the turn of the century, scientists identified that regions of the cortex or the 'thinking' part of the brain increase in size when exposed to stimulating conditions and the longer the exposure, the more they actually grow.[26] This area of research has also identified that stimulation enlarges the overall number of dendrites in each neuron and in turn enlarges or thickens cortical cells.[27] It therefore appears that enriched environments can boost the number of synapses a child forms and, equally important, an environment devoid of appropriate stimuli has been shown to thin out dendrites and reduce cortical thickness.[28]

What does research into 'sensitive' periods and experience suggest in terms of the day-to-day interactions parents, caregivers and educators have with children? First, while it appears that the brain has a remarkable ability to change due to its neuroplasticity, for some aspects of development the timing of particular stimulation is crucial. In other words, environments which are extremely deprived of stimulation can hinder brain development. Problematically, notions of deprivation are often used to promote doing more with children to ensure they do not miss out. This then leads to the term 'enrichment' being used as a descriptor for optimum environments. However, 'enrichment' should not be taken to mean that we should do more with children; instead, quality is better than quantity as is ensuring that activities and learning opportunities are developmentally appropriate. Second, while there appear to be optimum times for certain types of learning to occur, some aspects of learning can occur beyond those timelines. In most cases only those experiences that have robbed the brain of important early stimuli, such as visual stimulation, appear irreversible. For most children, the day-to-day experiences of life are often enough to ensure a healthy start to development. Finally, while there are sensitive periods for experience expectant growth, there are also 'windows of opportunity' when a child's brain is primed for to receive sensory input via experience dependent growth. Figure 2.3 maps the typical points at which some of these learning windows open.

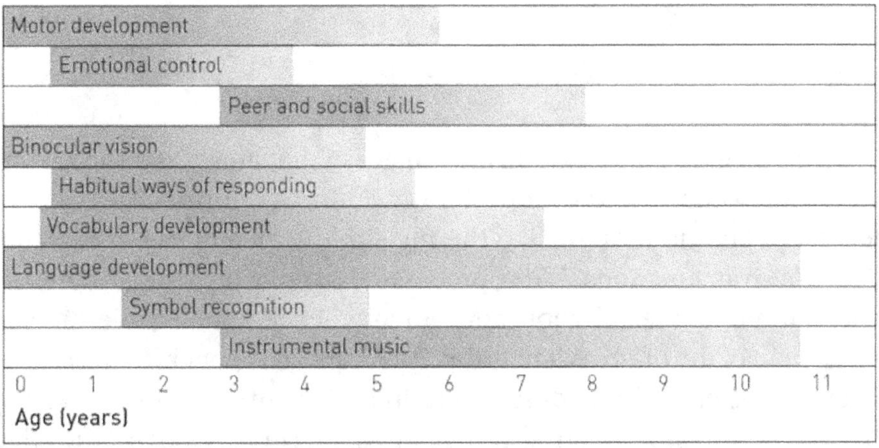

Figure 2.3 Learning windows: Key periods of neural connectivity.[29]

As illustrated in the chart above, learning windows never fully close. This is because neuroplasticity allows for learning beyond the periods identified; however, it might be somewhat more difficult to achieve certain skills later in life (i.e. second language acquisition).[30]

Learning windows and myelination

Although stimulation is crucial to brain development, there is also another important consideration when looking at the developmental timelines of the brain. This has little to do with outside stimuli and everything to do with the brain's production and accumulation of a fatty material called 'myelin'.

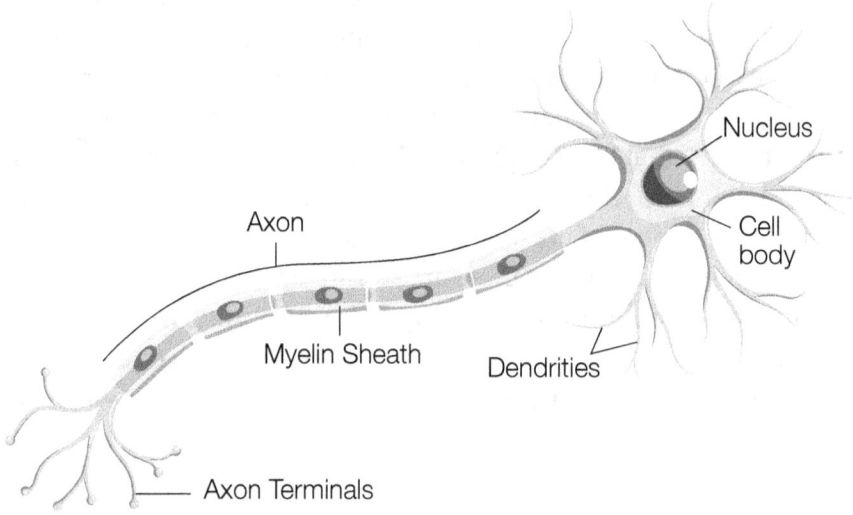

Figure 2.4 Myelin wrapped around an axon

Myelin is essentially a white fatty material that grows as a sheath and acts as an insulator and conduit for transmitting information from one neuron to another; the thicker the myelin, the greater the expediency of neural transmissions.[31] The process of myelin build-up, known as myelination, is a lengthy journey which will eventually triple the size and weight of the brain as it matures.[32] Myelin also appears to develop in certain areas of the brain during certain periods of time, further adding to the phenomenon referred to earlier as 'learning windows'. In other words, when the brain has greater myelinated axons in a particular region, the circuits in this region work faster and consequently there is greater neural efficiency and greater opportunity to learn.

The process of myelination occurs in different neural regions during development. The neural connections in the brain stem and in major nerve areas running to the face, limbs, various areas of the abdomen and the organs receive substantive increases in myelin before birth and during infancy,[33] which ensures that a baby's basic survival functions (i.e. breathing, heartbeat, vision) become quite efficient early in life. Myelination in regions of the brain that influence complex motor control such as the cerebellum and areas of the limbic system begin to reach adult levels around the age of two, which is evident in a child's growing ability to walk and run with increasingly improved motor coordination. We will examine these and other important structures of the brain in greater detail later in this chapter.

Finally, the areas of the brain responsible for some of our highest cerebral functions take the longest to myelinate. The hippocampus, the layers of the cerebral cortex and various areas of the brain stem that allow you to wake up and stay alert can take up to ten years to fully myelinate. During adolescence, myelin production continues at a phenomenal rate, increasing up to 100 per cent,[34] and it appears that a girl's brain generally myelinates faster than that of a boy This is especially evident in the hippocampus and cingulate; areas where emotion and intellect often meet.[35] Therefore, even at a cellular level we can identify differences between boys and girls which are worthy of consideration and which we will return to in later chapters.

Fine tuning the brain

When children enter pubescence and move through stages of adolescence, the brain begins to go through a process of pruning unused synapses.[36] As noted throughout this chapter, brain maturation occurs over an extended period of time and goes through a number of stages where it continually changes and remodels itself. A great deal of this restructuring actually occurs during adolescence.

As in childhood, the brain is very 'plastic' during adolescence and shaped by the experiences around it.[37] Part of this plasticity is effected through a process of eliminating or 'pruning' a substantial proportion of synaptic connections; it is estimated that only 60 per cent of the synapses produced in the first few years of life are ultimately retained into adulthood.[38] During adolescence the brain eliminates those connections that are not used on a regular basis, and leaves those that have become hardwired into our neural circuitry.

Synaptic pruning changes the brain markedly. These changes can be both quantitative and qualitative in nature; the overall number of synapses are reduced while many connections are refined.[39] What stays and what goes is significantly influenced by interactions with the outside world and therefore could be described as an 'experience-dependent' neural reorganisation.[40] Compared to an adult brain, an adolescent brain is highly malleable and shaped by experience where some connections become permanent features of our respective minds and those 'connections rarely used and not welded into permanent circuits become cortical dead wood to be pruned away.'[41]

Synaptic pruning appears to vary by region and the elimination of all but the most important connections is believed to improve the speed and efficiency of overall synapses.[42] The rate and location of pruning, guided by the 'use it or lose it' approach, has the capacity to influence all aspects of the brain's structural and functional architecture and have a profound impact on adolescent emotions, behaviour, thought processes and by extension, learning.[43] In practical terms this tells us that what a girl says and does is not only a product of experience and context but also the developmental milieu of her brain and mind. Nature and nurture work in tandem and our understanding of the developmental changes in the brain through adolescence give us greater insight into why adolescents may do the things they do. Having some understanding of the changes that are occurring beyond what we can openly observe, helps us to better unpack and understand the young girls around us as they grow and mature.

After looking at the information above there can be little denying the important nexus between stimulation and early development. There is also no denying that after the wondrous years of early childhood there is still substantive developmental work to be done in the brain and most of this occurs through adolescence. Neuroscientists continue to explore these important developmental milestones and there exist volumes of research looking at those important ideas. There are also numerous books that provide more detailed explanations of the developing adolescent brain. This volume of work however, focuses on those aspects of the developing female brain that may help shape how teachers and parents support and nurture their students and daughters. To that end, we now shift from developmental aspects of the brain to examining the interplay between the responsibilities and roles of various structures of the brain.

Structures and systems

Now that we have taken a brief look into how the brain develops and operates on a cellular level, we can identify how this cellular activity relates to brain functions at a structural level. The brain can be usefully divided into three regions: the brain stem at the bottom; the limbic system in the middle; and the cerebrum or cerebral cortex at the top. While these regions are best understood by describing their distinct functions, it is important to remember that they are intimately connected as a unified structure and each will influence the other.

Located at the base of the brain, the brain stem is often referred to as the 'reptilian' brain as it evolved more than 500 million years ago and is the most ancient part of the brain.[44] The command centres of survival reside here, such as our fight-or-flight response, and the majority of body functions not under conscious control: breathing, heartbeat, blood circulation, temperature regulation, tongue movements, vocal sounds, and movement of the muscles in the face and throat are all part of the brain stem's responsibilities. A small part of visual, tactile and oral stimuli are also processed via the brain stem where they are then passed on to the thalamus which acts a relay station between the brain stem and other areas of the brain including the limbic system.[45]

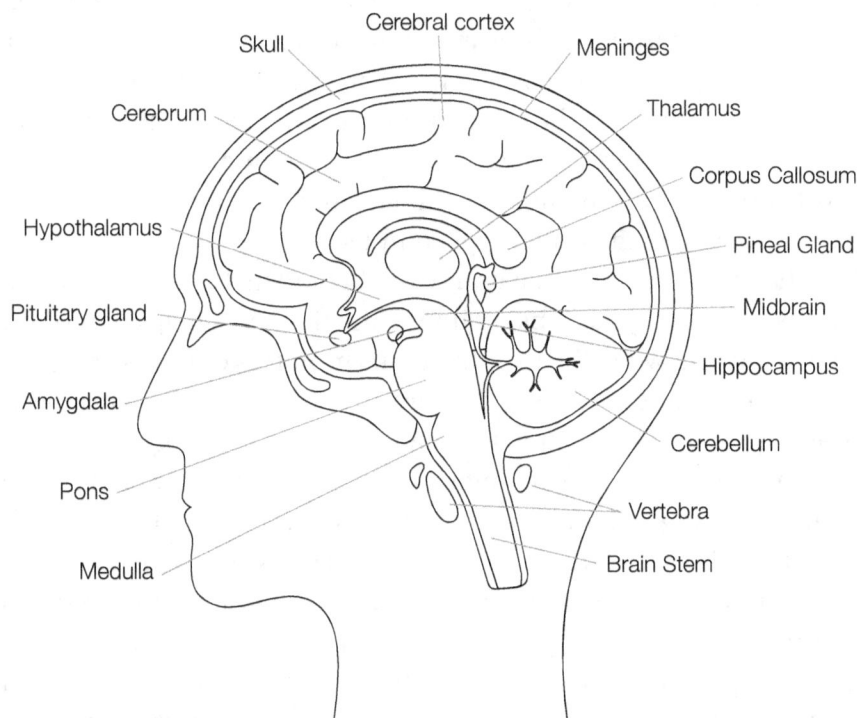

Figure 2.5 Structures of the brain

Positioned at the very back of the brain, bordering closely on the brain stem, is the cerebellum. While it makes up only about one tenth of an adult brain's weight, it has more neurons than any other part of the brain; some estimates suggest that the cerebellum contains about 50 per cent of the brain's neurons.[46] Overall, the role of the cerebellum is very diverse and complex: it not only plays a significant part in motor coordination but also helps to coordinate cognitive functions and thought processes.

The limbic system sits above the brain stem and is best known as the emotional centre of the brain, although it also processes memories and connects the lower regions of the brain responsible for motor and automatic functions and survival with the higher regions responsible for cognitive thought.[47]

The limbic system represents about one-fifth of the brain's volume and is not only responsible for generating and processing emotions but also initiating most of the many appetites and urges that direct us to behave in ways that usually help us to survive.[48] Indeed, the limbic system's physical position and close alignment with the brain stem indicates the importance of our emotions to our survival.[49] The limbic system also plays a role in sleep, attention, regulation of bodily functions, hormones, attention and the production of most of the chemicals found in the brain.[50] Structures in the limbic system that appear to have the greatest influence on learning and behaviour include the amygdala, thalamus, hypothalamus and hippocampus.

The thalamus and hypothalamus work in tandem to regulate the vital functions of the body via sensory input. The thalamus helps to monitor the outside world while the hypothalamus monitors our internal states, and damage to either of these structures would most definitely put our lives at risk.[51] More succinctly, the thalamus acts as a type of filter and relay station by taking sensory information from the body and directing it to other key areas of the brain for processing. The hypothalamus, on the other hand, releases hormones in response to stress signals from the brain and operates primarily as a feedback mechanism. Along with the pituitary gland, the hypothalamus also plays a key role in maintaining homeostasis.[52] Both the thalamus and hypothalamus are integral components of the limbic system but they must rely on the amygdala, hippocampus and other areas of the brain to fulfil their neurological functions adequately.

The amygdala has been described as the neural basis of emotion and has long been the object of interest in most brain-referenced theories of emotion.[53] Shaped like an almond (amygdala is the Greek word for almond), there are two of these important structures located in the lower area of the temporal lobes. The amygdala is a critical component in responding to danger, acting as the brain's alarm system, and operates by receiving information about the outside world from the thalamus and setting in motion a variety of bodily mechanisms.[54] If, for example, the brain senses fear or stress, the amygdala acts to ensure that the endocrine system responds by sending out the appropriate hormones to raise the heart rate, blood pressure and prepare the muscles for activity.[55] The amygdala, then, is a very important mechanism in ensuring a person's survival.

A further interesting characteristic of the amygdala is that our feelings are dependent upon which parts of it are activated. Stimulate one part and you get the type of fear reaction noted above; however, stimulate another region and you produce what is best described as a warm floaty feeling while a third region can result in outbursts of sheer rage.[56] This important feature of the amygdala is yet another example of the brain's ingenious design. Packing all of these types of mechanisms in one area allows us to shift between flight, fight and appeasement very swiftly when necessary ... if a smile won't ward off a bully or aggressor, then flight or attack is easily triggered.[57] The decision whether to fight, flee or appease is generally facilitated by the brain's prefrontal lobes, which are the last regions of the brain to fully mature. This is important when considering adolescent behaviour, as the prefrontal cortex will often receive the emotional stimuli from the environment after the amygdala has already begun to respond to the situation at hand. In other words, an adult's facial expression might be misinterpreted and elicit a negative emotional reaction via the amygdala in an adolescent girl before her frontal lobes can provide a more measured analysis of what is actually being conveyed.

Finally, the amygdala also plays a significant role in the consolidation of long-term memories. Generally speaking, the amygdala adds some measure of emotional significance to an experience and works in tandem with the hippocampus to assess the emotional relevancy of an event and then store the memory of that experience.[58] An interesting point for parents and educators to remember is that because the amygdala responds to stress and fear, memory and learning can actually be impeded by these emotions. There is a great deal of evidence indicating that stress, fear, anxiety, and other emotional responses to environmental stimuli can directly impact upon cognition and learning.[59] When we look at the emotional lives of the girls around us later we will continue to unpack the intricacies of the amygdala. At this stage however, let us look at one final important component of the limbic system: the hippocampus.

The hippocampus also plays a vital role in consolidating learning and converting information from working memory to long-term storage in various regions of the cerebrum. Working memory involves both the storing and processing of stored information and brings the present, past and future together in a moment-by-moment whiteboard of the mind.[60] The hippocampus has been described as the brain's 'workhorse' for it is here that the memory of an immediate past experience is compared to those experiences stored in long-term memory in order to illicit meaning.[61] In essence, the hippocampus acts as a type of way station binding memories together until they can be transported to long-term storage in various regions of the cortex that surround it. Interestingly, this storage process may take three years or so before a memory is firmly lodged in cortical regions.[62]

As noted earlier, the formation of memories also relies on the amygdala:[63] the hippocampus reads the emotional tags attached to events by the amygdala and then acts as a filter deciding which information goes where. In making these decisions, the hippocampus determines the level of engagement an individual has in the activities around them by monitoring events as either novel or ordinary. Learning experiences that excite these parts of the limbic system due to their novelty or emotive content have a greater possibility of being stored in the brain's memory. For parents, novelty or connecting with the emotional centres of the brain and not some measure of extrinsic reward may provide the greatest catalyst for motivating children and teens. To this end, we must always remember that emotion and cognition are intimately linked as the limbic system engages with the grey matter of our psyche most commonly referred to as the cerebrum.

The cerebrum: a uniquely human structure

The region of the brain that is perhaps uniquely human in its function and abilities is the cerebrum. It is the largest and topmost part of the brain, and contains the cerebral cortex, or 'grey matter': the glial cells that act as protective and structural supports for neurons.[64] This uppermost grey layer of the brain is where thinking, consciousness and further responses to environmental stimuli take place.

The cerebrum is often described as the 'thinking' centre of the brain and is made up of four lobes across two hemispheres that are connected by a thick bundle of nerve fibres called the corpus callosum. Before looking at the functions of each specific cerebral lobe, we need some understanding of what takes place in each hemisphere. While most cognitive and affective (affect refers to emotion) activities involve both hemispheres, there are certain functional differences between the two sides of the brain. By design and function, the hemispheres are not simply mirror images of one another: hard-wired into each hemisphere are some quite specific functions.[65]

The left hemisphere has been described as being the analytical heartland of the mind. Language, logic, interpretation and mathematical competencies appear to be predominantly situated in the left side of our brain which is also often characterised as being precise and time sensitive; some might say it is the pedantic side of the brain. The right hemisphere, however, is often acknowledged as being more holistic in how it processes information and is more involved with sensory perception and abstract thinking. Spatial awareness, geometry, nonverbal processing, visual pattern recognition and auditory discrimination have all been associated with the right hemisphere.[66]

Another interesting aspect of the differentiation between hemispheres is that the human brain is contralateral: the left hemisphere governs activity on the right side of the body while the right hemisphere manages activity on the left. Researchers have also identified that approaching others, cheerfulness and general positive behaviours result in greater activity in the left hemisphere while the right hemisphere has been identified with avoidance behaviours and negative emotions.[67] And finally, we also know that a number of differences exist between the hemispheres of males and females, including how the hemispheres process language and aspects of spatial awareness.[68] These important considerations are explored in later chapters.

Despite these differences between the hemispheres, we must remember that they are intimately connected with one another, and with other regions. The hemispheres' overall functioning does not happen in isolation from one another, nor does it happen without some measure of influence from the limbic system or the brain stem. Consequently, when we look at the cerebrum and its hemispheres it is equally important to look at the overall structures or lobes of the 'thinking' part of our brain: the occipital, parietal, temporal and frontal lobes which occupy the same space across each hemisphere. Each of these areas has a number of very important responsibilities.

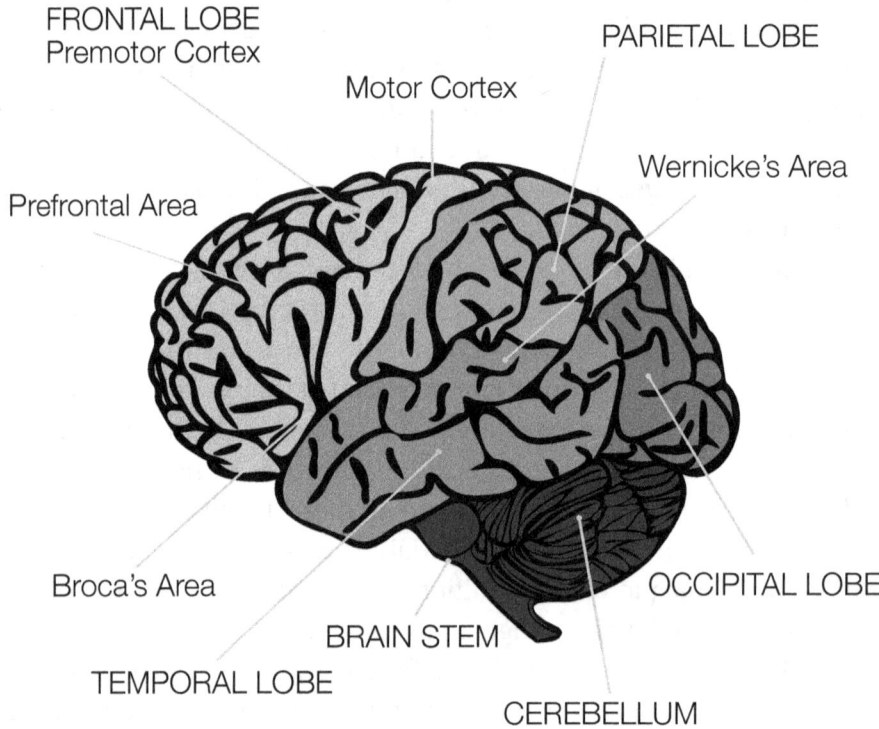

Figure 2.6 The brain's lobes and functions

The occipital lobes lie at the back of the cerebrum and appear to rest on the cerebellum. They focus primarily on processing visual stimuli including shape, colour, movement and depth.[69] As visual information is processed through the thalamus, it is sent to the occipital region of the brain where it is matched with previously stored memories. Therefore, it is important to note that the visual stimuli that each individual might attend to is highly dependent on several other brain systems as well as previous experience.[70]

The temporal lobes are located just above the ears and are primarily responsible for processing auditory stimuli and for recognising dangers and opportunities. They are also responsible for focusing on music perception and comprehension, higher visual processing, memory and language comprehension. The left temporal lobe also contains Wernicke's Area, a structure vital to language comprehension. Named after the German neurologist Karl Wernicke, it comprises a number of smaller systems that process specific elements of language and also convert thoughts into language.[71] When we learn to read it is Wernicke's Area that deciphers the meaning of the visual data obtained through the occipital lobes.

The parietal lobes can be found at the top and along the sides of the head. Within the parietal lobes is a region called the somatosensory cortex, which is the primarily responsible for receiving any incoming sensory stimuli. The parietal lobes process information regarding body awareness (touch, sensations of pain and positions of the limbs), spatial orientation and awareness and some language functions. The ability to locate objects in relation to our bodies and focus our attention on stimuli in the environment is dependent on the parietal lobes.[72] Simply stated, the parietal lobes allow us to touch and feel the sensation of being touched which is one of the early primary mechanisms of learning.

Finally, the frontal lobes, or the brain's thinking centre. The frontal lobes allow humans to be consciously aware of their thoughts and actions and are responsible for aspects of memory, emotional regulation, higher order thought processes, problem solving, decision-making, planning, responsible thinking, creativity, judgment and language.[73] All of these activities fall under the umbrella term 'executive functions' and are critical for all aspects of development and learning.[74]

The frontal lobes also contain Broca's Area, another important region for speaking and written language. While Wernicke's Area works at comprehending language, it is Broca's Area which synthesises language and articulates our thoughts through the regulation of face and hand activity including speech and writing.[75] And while both of these regions are important in terms of language, in girls Broca's area matures sooner than in boys.[76] This gives girls a distinct language advantage early in life and is something explored in more detail in later chapters.

Perhaps the most important component of the frontal lobes is the prefrontal cortex. As well as helping to weigh consequences and thus determine strategies for action, this area of the frontal lobes coordinates and integrates most brain functions due to its interconnectedness with every distinct functional unit of the brain. It is responsible for most higher order functioning and the capacity for thinking through the results of one's actions or the responsibilities attached to those actions.[77] For these reasons, while the centre for executive functioning is the frontal lobes, the prefrontal lobes are often referred to as the brain's chief executive officer.

The prefrontal lobes are very important in the context of understanding and educating young minds for a number of reasons. Firstly, and as noted above, this region is integral in terms of weighing up the consequences of our actions and thinking though our responses to various situations. Secondly, as noted earlier in this chapter, we now know that 'the most advanced parts of the brain don't complete their development until adolescence is pretty much over.'[78] That is, the areas of the brain responsible for emotive and survival responses (the limbic system and brain stem) mature and develop sooner than the areas responsible for thought processes and logical thinking. In practical terms this tells us that the brain's CEO, which is not only responsible for deciding particular courses of action but also for behavioural inhibition and the ability to control emotions and impulses, is the last region to mature. Concurrently, as this area of the brain matures the ability to reason better, develop more control over impulses and make better judgments also matures.

The different maturational timelines for the brain's thinking, emotional and survival centres present very important considerations for parents and educators alike. Knowing that the regions of the brain responsible for survival and emotion are in full swing long before the regions responsible for logical and moral reasoning can follow suit gives us a better understanding of why teenagers may do things that often fall short of our own adult expectations. Adolescents are at an interesting and paradoxical juncture in their lives – they can confront us with the physical and intellectual stature of an adult one minute and then act like a defiant and stubborn infant the next. Parents and educators will often need to stand in for the adolescent's developing prefrontal cortex and carefully monitor the freedom that teenagers long for; too much responsibility and independence may not necessarily be in the best interests of the adolescent brain and growing child.

One final and very significant consideration in all of this discussion on neural structures and development is that the entire process of neurological maturation appears to occur at a different rate for boys and girls. Not only does the female brain mature sooner but there is a great deal of research to suggest that the male and female brain maintain significant anatomical, functional and chemical differences,[79] which are explored in the next chapter as we continue to uncover how best to educate and raise girls.

Summary

This chapter has offered you an opportunity to imagine the unimaginable! We now have a basic understanding of how the brain develops from birth through adolescence, the various structures within the brain and where certain important functions such as emotional processing and thinking occur. The importance of experience in shaping much of the brain's neuro-architecture was also explored. Parents and teachers alike need to remember that full development of the brain is more a marathon than a sprint, with full maturation occurring well into the third decade of life. A young person's brain is actually a work in progress, and the role of parents and teachers is to help establish the best environments possible to support and foster healthy neuro-development.

3 Boys and girls *are* different

The bias against biological explanations [of gender differences] seems to have risen from egalitarian ideologies that confuse the Western concept of equal treatment before the law – the societal application of the idea that 'all men are created equal' – with the claim that all people are in fact equal. People are not born equal in strength, health, temperament, or intelligence. This is simply a fact of life no sensible person can deny.[1]

— *Professor Doreen Kimura*

Discussions related to gender, and in particular the differences between males and females, evoke great debate and great passion, and no area of potential gender difference attracts more controversy than the human brain. After all, the brain is integral in who we are and who we become; it is our source of intellect and emotion and some might suggest our soul. Therefore, to suggest that men and women or boys and girls might indeed have any measure of difference related to the gelatinous mass between their ears is very risky business. Yet, males and females alike seem to have little difficulty in accepting that:

- Women's hearts beat faster than men's, even during times of rest.
- Men and women metabolise drugs differently.
- During adolescence the basal metabolic rate is about 6 per cent higher in males and that difference increases to about 10 per cent after puberty. Girls also convert more energy into stored fat while boys convert more energy into muscle.

- Men, on average, have larger windpipes, 30 per cent greater lung capacity, relatively larger hearts, higher red blood cell counts, higher haemoglobin readings and consequently higher oxygen-carrying capacity.
- Women, on average, have more stored and circulating white blood cells, produce more antibodies and have a more rapid and effective response to infection.
- Smoking damages a specific gene in women, resulting in a fourfold increase in the likelihood that a woman who smokes will die of cancer.
- The respiratory system differs between males and females in both structure and aspects of function.
- Stomach bile has a different composition in men and women.
- Men's stomachs empty more quickly than women's.[2]

The list above is certainly not exhaustive of the many physical and physiological differences evident between males and females.[3] As a society we seem to have little difficulty in accepting those differences or the physical characteristics that distinguish us as male or female. This then begs the question as to why, when we look at the brain, or the possible gender differences that appear to exist in our neuroanatomy and physiology, that controversy arises?

Western society has a long history of disadvantaging individuals based on differences in race and ethnicity, culture, social class and gender. In particular, science has been used to justify and reinforce social and political power structures, as evidenced by the dubious assertions made in the past related to gender and sex differences in the brain where women were labelled somewhat lacking or deficient. Such assertions and beliefs about female neuroanatomy mirrored those raised against people of colour and notions of inferior biology were used to deny many aspects of equal opportunity.[4]

Given the past treatment of women based on unfounded 'scientific' assertions, the scepticism and caution that still exists today when considering the neurological differences between males and females is understandable. And while due consideration must be given to the role of environment and social learning in shaping our gender attributes, neuroscience continues to uncover a growing list of differences in the brains of males and females.[5] As Rockefeller University's Professor of Neuroendocrinology Bruce McEwen noted some years ago, 'we now are beginning to understand that the entire brain is, to varying degrees, a target of gonadal hormones and a potential site of developmentally programmed sex differences.'[6] That being said, there are also a few important considerations to be mindful of before identifying all that is neurologically *different* between girls and boys.

First, the male and female brain share greater similarities than differences. Nonetheless, we cannot disregard those areas that are different and consequently impact on health, emotion, cognition, behaviour and learning. For example, sex differences in the brain are present in the prevalence and onset of many neurological disorders including autism (4:1 ratio male to female), schizophrenia (higher incidence in males), depression (higher incidence in females), Parkinson's disease (more common in men) and multiple sclerosis (more common in women).[7] In terms of intelligence, contemporary science is quick to note that there are no significant differences between males and females, but while many neurological differences between men and women may appear tiny, they are no less real than other, more easily seen, gender attributes.[8] Moreover, it is important to bear in mind that 'even small differences between male and female brains can have major effects on gender differences in behaviour and cognition.'[9]

Second, we must also acknowledge that while structural and physiological differences exist *between* each gender, they also exist *within* each gender. Not all girls will be the same and this book is not attempting to suggest that there is some measure of a scientific 'absolute' regarding the female brain. The intent is to uncover a range of tendencies, or what Professor Simon Baron-Cohen refers to as 'statistical averages' that appear in the neurological make-up of the female brain that will aid parents and teachers in developing a better understanding of how to engage with girls in a positive and meaningful way.[10]

Third, although this book looks to identify the important neurological differences that set boys and girls apart, it also acknowledges the important links between neurological development and the social and environmental contexts that influence all mechanisms of the mind. Looking at the neurological differences between boys and girls cannot negate the reality that nature and nurture are intimately related. Research continues to identify the importance of the environment in relation to brain 'plasticity' and development and the interplay between heredity, biology, life experiences, cognition and neurodevelopment.[11]

Consequently, any discussion of brain difference must take into account how nurturing influences nature and how nature impacts upon the nurturing process. Such an approach affords a more holistic view to understanding the female brain and its interconnectedness with the familial, social and educational environment around it. It also forms the fundamental premise of this book which sets out to offer avenues for positively supporting and nurturing girls.

Finally, while I am continually amazed by all that has already been researched and written about the brain, that amazement is compounded by the knowledge that what we know about the brain is infinitesimal in comparison to what we don't know. Advancements in neuroscientific research and technology have created more questions than answers, and it may even be the case that many real differences between the male and female brain are not yet detectable with the brain-imaging technology that currently exists.[12] Therefore, we must be willing to accept new information as it arises and examine new findings with an open and yet analytical gaze. Interestingly, an open view to the type of information being presented tells us that no matter how much we want to believe that men and women are similar in various attributes and abilities, the human brain presents us with a different story or, perhaps, a story of difference.

Girls are different ...

> *... the more we look, the more we discover real differences in human organs as a function of biological sex. The brain is no exception. The shape and size of the brain, as well as the numbers of cells and the extent to which they are interconnected, differ between men and women. Scientists call these differences in anatomy sexual dimorphism (di means 'two' and morph means 'shape').*[13]
>
> — *Dr Marianne J. Legato*

In 2005, then President of Harvard University Professor Lawrence H. Summers made some rather interesting claims at an economic conference regarding what he referred to as innate cognitive and temperamental differences regarding the mathematical and scientific abilities of males and females. In essence Summers was suggesting that those innate differences might be one reason why fewer women show interest, or succeed in, careers like engineering. Needless to say, the uproar from his assertions went from some audience members walking out of his keynote to newspaper headlines and media coverage throughout the United States. And while Summers was also quick to acknowledge other factors impeding women in these fields, the genie was well and truly out of the bottle.

Fast forward to 2017 and the related downfall of Google senior software engineer James Damore. After attending a 'Diversity and Inclusion' summit, at the behest of Google, Damore provided feedback to his employers on aspects of the content he received during this experience. His feedback noted that men and women, on average, find different types of occupations interesting, that such differences in interests were underpinned by biology, and perhaps this was a reason for any hiring gap as opposed to discrimination or bias.[14] Unfortunately for Damore, his memo was leaked to the public and after much outcry from commentators, social justice advocates and others via social media, he not only lost his job at Google. Yet if we look at contemporary scientific evidence (which is, ironically, available on Google), we find that there may be some merit in their assertions.

One of the things that stands out across numerous studies and multiple data sources is that boys' interests tend to tilt towards things while girls appear more interested in people.[15] Such findings are consistent across cultures and are demonstrably evident in Scandinavian societies where years of egalitarian policies have reduced social and systemic barriers to female inclusion in traditionally male-dominated fields: there are still far more female nurses than male nurses and far more male engineers than female engineers in countries that have done the most to ensure equality of outcomes.[16] In other words, in spite of any attempts to socially engineer outcomes, males and females will likely engage in what interests them most and what they are innately driven towards doing.[17] Furthermore, linking the above with research in the field of neuroscience suggests we may need to rethink how we work with girls to enhance their capacities, skill sets and goals across any subjects and areas of interest in which they choose to participate.

At the risk of sounding repetitive, during the last few decades some of the scientific evidence acknowledging sex differences in the brain has been quietly understated or misrepresented due to its potentially contentious nature. Looking at sex differences in the brain allows us an avenue for discovering how biological, social and environmental influences act on males and females in different ways but it does not purport to be prescriptive for each and every individual.[18] Keeping that in mind, we can examine what the research does tell us and then consider how this may influence our own decisions and behaviour when educating and raising girls.

From the beginning, it is important to recognise that from conception, and for a few weeks, all brains have the same biological template and that template is female. At about six weeks after conception the endocrine system dictates the neural architecture of a human embryo through the level of pre-natal testosterone in the womb and pouring out of the testes if you are genetically male or dripping out of the adrenal glands if you are genetically female.[19] In other words, if the baby is a female (genetically XX) then the reproductive system produces no significant amount of male hormone. However, if the baby is male (XY), then his brain will be exposed to massive doses of testosterone (about four times the level experienced through infancy and boyhood).[20] It is this hormonal influence in utero that sculpts a female or male brain with all of the subsequent differences associated with growing up female or male. There are of course variations and exceptions to this which are touched on throughout this book, but generally speaking there is a specific biological foundation for sex differences in the brain.

Neuroscientists tend to agree that the shaping of the female brain is not as problematic or prone to challenges as that of the male brain because it is the 'default' patterning: as noted above, all brains literally start out female and it is high levels of testosterone that facilitates a change in much of the brain's physiology and neuro-architecture. The patterning of the female brain does not undergo as drastic a change as the patterning of the male brain. Some researchers also believe that it is this bathing of testosterone and shift in architecture that is responsible for differences in social behaviour and the number of genuine learning difficulties we see in boys.[21] Thus, the female brain appears to have a genetic predisposition towards a smoother progression of development than its male counterpart.

It is possible for the female brain to take a different pathway more in line with the development of a male brain. While androgens such as testosterone are perhaps the most significant determiner dictating the sex of the brain in early neural development, research also suggests that the neuroanatomy of the brain is also influenced by genetics and various hormonal factors including the proportional mix of estrogen and testosterone.[22] For example, girls who receive too much testosterone in the embryonic stage of development demonstrate some very interesting characteristics as they grow and mature.

Congenital Adrenal Hyperplasia (CAH) occurs in about one out of every 10 000 infants and appears to arise out of a genetic predisposition involving the adrenal glands resulting in embryos being saturated with unusually high levels of androgens or male sex hormones.[23] The physiological and physical results of this in terms of reproduction and the formation of genitalia can vary, however, even if a child's physiological and physical makeup remains markedly female, the brain appears to become masculinised. Girls who receive high levels of androgens in utero due to CAH tend to demonstrate behaviours and attributes more generally associated with boys. Girls born with CAH will be more inclined to participate in rough and tumble or physical play, be highly competitive, prefer stereotypical 'boys' toys', engage in substantially less play-parenting or nurturing activities, and have a better ability at solving spatial problems than unaffected females.[24] Quite simply, CAH girls act more like boys than girls and this is evident across cultures, thereby limiting any notion of socio-cultural influence.[25] Relatedly, many generations have often labelled CAH 'tomboys'.

Consequently when a young girl comes into this world with a 'female' neurological makeup, we must remember that this is the biological tendency, not the absolute rule. Internationally acclaimed author and therapist Michael Gurian also eloquently reminds us that 'brain development is best understood as a spectrum of development rather than two poles, female and male' and as such we will witness children 'who possess nearly equal qualities of both the male and female brains' or what Gurian refers to as 'bridge brained'.[26] If, however, all goes according to plan, when a girl arrives into the world her brain will possess a number of attributes that will develop and mature differently than those of the males around her.

Perhaps Moir and Moir provide a more succinct analysis of the significance of differences in noting that 'differences in the brain lead to sex differences in abilities, interests, levels of aggression, motives and emotional characteristics, and these in turn will influence what boys and girls choose to do in school.'[27] A look at some of the most recognisable differences thus provides us with some understanding of what it might mean to grow up female.

Viva la difference!

> *More than 99 per cent of male and female genetic coding is exactly the same. Out of thirty thousand genes in the human genome, the less than one per cent variation between the sexes is small. But that percentage difference influences every single cell in our bodies – from the nerves that register pleasure and pain to the neurons that transmit perception, thoughts, feelings and emotions.*[28]
>
> — *Professor Louann Brizendine*

It is not yet possible to identify the total number, and nature, of differences between male and female brains. For parents and educators, it is perhaps most helpful to examine a few noteworthy examples followed by an overview of what the research tells us. In the rest of this chapter we'll uncover a few areas which have immediate familiarity and offer some sense of how male and female brains are different. To better educate and raise our girls, we need to understand and celebrate these differences. However, it is important to reiterate that we use the phrase 'female brain' as a descriptor of those systems, structures, features and chemicals of the brain that appear different to its male counterpart and that males and females share more similarities than differences. Therefore, let's examine some of the things that we have known intuitively and anecdotally for some time and later move towards a deeper analysis of what it might mean to grow up with a 'female' brain.

In Chapter 2 we looked at current understandings of development and structures of the brain. For the most part this pattern of development is identical in boys and girls; however, what is different are the timing and stages of this process. A female brain does not mature along the same timelines as its male counterpart, nor does it follow the same developmental schedule. Indeed, the research continues to confirm that girls' brains mature earlier than boys' brains, and the male brain also ages and deteriorates faster.[29] Furthermore, brain development is best conceptualised as a process lasting from early periods of prenatal life through adolescence and into old age that varies for different neurological regions at different times and affecting different behaviours.[30] There also appears to be a lifelong relationship between neural development and functioning and the levels of various hormones.[31]

From the very beginning and throughout our lives, the neurological maturation of both boys and girls goes through a series of stops and starts and, as discussed in Chapter 2, much of this is attributable to the proliferation and growth of myelin. Of course, the chronological development of the brains of all children, or indeed all girls, will not be identical; genetics and the environment also have a role to play and will impact on the brain's development. Nonetheless, there are significant differences in neuro-developmental timelines between boys and girls that impact on cognition and emotion and may in fact work to disadvantage both genders in a one-size-fits-all approach to educating and raising children.[32] We explore aspects of this throughout the book, more specifically in Chapter 8, but we'll unpack some of the differences from this point forward.

Language, literacy and numeracy – and the brain

One of the first notable developmental differences between male and female brains is early language development. Girls will, on average, speak earlier and better than boys, produce longer sentences and also tend to have larger working vocabularies at younger ages.[33] Girls will also generally outperform boys on spelling, capitalisation, punctuation, language usage and reading comprehension tests.[34] Even as adults, women tend to do better on tests of verbal fluency and other related language tasks.[35] Consequently, girls tend to have an early advantage in communication and a distinct advantage in the early years of schooling where language proficiency becomes increasingly significant.

So, what is it about the female brain that differs from the male brain in terms of development, specifically in something as important as language development? While the neural basis for sex differences in language is only beginning to be understood, there are some interesting structural and functional differences that may have an impact on language development.

To begin with, the communication centre of the brain appears larger in girls and has a greater neural density. Language-based tasks are also processed in different regions and in different ways,[36] with one of the most striking differences noted by many researchers being that the function of language appears to be lateralised differently in the hemispheres of the female and male brain. Continuous bodies of research reveal that the left and right hemispheres of the brain are, to some extent, dominant or lateralised for different cognitive functions.[37] Significantly, only the brains of human beings have two hemispheres that differ significantly in structure and function and language appears to be our most lateralised function.[38] While neither hemisphere is completely responsible for language function, in females language processing tends to be equally distributed between both hemispheres, while the male brain predominantly uses the front and back of the left hemisphere.[39] Furthermore, the dominant language areas of the brain located in the left hemisphere actually mature earlier in the female brain. There are also differences in how language is lateralised between the hemispheres in girls and structural differences in the female brain that give girls a language advantage.

One of the structures that appears to be different between the male and female brain is the corpus callosum – the band of tissue that connects the right and left hemispheres. Specifically, the corpus callosum is a band of myelinated axons that acts as a bridge between each hemisphere and allows for the flow of information from one hemisphere to the other.[40] It is the primary pathway for communication between the left and right side of the brain and estimates put the number of fibres that transfer information between 200 and 800 million.[41] Not surprisingly, the greater the number of connections between the hemispheres, the greater the likelihood of better language function.[42] While a female brain is physically smaller than a male brain, the corpus callosum appears to be the same size or somewhat larger, suggesting that females likely have greater connectivity between the two hemispheres.[43] The corpus callosum in females is also more bulbous in certain regions than its male counterpart and is synaptically denser, resulting in greater connectivity between the hemispheres in females and by association greater efficiency and cross talk between each hemisphere.[44] Numerous studies also identify that in males the two hemispheres appear to be more lateralised and 'tend to function more autonomously and task dependently than in females.'[45] In simpler terms, the female brain seems better suited to process information and talk to itself.

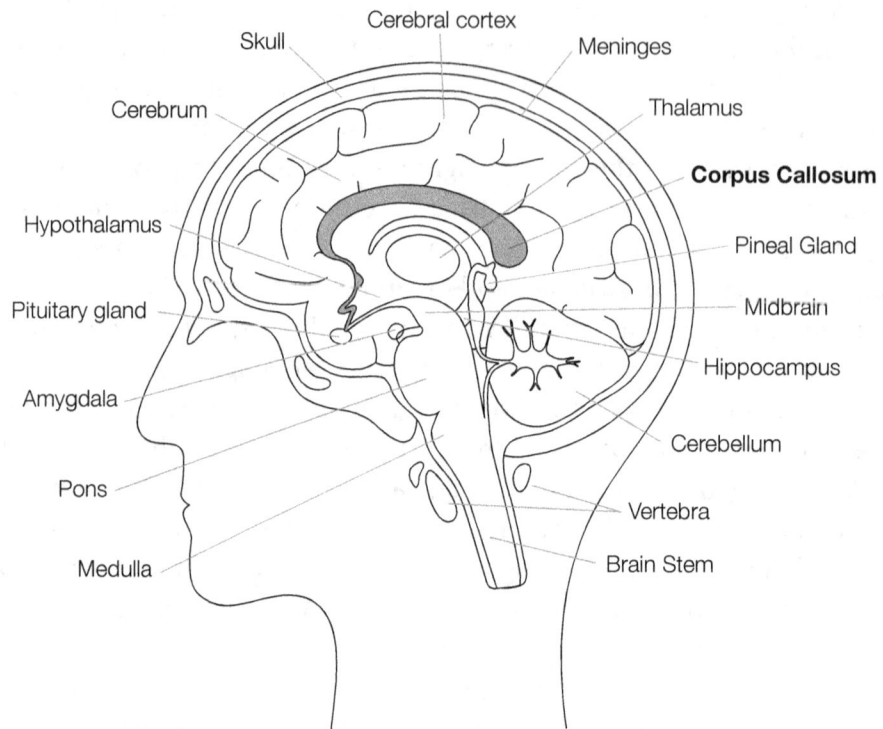

Figure 3.1 Corpus callosum

While the degree of connectivity between the hemispheres may not correspond to better performance in all cognitive function, it has been shown to be significant in terms of fluency, coherences and articulateness in language. Moreover, the evidence regarding language speaks for itself; women typically outperform men in tests of verbal IQ, demonstrate superior verbal fluency and are more proficient in a range of language related tasks.[46]

In addition to the lateralisation of language, there are other important regions of the brain that mediate language and are proportionally larger in females than males, including Broca's and Wernicke's areas.[47] As noted in Chapter 2, Broca's area is the area of the brain that helps to produce fluent spoken and written language: it is the grammatical and syntactic centre for putting language together in a coherent fashion. Wernicke's area is the region of the brain that processes specific elements of language – the place where language is understood. In addition to being proportionally larger in females, close analysis of Wernicke's area in women has identified that the neurons in this region are more densely packed together and have longer dendrites than those of men.[48] The extent to which structural differences contribute to language proficiency is an area of continued debate and research interest, but given the importance of neurons and dendrites outlined earlier, in other words, a female brain likely has greater expertise and ability in the verbal arena due to its neural architecture.

In practical terms, teaching literacy the same way to boys and girls may not be meeting the needs of either group. If girls possess some measure of an advantage in language and literacy, then they need opportunities to both extend those strengths in that area as well as opportunities to engage other subject areas using those inherent capacities. As research continues to advance, it will allow us to design learning experiences that better differentiate for girls and boys, for while girls may have some measure of advantage in language related tasks, similar advantages are not always evident in other areas especially those related to science and maths.

The participation of girls and women in fields involving particular aptitudes in mathematics is still a cultural concern, and as Professor Summers learned, remains controversial. The underlying reasons for the gender difference are many and complex, and we'll explore them in greater detail in Chapter 8, but for now we'll examine the neurological differences that may influence cognitive capacities. As mentioned earlier, there is a fairly robust corpus of literature identifying sex differences in temperament and interests, and an equally substantive amount of research suggesting some aspects of mathematical and scientific reasoning also differ between males and females.

Doreen Kimura, a world-renowned expert in gender and cognition, spent most of her life looking at the biological influences that impact on human cognitive and motor skills, and her work includes findings that males typically perform better on spatial and mathematical reasoning tasks, and are thus over-represented at the higher end of advanced math aptitude tests.[49] In addition, Kimura acknowledged the plethora of research across various continents and cultures identifying a universal male advantage on various aspects of maths;[50] something that is yet to be disproven. This further substantiates the idea that sex differences exist in the brain that can impact on behaviour and learning. These differences may not be confined to structural aspects of the brain, but may also include sex differences in grey and white matter composition, cerebrospinal fluid in the brain and hormone types and levels.[51] This research may suggest that while girls have made great leaps in closing a 'maths' gap resulting from past cultural or societal biases, the gap in some areas of maths remains constant and may have a biological basis. We will look at this in more detail when we look at how we might enhance aspects of 'schooling' for girls in Chapter 8. In the meantime, let's examine other neurological differences between boys and girls that impact on behaviour and learning. Specifically, let's take a look at differences in how the male and female brain deal with emotion.

Emotions: the heart of the brain

In 1992 John Gray released a book that became a best seller and fodder for talk show hosts, comedians and self-professed relationship gurus. Almost three decades later, *Men are From Mars, Women are from Venus* continues to attract legions of supporters who can relate to Gray's observations. And while Gray's work is a fairly light-hearted and simplistic approach to sex differences, a great deal of research has identified differences in the processing of emotions and the operation of the limbic system in males and females.

As noted in the previous chapter, the limbic system includes the hypothalamus and amygdala and several other important areas of the brain. If the frontal lobes are the CEO of the brain then the limbic system is the 'heart' of the operation. Hunger, thirst, sex, pleasure, fighting, and fleeing are moderated in the limbic system. The limbic system also drives our responses to various stimuli; it regulates our moods and physiological responsiveness to various situations and in many circumstances can actually shut down thinking. And research has shown that men and women differ in how they process emotion, how they perceive emotionally evocative cues, how they express emotion and how their respective brains activate various limbic structures.[52] There is also evidence of these differences in children from a very young age, which have implications for how we work with both girls and boys.[53]

One of the first differences related to emotion and also to learning occurs in utero. In 1925, Albrecht Peiper, a Leipzig University pediatrician, conducted a series of experiments to determine whether or not a baby could hear while still in the uterus. Peiper found that not only could they hear but they also exhibited 'habituation'– a type of learning in which the repeated exposure to a particular stimulus decreases the strength of a response. Simply stated, the brain will recognise a repeated non-threatening or seemingly unimportant stimulus and ignore it.[54] Peiper monitored fetal movement by visually confirming a prenatal response to outside stimuli (he observed 'kicking' movements in the abdomen after an automobile horn was sounded),[55] and while somewhat crude, Peiper's research is now verifiable via ultrasound and fetal heart rate monitors which have confirmed that babies begin to respond to sounds at around five months of age. Interestingly, 'habituation' appears in girls earlier than boys, demonstrating that even prior to birth a girl's neural system is on a different developmental schedule than that of a boy.

Post-birth, a baby girl's limbic system continues to mature and work differently than that of a boy. Obviously, at this stage nurture begins to play a powerful role in the expression of emotional characteristics, but it is significant to note that many of the differences between boys and girls are evident too early in life to be associated with nurturing. Among infants as young as one to three days old, girls will respond with greater frequency and attention to various social stimuli including a human voice or face.[56] Girls will also make eye contact sooner and for longer periods of time, demonstrate greater degrees of empathy and by the age of four are better at recognising facial expressions and reading the emotional signs associated with various facial gestures.[57]

These differences are but a small sample of how girls and boys respond differently to the world around them at a very early age. While one of the least understood aspects of sex differences in the brain is sensory stimulation and how the brain processes emotion, research has shown that females tend to be much more efficient at processing and dealing with their own emotions as well as the emotions of others. In his groundbreaking work entitled *The Essential Difference: The Truth About the Male and Female Brain*, Professor Simon Baron-Cohen of Cambridge University describes how the female brain is predominantly hard-wired for empathy and emotion and therefore better at dealing with emotion and emotive responses. He notes how the amygdala of boys and girls show a different pattern of responsiveness to emotive stimuli, and how structural differences in the corpus callosum and massa intermedia (an area which connects the two sides of the thalamus) allow for better overall processing of emotion in the female brain.[58]

Neuroscientists Ruben and Raquel Gur of the School of Medicine at the University of Pennsylvania and their colleagues have conducted research showing that the processing of emotional stimuli and the verbal articulation of emotions happens with greater proficiency and expediency in the female brain.[59] Dr Leonard Sax has elaborated further by demonstrating that as girls mature, a larger fraction of the brain activity associated with negative emotions shifts from the amygdala to the cerebral cortex (the area of the brain associated with higher order cognitive functions).[60] This does not happen for boys, and as such during mid-adolescence we see teenage girls able to use, with greater ease, the area of their brain responsible for reflection, reasoning and language to articulate feelings and emotional status.

This apparent facility for processing emotion that girl's display can also be a curse as well as a gift. The emotions of girls are often played out in very problematic arenas ranging from depression to self-harm to relational aggression, and as such need to be a central focus for enhancing the lives of the girls around us. We will explore this in greater detail in chapters 5 and 6, but for now let us examine one final difference which will help to further substantiate sex differences in the brain.

Size doesn't really matter ... but other things do

One of the most easily discernible differences between male and female brains is size: the male brain is larger than the female brain. As children grow and mature into adults, brain size and mass generally parallel that of body size; men are generally larger than women and thus tend to have bigger brains.[61] Size doesn't really tell us much about whether the brain works differently, or indicate greater cognitive ability,[62] but a bigger brain may in fact be one of the reasons boys appear more susceptible than girls to various developmental and cognitive disorders.[63]

As noted earlier, the female corpus callosum appears to have a greater number of connections between the two hemispheres of the brain. The female brain also appears to have a greater volume of grey matter in certain regions and more extensive and intricate communications between brain cells, particularly in the prefrontal cortex (the executive centre or CEO of the brain responsible for decision making and judgment). There is also a faster rate of blood flow in the female brain and some scientists believe that this is a direct result of the intricate web of neural connections found in the female brain.[64] The flow of blood to the brain is an important consideration, as the brain requires a great deal of energy in the form of glucose metabolised from the nutrients in the bloodstream.

As well as blood flow, male and female brains differ in the timing of the important developmental stage of synaptic pruning. As discussed in the previous chapter, the vast majority of the brain's work in pruning back unused neural connections occurs during adolescence and this in turn affects, and is affected by, other developmental factors such as hormones.[65] Studies have shown that significant differences exist between males and females in the timing of both synaptic pruning and expansion, and that the female brain matures earlier than the male brain.[66] This discrepancy in the schedule of synaptic pruning is another reason why developmental timelines and emotional maturity can vary significantly between boys and girls.

While brain size, synaptic pruning, neural density and the extent of communication between the hemispheres offer examples of structural and functional differences between the male and female brain, there are many other differences which I've summarised in the following table. The table is a broad overview of the important aspects of sexual dimorphism (structural physiological differences according to sex) in the brain as identified by medical and scientific research that serves as a foundation for the more detailed discussions later in the book.

Table 3.1 The sexually dimorphic brain[67]

Prominent structural considerations	Function	Gender differences	Significance
Amygdala	Part of the limbic system involved in emotional processing.	Larger in males. The amygdala in males has also demonstrated a different pattern of neural responsiveness to emotional stimuli as compared to females.	Some research suggests a larger amygdala helps make males more aggressive; this may be due to the fact that the amygdala is rich in testosterone receptor cells.
Anterior cingulate cortex	Acts almost like an assistant to the prefrontal lobes and helps to focus attention and tune in to our own thoughts. It's also the worry wart, fear-of-punishment area and centre of anxiety.	Found to be proportionally larger in females and with greater neural density.	Females better equipped to process emotion and focus attention and motivation while also being prone to anxiety and ruminating over negative thoughts.
Cerebellum	The cerebellum contains neurons that are extensively connected to other parts of the brain and spinal cord. This region coordinates smooth, precise movement and balance. It also coordinates thought processes.	Stronger connecting pathways in female brain between brain parts.	Females have superior language and fine motor skills.

Corpus callosum	Primary pathway for communication between the two hemispheres of the brain.	Given relative brain size, the corpus callosum appears proportionally larger in females with greater synaptic density.	Females able to coordinate the two sides of the brain better and use the entire cerebrum more efficiently. Female superiority at language-based tasks and the processing of emotion partially attributable to this region.
Frontal lobes	The 'CEO' of the brain. The prefrontal cortex is directly connected to every distinct functional region of the brain. The prefrontal lobes also help to mediate and inhibit emotional responses.	This region develops and matures earlier in females and is generally more active. Recent research has identified that these regions are functionally different in males and females.	Verbal communication skills are significantly improved in females as is the likelihood of girls being able to reflect and make responsible decisions at an earlier age.

Hemispheres of the brain	The brain's hemispheres are often characterised by functions performed in particular regions.	Differences in size, number of neurons in particular regions, and where particular tasks are performed. Left hemisphere larger than right in females.	In females the left cerebral cortex is thicker. The mechanics of language engage front of left hemisphere, while vocabulary work engages front and back of both hemispheres. Visual or spatial perception engages front and back of both hemispheres and emotions are activated in both hemispheres of the female brain.
Hippocampus	A pair of curved structures under the inner surface of the temporal lobes that run along each lateral ventricle of the brain. The hippocampi play a key role in the formation and retrieval of long-term memories stored elsewhere in the brain.	Significant difference in size: larger in females. Functional difference between males and females, with the number and speed of neuron transmissions higher in females.	Increased memory storage in females.

Hypothalamus	Often called the brain's 'brain', the hypothalamus is important for emotional and homeostatic regulation. It is connected to the hippocampus and seems to be involved in everything including thirst, sleep, hormonal secretion, heartbeat, breathing and temperature; also controls arousal and attention to stimuli.	Female and male cell structures and patterns significantly different: denser in males. This structure also starts the flow of reproductive hormones earlier in females. Testosterone required to enhance libido via the hypothalamus.	Males possess a greater and more constant sex drive due to larger and more constant amounts of testosterone.
Pituitary gland	Secretes hormones influencing growth, metabolism, and activity of other glands. The pituitary gland activates the adrenal gland in response to stress or fear as well as producing fertility hormones.	Likely more strongly relays fight-or-flight data from hypothalamus to endocrine gland in males. Activates the maternal instincts in females.	Males' fight-or-flight response is more rapidly engaged while females rely on this region for enhancing nurturing and bonding behaviour.

Thalamus	Regulates emotional life and physical safety; processes incoming sensory information from all senses except smell; directly or indirectly involved in almost every regulatory activity in the body	Processes data faster in females, especially at certain times in menstrual cycle.	Greater stress and activity in female thalamus at varying times during menstruation.
Cortisol	Hormone secreted by the adrenal gland during stressful situations. Helps to activate fight or flight responses.	Levels will vary between males and females where females often have elevated levels of cortisol through the day.	Gender differences demonstrated in emotional processing and behaviour. While cortisol is often elevated in females they tend to process it better and tend and befriend rather than fight or flee.
Estrogen	Generally described as the female sex hormone. Helps shape gendered neural architecture of brain in utero.	Much more functionally present in females.	In females, estrogen lowers aggression, competition and self-reliance. Also promotes brain cells to be more active when levels are high allowing the brain to be more alert and absorb a greater amount of information.

Metabolic rate	Part of the biological process of converting food nutrients to energy.	Female expenditure of energy is lower than male's. Glucose metabolic activity in regions of the brain varies between males and females.	Females appear to expend less energy when activating regions of the brain responsible for processing emotions: ie. Females process emotional stimuli more efficiently.
Melatonin	Hormone synthesised from serotonin in the pineal gland. Regulates sleep and circadian rhythms and therefore can impact on moods.	At various times of the day, particularly in the evening, females will have higher concentrations of melatonin.	Impacts male and female moods and can also impact sleep patterns especially during adolescence; elevated melatonin makes falling asleep easier.
Neuro-transmitters	Neurotransmitters are the chemical messengers of the brain. They facilitate or inhibit impulses at the synaptic level of brain functioning. Commonly known neurotransmitters include serotonin and dopamine.	Prevalence and availability of certain neurotransmitters varies in males and females.	Differences in how each gender processes data and regulates mood.

Oxytocin	Hormone secreted by the pituitary gland. Promotes bonding and attachment.	Much more functionally present in females. Testosterone in males blocks the effects of oxytocin while estrogen enhances the effects of this hormone	Assists in childbirth and lactation and likely strengthens bonds between an infant and mother. Females have greater sensitivity to touch due to the effects of oxytocin and high levels of estrogen. May also be involved in bonding aspects of relationship building.
Prolactin	Hormone secreted by the pituitary gland. Associated with the production of tears as well as bonding and milk production.	Boys and girls have equal amounts until about age twelve when levels plummet in boys as testosterone levels rise.	Grieving patterns and behaviours different between males and females.
Testosterone	Male sex hormone. Principal factor in shaping sex differences in brain organisation.	Much more functionally present in males.	Range of influences, most notably that of exacerbating aggression when levels are high.

Summary

Boys and girls are different! The preceding chapter has provided some insights into the structural and functional differences between male and female brains, and while neuroscientists continue to uncover further differences and their effect on haviour and learning, we can what we know now to better understand and educate our girls. These insights are not exhaustive but instead are representative of some of the differences parents and teachers encounter when educating and raising girls. They help to establish a framework for examining how differences play out in the environmental milieu we call 'girlhood'. The following chapter more closely examines the passage from infancy through childhood to adolescence, and how the differences in a girl's brain influence the process of growing up female.

4 The developing brain and growing up female

New sciences that will not be submerged in politics any longer have made it very possible to know our daughters from the inside out. Distinctions like nature vs. nurture become relatively trivial ... what comes to matter most is the knowledge of how a girl's brain, hormones, physiological development, within her everyday environment, are affecting her life.[1]

— Dr Michael Gurian

I have a beautiful daughter whose move from infancy to childhood to adolescence and now adulthood seems to have happened in a heartbeat. She is the eldest of my two children and from the moment she arrived she began to teach me many things about what being a father was all about, but more importantly, what fatherhood meant in terms of raising and caring for someone growing up female. I only wish that from the beginning I had known what I know now, as I think the road we have travelled together thus far may have been smoother. I hope that the information I present in this chapter, and indeed throughout this book, might make your journey of educating and raising girls less bumpy.

As I noted earlier, it is somewhat challenging for a male to describe what it might be like to grow up female; that has not been my personal experience so I am bound to comment as an observer. However, I am also a researcher and have spent most of my life studying child development, so the framework of this book is informed by taking those experiences and levels of expertise and linking them with what neuroscience tells us about the interplay between the brain, hormones and developmental stages in a young person's life.

Most of us are generally aware of the physical and emotional changes we see as girls move through various stages of life. However, scientific and technological advances have provided us with greater insights into how the brain changes and the impact of this on various aspects of thinking, feeling, behaviour and learning. Therefore, if we pay attention to the quote above and take the opportunity to look at what science has to tell us about what happens to girls neurologically and physiologically as they grow and develop, then we may have a greater understanding of how we can influence their lives in a positive manner.

Infancy and toddlerhood

As we noted in Chapter 3, differences between male and female brains are evident from the first trimester, and this translates to differences in behaviour that is noticeable not long after birth. As explored in the previous chapter, one of the most immediate things a female brain compels an infant to do is study the faces of the people she encounters.[2] For many years it was insisted that all babies are born with a need for mutual gazing with the people around them, but research now suggests that from the earliest stages in life, boys and girls are pre-programmed for temperamental differences and different responses to the world around them. Before any significant measure of socialisation can take place, males and females demonstrate distinctive behaviours, with infant boys tending to show greater interest in their surroundings and things while girls focus on the people around them.[3] And while as children grow, nurture begins to play a role in such observed differences, there are a number of neuroscientifc reasons why there is more than nurture at work here.

First, as we said in the previous chapter, the brains of boys and girls grow at dramatically different rates. Girls' brains mature much earlier than boys' by anywhere from two to four years depending on which brain structure we are talking about.[4] It also appears that the hemispheres of the female brain grow more quickly, with the left hemisphere in particular developing much faster in females.[5] The left hemisphere of the brain will also grow to be larger than the right in females while the right side of the male brain will become larger than the left.[6] The potential significance of this lies in what neuroscientists refer to as the *lateralisation* of brain function.

Brain lateralisation is still a relatively new field of research and the day-to-day implications of lateralisation are not yet well understood. However, scientists do know that certain regions within the brain are responsible for various functions and gender differences manifest themselves in how males and females engage with the world around them.[7] For example, the left hemisphere has been identified as the fundamental region for comprehension and processing language. In early infancy girls show left hemisphere dominance for speech perception and as they mature they begin to use both hemispheres for most language activities.[8] Such early dominance in this area is evident in that girls' oral language skills and the associated capacity to communicate occurs considerably earlier than most boys. Couple this with the knowledge that a fetal girl's brain develops greater neural connectivity in the communication centres and areas that process emotion and it should not come as a surprise that for an infant girl, people and connecting to those people are primary behavioural characteristics and social imperatives.[9] It therefore follows that for infant girls, connecting and bonding via facial expressions is of paramount importance for nurturing happy, healthy girls. As neuropsychiatrist and author Louann Brizendine states, 'take away the signposts that an expressive face provides and you've taken away the female brain's main touchstone for reality'.[10]

These visible early differences in communicative abilities, emotional processing, brain lateralisation and a young girl's sensitivity to facial expressions has been linked to her naturally lower levels of testosterone. Studies have shown that because the female brain is not immersed in high levels of testosterone in the womb, a girl arrives in the world better at reading faces, hearing human vocal tones and empathising with others.[11] Long before any measure of socialisation has taken place, infants and toddlers identified as having lower fetal testosterone have demonstrated higher levels of eye contact, better communication skills and larger vocabularies.[12] Again, we are outlining 'tendencies' here, not biological absolutes: boys do of course show these types of skills, but girls demonstrate them more frequently and to a measurably greater extent.

Michael Gurian describes this need for connecting with people as an 'intimacy imperative'. He suggests that while boys also need to forge connections with people, the female brain is programmed for social contact and fostering relationships, and connecting with others is perhaps the most important aspect of a girl's emotional wellbeing.[13] Others have echoed such sentiments and noted that the successful and healthy development of a girl's sense of self is underpinned, even in the earliest days of life, by a connection with and response to the emotional lives of others.[14] This extends into adulthood, where multivariate analyses of sex differences in personality traits have found females to be more nurturant, warm, altruistic, tender-minded and open to feelings and aesthetic experiences.[15] These are all important characteristics for fostering relationships which are explored in more detail in Chapter 6.

As a girl moves through infancy into toddlerhood, her need for connecting with people becomes ever more apparent. A primary factor in this early deep-seated move towards bonding and connecting with others possibly lies in a developmental phase known as *minipuberty* or *infantile puberty*.[16] During the first couple of years of life, the brains of both boys and girls are marinated in high levels of sex hormones. For boys this time of neural testosterone saturation lasts about nine months, while in girls, the ovaries will produce adult levels of estrogen for about twenty-four months.

Simply stated, high levels of estrogen stimulate the growth and development of neurons that further enhance a girl's neural circuitry and capacities for observation, communication, emotional processing, empathy and relationship building.[17] In other words, there appears to be a genuine developmental and neurological foundation for a girl's desire for social bonding and connecting with others which is often demonstrable through her play behaviour and how she engages with people and the environment around her.[18]

It should come as no surprise that boys and girls engage with the world differently as toddlers. Anyone who has ever raised, lived or worked with small children has witnessed differences in how boys and girls play. Given that much of children's play involves communication, role-taking and cooperation, it is not surprising that differences in play mirror the sex differences in the development of socio-cognitive skills that we have discussed. Boys are more likely to be aggressive, competitive, boisterous and prefer toys that make noise and can be manipulated (a diplomatic way of saying pulled apart or destroyed),[19] while girls tend to be more sociable, passive, talkative and show greater capacities for listening, concentrating and paying attention.[20]

Plenty of research also suggests that these variations in attributes of play help to explain gender segregation in playmates.[21] In all settings where social groups are large enough to permit choice, boys will mainly choose to play with boys and girls will choose to play with girls. This is a widespread phenomenon across cultures and also many primate groups, suggesting that such differences are innate and not solely determined via socialisation.[22] Moreover, in the instances where studies have attempted to disrupt same-sex play groups, the preferences appear difficult if not impossible to change.[23] Considering these innate differences, we should be mindful of the social and physical wellbeing of boys and girls in mixed play groups.[24] Again, this isn't anything new for most parents and teachers. Decades of evidence suggests that we reconsider any misguided notions of play as nothing more than a cultural construction and rethink how we organise, and what we expect, from learning and play environments for young children. Remember, there is strong evidence to suggest that differences in patterns of play between girls have biological and neurological foundations.[25] Indeed, even when girls use fantasy as a modus operandi for playing we see gender differences in how they engage in the world around them.

Pretend play is another aspect of normal child development where the differences between boys and girls are evident, with girls' pretend play involving more cooperative role playing and relationship building with imaginary companions.[26] To this end, it should be apparent that girls require appropriate responses and attention from parents, caregivers and teachers from the earliest stages of life and that these responses will have gender specific attributes, something we will turn to in more detail in further chapters. Now, however, we'll consider adolescence, and the gender specific behaviour and needs that arise then as a result of sex differences in the brain.

Childhood

What, in age terms, do we mean by childhood? Depending on the disciplinary field, childhood has different benchmarks. In neuroscientific terms, the first few years of life involve a great deal of developmental activity which, barring any measure of trauma or disease, plateaus somewhat between the ages of four and five for all children.[27] We can therefore use this timeframe to demarcate a shift from the early days of toddlerhood to childhood.

In neuro-developmental terms, most of the hard work of brain development occurs before a child's fourth birthday, and is followed by a time of continued growth and consolidation through the childhood years until the onset of pubescence. In essence, the early years are a crucial time for brain development where the foundations for future maturation and growth are put in place. As a girl moves into childhood these foundations require further development given that the limbic system or emotional part of the brain is in full swing and driving a great deal of her behaviour and interactions with the people and environment around her.

There is possibly no greater evidence of sex differences in the brain than that which exists in the limbic system. The last few years of research have provided us with the knowledge that much of the emotional part of the female brain operates differently than its male counterpart,[28] and childhood is a time when a girl's limbic system plays an important role in shaping her responses to the world around her.

In Chapter 2 it was noted how the brain is hardwired for survival and emotional responses from birth. Between a girl's fourth and fifth birthday, the limbic system becomes much more developed and makes greater connections with the cerebral cortex, the region of the brain responsible for cognition or thinking. And as we've seen, important components of the limbic system are different in males and females.[29] For example, the hippocampus is not only larger in girls than in boys but it also appears to have greater frequency and expediency in terms of neural firing.[30] As one of the hippocampus's functions is memory storage, these structural and functional differences mean a girl may have better memory capacities than a boy early in life. Though there are other factors influencing memory, there is little doubt that the hippocampus plays an integral role in this ability. While the hippocampus presents us with one difference, there are many other differences in girls' and boys' childhood behaviour that can be linked to the brain.

As mentioned earlier, for most boys competition is an important part of their play behaviour, while girls tend to focus more on cooperative endeavours. Differences in these aspects of behaviour can be linked to the limbic system, as well as to various hormones and neurotransmitters. Developing relationships often relies on an individual's capacity to be cooperative, empathetic and sympathetic, prominent behavioural traits found in girls and resulting from characteristics of female neuroanatomy.[31] Studies have even shown that girls are twenty times more likely than boys to take turns.[32] On the occasions when boys and girls do play the same games, boys will have a tendency to compete with everyone while girls form cooperative friendship groups. Other research examining same-sex and segregated gender competition among children have also found that boys displayed more physical behaviour while girls were more verbal.[33] Sometimes, however, girls' ability to form connections can turn sour, and paradoxically be used to sever such connections.

Not unlike the infant years, much of a girl's childhood focuses on forging connections and building relationships. Her play patterns maintain important aspects of bonding and demonstrate greater emotional intelligence, and better skills at empathising and socialising, than those of boys. Girls also appear to develop greater inhibition skills and self-control, which researchers have attributed to early development and maturation in various regions of the cortex, and lower levels of testosterone.[34] This helps to explain a girl's capacity to engage in relationships with more apparent maturity and sophistication than that of boys, who tend to act impulsively and function within a 'dominance hierarchy'.[35] But this doesn't mean a girl's pathway to relationship building is unproblematic, for although she is looking to forge new relationships, a girl often walks a fine line between developing bonds with others and ensuring she is at the centre of those relationships.[36] This fine balancing act often sees girls use their emotional and language capacities as tools for subtle forms of aggression.

It seems odd to think of young girls as aggressive, but that has more to do with our conceptual framework for the word 'aggression' itself rather than anything else. All too often 'aggression' is painted blue and perceived in terms of fisticuffs, sporting prowess or even masculinity itself. The word itself comes from the Latin '*aggredi*', meaning '*to attack*', and it describes *injurious or destructive behaviour* more broadly, not just in a physical context. Moreover, while boys have more neurons in their motor cortex and will therefore react more readily to anger with physical responses, girls appear to have enhanced interconnections in the frontal lobes and verbal regions allowing them to use verbal responses ('You're not playing with us or coming to my party') as a mechanism of unleashing anger responses.[37] Therefore, we should remember that aggression comes in shades of pink as well as blue and *aggression in pink* is often perpetrated using emotion and language. This type of aggression comes far easier to girls than boys and can be at its worst when puberty sets in and girls move into adolescence.

Adolescence

Adolescence ... It is the best of times; it is the worst of times. There is arguably no time in our developmental history that presents as many opportunities and difficulties as adolescence. Parents and teachers have long lamented the difficulties they have faced with children as the move into the teenage years, and now neuroscience offers us some very interesting insights into why this time in our lives can be so challenging.

The term *adolescence* itself can be problematic as it is open to so wide an interpretation. In the context of this work, the word *adolescence* is placed alongside the word *pubescence*, which is actually a medical term denoting a change in an individual's reproductive organs. Interestingly, a change in reproductive capacity closely aligns with changes to the brain and as such signals the beginning of adolescence. Moreover, changes to our neuroanatomy further help to signify a transition from childhood to adulthood.

It is also important to note that for some girls, puberty begins much earlier in life than it did decades ago, and it is not always accurate to associate adolescence with the teenage years: girls younger than thirteen may find themselves in the midst of hormonal and bodily changes. That being said, the biological tendency for most girls sees puberty kick in somewhere between the ages of ten and twelve, with neurological changes gathering momentum into the teens.

And finally, it is also important to remember that while the body may change drastically following puberty, the brain will also change during adolescence, but much of this work is not complete for girls until the mid-twenties. This is not a uniform pattern for all girls and maturational processes will vary in duration between individuals, but for the most part a girl's brain will go through much of its restructuring during the teens and into adulthood. Therefore, while bodily changes as a result of pubescence generally take around four years, neurological changes extend beyond that time and girls who may look like grown adults are still undergoing extensive development in their neurological make-up. In other words, *what you see is not what you get!*

In Chapter 2 we looked at how the brain matures and actually restructures itself during adolescence, but it is timely to reiterate the following:
- Brain maturation occurs from the bottom up and around to the front so the last regions of the brain to mature are the prefrontal lobes.
- The limbic system (or emotional centre of the brain) will mature long before the prefrontal lobes and it will mature sooner in girls than in boys.
- Because the brain prunes itself and gets rid of unused neural circuitry, it is highly malleable and in a state of experience-dependant neural reorganisation. Simply stated, the environment and experiences girls surround themselves in can have a direct impact on how the brain shapes itself.

As we can see, adolescence is a time when the limbic system, and thus emotion, has an overriding influence over the prefrontal lobes. During the time of life when adolescents are striving to become independent, receive greater autonomy and responsibility and are in the midst of shaping their own identity, the very region of the brain responsible for many higher order skills such as analysis and responsible decision-making is not operating to its fullest capacity.

For parents and teachers alike, this suggests the need for careful consideration of the boundaries we set for young people: in some ways, adults need to act as the prefrontal lobes of adolescents and ensure that the balance between what adolescents want to do and what they can do is responsibly met. In terms of the developing female brain and adolescence, Dr Louanne Brizendine acknowledges the importance of this when she states that 'teen girl reality will explode, and every trait established in the female brain during girlhood – communication, social connection, desire for approval, reading faces for cues as to what to think or feel – will intensify.'[38]

Along with structural changes in the brain, a girl's changing body chemistry will influence the brain, and thus learning and behaviour, during adolescence. The primary chemical instigators are the hormones estrogen and progesterone, which turn the wave of pubescence into a tsunami of change. Hormones are literally mind-altering chemicals, and for the first time since infantile puberty, the female brain will be marinated in high levels of estrogen coupled with a rising tide of progesterone. This will resolve into repeated monthly surges of chemical upheaval that will render female-specific brain circuits far more sensitive to emotional nuance, often resulting in extreme emotional fluctuation. In essence, the level of estrogen and progesterone during monthly cycles will alter a girl's levels of confidence and self-esteem as well as impact on her hippocampus (memory and learning), hypothalamus (control of body functions) and amygdala (master control centre for emotions).[39] Citing an important study in the United States, Moir and Jessel note that:

> *It is essential to recognize that the hormones which induce bodily growth, breast development and menstruation are, at the same time, exerting their influence upon the brain, and therefore the girls' emotional and intellectual reactions.*[40]

The widespread impact of estrogen and progesterone on the brain during adolescence causes changes in how girls see the world and how they believe the world sees them, and also plays a role in a girl's resilience and capacity to deal with stress. A great deal of research tells us that for girls, relationships and relationship conflict are primary conspirators in sending a girl's stress system off the rails. We will look at this in further detail when we unpack the links between the female brain and emotions in Chapter 5 and relationships in Chapter 6. For now, we'll look at one last structural difference in female brains that influences behaviour in adolescence: the production of myelin.

If you recall from Chapter 2, myelin is a fatty material that acts as an insulator for the axons of neurons. The more myelin present, the more efficient neurons are at sending chemical messages to one another. Myelin will increase about one hundred per cent during adolescence and this increase will occur sooner in the female brain and most notably in the emotional parts of the brain first, giving girls greater emotional maturity than boys.[41] That being said, this advantage in emotional maturity occurs at a time when the inhibition and mediation of emotional responses through the prefrontal cortex is compromised; the higher order thinking areas of the brain mature last. The end result of this growth in myelin at the time of increased hormonal influence is often evident in adolescent girl's heightened emotional responses to seemingly mundane situations, as well as the use of emotions as a platform for aggressive behaviour.

The following table summarises the changes we have examined in this chapter, and offers an overview of what might be expected during this time of neurological maturation.

Table 4.1 A summary of neurological changes

Neurological changes	Significance of changes
Change in levels of estrogen and progesterone.	As noted above, estrogen and progesterone will directly impact on the hippocampus, hypothalamus and amygdala. Estrogen will impact upon almost everything in the adolescent female brain including responsivity to light and the daily light-dark cycle and bodily rhythms involving breathing, sleep, temperature and mood. Researchers have also found that high levels of estrogen result in: • Girls being socially interested and more relaxed with others. • Lower stress levels. • Sharpened critical thinking skills and emotional responsivity. • The activation of **oxytocin** (bonding chemical) resulting in more talking, flirting and socialising. • Higher levels of **dopamine** (pleasure chemical) and oxytocin. • Heightening of **serotonin** levels (calming chemical).[42] Conversely, low levels of estrogen have been found to: • Result in increased irritability. • Heighten stress levels. • Result in 'brain fog' or forgetfulness.

Changes to structures in the limbic system and cerebral cortex due to maturation.	• Heightened emotional responses. • Greater capacity for abstract thinking. • Drive for independence, privacy, self-sufficiency and autonomy. • Experimentation in social, moral, physical and emotional arenas. • Fluctuations in various neurotransmitters including dopamine and serotonin which will influence behaviour (attitude, confidence, self-esteem, self-judgment) and relationships. • Difficulties in areas related to judgement and responsible decision-making. • Acting on emotional impulse. • Greater capacity to process and verbalise emotions.

Adapted from various sources.[43]

Summary

In utero and into adulthood the brain is a work in progress. Much of this work happens in the early stages of life to early childhood and during adolescence. The timeline for much of this journey varies between males and females with most aspects of maturation occurring sooner in girls than in boys. This presents many opportunities but also some challenges along the way. By most measures girls are more proficient in oral language development and therefore aspects of literacy. And while the emotional regions of the brain mature sooner than they do in boys, the part of the brain that can put the brakes on those emotions will not fully develop until the third decade of life. Therein lie some of the challenges – an inability to temper those emotions can lead to an array of issues for girls and their parents and teachers alike. Couple this with the impact of changes in the levels and fluctuations of hormones and neurotransmitters and it should be apparent that early maturation is not without its pitfalls. Some of these are explored in greater detail in the next three chapters where we look, in greater detail, at emotions, relationships and contemporary problems for adolescent girls respectively.

5 'I love you': emotions and the female brain

> *... there's no getting around the fact that women have different emotional perceptions, realities, responses, and memories than do men, and these differences – based on brain circuitry and function – are at the heart of many interesting misunderstandings.[1]*
>
> — *Professor Louann Brizendine*

When I first entered the field of education as a teacher over thirty years ago, I taught in a coeducational public school in Canada. This school was in a neighbourhood of middle-class families and my students were in Year 7. I was green and lacking in experience, and the students knew it, but we got on very well. I will never forget an incident that I can reflect on now with greater clarity and understanding.

One day, a girl in my class approached me during a lunch break when I was on playground duty. She was very upset with another girl, described as one of her closest friends, who had caused her some measure of embarrassment and distress over something she said to another group of girls. I listened intently to the details of the story and was considering how to deal with the situation, when I asked a question that left me dumbfounded by its response: 'Can you tell me when all of this happened?'

'Oh yes,' she said. 'It was when we were in Year 5!'

Many parents and teachers have similar stories and as I visit schools and work with teachers and parents, one of the things I am most commonly told is that when girls become angry or upset, their memories are poignant and enduring. For boys, anger and frustration is often mediated immediately and physically. This difference in emotional responses is not only visible in times of frustration and anger, but also with other emotional responses and as such an understanding of emotions and the female brain is integral to enhancing our capacities to raise healthy and happy girls.

We have already discussed many of the differences between males and females in the limbic system, or emotional centre, of the brain. We noted how, from the earliest stages of life, the emotional part of the female brain matures sooner than its male counterpart, processes emotive stimuli with greater proficiency and expediency, and how superior language skills allow girls to articulate their emotions better than most boys. We also looked at how differences in the amygdala and other components of the limbic system operate in girls. The limbic system is an incredibly influential part of a girl's neuroanatomy, and so in this chapter we will look more closely at various emotional states, other important hormones, and the wider impact on girls both physiologically and psychologically.

If you recall from the last chapter, from birth females are actively reading faces and, by association, the emotional climate around them. Males do not seem to have the same level of ability to read faces, nor are they as proficient at identifying tones of voice for emotional nuance.[2] And while there is some disagreement as to the cause of these differences, studies of other mammalian species mirror human studies, suggesting that nurture is not the only factor at play.[3] Researchers have also found that males tend to have higher activity in regions of the limbic system involved with the perception of motion and action, while females tend to have far greater activity in areas involved with the interpretation of expression and the nuances of speech.[4] Moreover, while neuroscientists continue to look for causal connections between the activity of the limbic system and the expression of that activity in the day-to-day reality of growing up, we do know that there is no shortage of research, across cultures, identifying that on many levels emotions and the processing of emotions is different for males and females.[5] Importantly, the processing of emotions is also intimately linked with other attributes of the female brain, especially language ability.

Emotions, language, neurotransmitters and bonding

Language proficiency in the female brain is not only an important part of a girl's cognitive capacities but also a major influence on her emotional state. Again this starts early in life and is arguably something that never diminishes in its importance as girls mature into adulthood.[6] As a girl moves through childhood her proficiency of language is then followed with increased sensitivity in verbal and emotional neural circuitry during adolescence and earlier maturation of decision-making and emotional control in adulthood.[7] On most measures it does appear that links between language and emotion play a far greater role in shaping the interactions of life in the world of girls as compared to boys, who tend toward verbal avoidance and greater physicality.

In looking at the links between gender, emotion and emotional expression, some researchers have noted that because girls develop their language capacities quicker than boys this leads them be more experienced at articulating their feelings and more skilled at using words as a substitute for emotional reactions.[8] Deborah Tannen, Professor of Linguistics at Georgetown University and author of *You Just Don't Understand: Women and Men in Conversation*, has identified that females tend utilise 'rapport-talk', while males are 'report-talkers'.[9] Rapport-talk, according to Tannen, is a communication style meant to promote social affiliation and emotional connection and as such concords with the importance of empathy and relationship building in girls. And, as noted earlier, the capacity to bond with others through language begins at birth and is prevalent throughout a female's lifetime.

On average, the language and linguistic abilities of girls surpass boys' very early in life, and this early maturation in language development is evident in how girls use language and how language is an important part of their emotional 'being'. On average, girls will speak two to three times more words per day than boys and while boys will eventually catch up in terms of their vocabulary arsenal, the female brain will continue to outgun its male counterpart in speed and proficiency of speech and is one of the factors related to girls' greater success in most aspects of literacy.[10] Moreover, there appears to be another neurobiological reason for a girl's superior language skills: the emotional connection achieved through talking with others appears to activate the pleasure centres of the female brain, resulting in increases in dopamine and oxytocin.[11]

Oxytocin and dopamine are very important chemicals that influence the limbic system, and in turn, how people feel. Oxytocin, a sex hormone, acts as a neurotransmitter in the brain and plays a key role in sexual and social behaviours.[12] Oxytocin appears to have a far greater impact in females, and part of this difference is due to how it combines with various sex hormones – estrogen tends to magnify and intensify oxytocin while testosterone neutralises its effect.[13] Interestingly, while oxytocin is associated with bonding and exclusivity in relationships, it appears to only enhance aspects of bonding in females and has been referred to by some researchers as the 'cuddle chemical' or the fuel for a 'tend and befriend' response.[14] The 'tend and befriend' response can be triggered by fear and stress and is one of the most robust gender differences in human behaviour: a desire to connect with others, as opposed to fighting as a survival mechanism, is engaged far more in females than males.[15] The effects of oxytocin also fluctuate with the cyclical levels of estrogen during a female's monthly cycle and we often see this in behaviour patterns. When estrogen levels are high, oxytocin levels are also high and bonding, socialising and relationships take on heightened importance. Conversely, when estrogen is low, oxytocin levels may drop resulting in increased irritability and social isolation.[16]

Dopamine is another very important component of our neurochemistry, especially in terms of 'feeling good'. The central location of pleasure in the brain is found in the hypothalamus, where dopamine seems to have its greatest impact. Dopamine is also associated with the reward systems of the brain and often referred to as the 'pleasure or feel-good' chemical due to its capacity to intensify endorphins (naturally produced opiates) resulting in heightened feelings of pleasure.[17]

In spite of the fact that both males and females can experience the pleasurable effects of dopamine, such pleasure effects are triggered by different cues. For example, girls are more inclined to experience a burst of dopamine, and a sense of pleasure, when rewards are shared or prosocial, while boys show greater dopaminergic activity when rewards are selfish or individualistic.[18] And not unlike oxytocin, dopamine levels tend to be at their highest when estrogen levels are also elevated.[19]

Given the impact estrogen has on oxytocin and dopamine, it is worth exploring how it influences other parts of the female brain and, by association, behaviour. Research continues into how exactly hormones do regulate or alter mood and behaviour, but results so far suggest that hormones influence the communication between neurons. Coupled with the structural differences that sex hormones cause in the brain, it seems that these hormones produce differences in male and female behaviour through several channels.[20] Areas of emotional behaviour of particular interest in girls include anxiety, depression and how girls deal with stress and much of this can be linked to structures in the limbic system.

Negative emotions

In Chapter 2 we examined the important roles of the amygdala, hippocampus and hypothalamus in the limbic system. In both males and females, the amygdala serves as the emotional gatekeeper of the brain, and acts in concert with the hypothalamus to coordinate responses to emotional stimuli. The amygdala also acts as an early warning station for the cortex to size up emotional scenarios, analyse their significance and determine what course of action, if any, should be taken. A great deal of evidence shows that male and female brains have different patterns of amygdala responsiveness, and that the female's amygdala is far more easily activated by emotional nuance.[21] Moreover, estrogen and the female brain's relatively larger hippocampus allows detailed recall of pleasant and unpleasant emotional experiences with greater clarity and frequency, and a greater capacity to move those memories into long term storage areas of the brain.[22] (Remember: *"Can you tell me when all of this happened? Oh yes, it was when we were in grade five!"*)

There is one situation, though, in which males appear to have an equally vivid memory of unpleasant experiences: when it involves an aggressive threat. But while males and females report feeling similar levels of anger when threatened, the expression of anger and physical aggression is greater in males – in heightened and stressful situations males tend to act out (fight and flight) while females tend to act in (tend and befriend).[23] This difference has been linked to testosterone and a larger amygdala in males.[24] The female brain appears to possess a built-in aversion to conflict and jeopardising relationships, which is often played out in regions of the prefrontal lobes where anger gets detailed scrutiny and analysis.

What constitutes an aggressive act has also been shown to be different between males and females – studies from the United States have identified that females typically list a range of variables that contribute to the perception of aggression that men do not acknowledge.[25] And once the female brain decides to act on anger, this is usually done verbally, with an onslaught of words that its male counterpart cannot match in terms of quantity and speed.[26] Female aggression, particularly in terms of relationships, is discussed in greater detail in the next chapter.

While anger appears to affect male and female brain with similar frequency, anxiety and depression are much more prevalent in females. Not unlike other mechanisms of the brain, males and females have different circuitry to deal with safety and fear.[27] Women tend to demonstrate a stronger protective or defensive orientation with increased fearfulness, and as noted earlier, are more disposed to avoid conflict.[28] Some have suggested that this is part of an innate mechanism for protecting one's offspring.[29] Whatever the case, the female brain does appear to deal with fear differently, and the female amygdala is far more sensitive to a variety of environmental stimuli that triggers a fear response than that in males. The end result of this heightened mechanism is a predisposition to anxiety and depression.

Anxiety is almost five times more prevalent in females and depression is anywhere from two to four times higher than it is in males.[30] The difference in rates of anxiety and depression between boys and girls begins to escalate from the onset of pubescence, and while cultural and societal expectations may be a factor in both frequency and the diagnosis of anxiety and depressive disorders, the sex differences that do exist have been found across cultures in all parts of the globe.[31] This is a troubling reality for many girls, and while researchers continue to search for answers to the problem of depression in females, there is substantive evidence that a major contributing factor to depression is hormonal fluctuations. Estrogen and progesterone are thought to be heavily involved, and they become more problematic when coupled with a female's sensitivities towards the nuances of social relationships.[32] Remember that the female brain appears to focus on people and relationships. In many circumstances this provides advantages in terms of emotional wellbeing and social connectivity, but such acuities towards relationships may also increase risk of internalising disorders such as anxiety.[33] This is even more worrisome for girls entering puberty, considering the changes that are occurring in the neurological architecture of the brain during adolescence.

Emotions and the adolescent female brain

As we examined in Chapter 2, the brain goes through some major restructuring and maturation during adolescence. Much of this restructuring occurs at a cellular level and impacts upon all parts of the brain. In other words, research supports what many parents and teachers have long suspected – the brain of an adult and that of an adolescent are different. The 'adolescent brain undergoes a massive remodelling of its basic structure, in areas that affect everything from logic and language to impulses and intuition.'[34] In addition, the brain seems to mature roughly from the bottom up and around to the front, and in different areas and at a different rate for males and females.[35] This has a profound impact on adolescent emotions and thought processes, as the greatest changes, which occur in the parts of the brain responsible for processing and mediating emotions, exercising self-control and judgment, making responsible decisions and organising one's life, start at puberty and last into adulthood.[36] As we noted earlier, the prefrontal cortex, which is implicated in behavioural inhibition and the ability to control emotions and impulses, is the last area to mature and the most important for comprehending the consequences of one's actions.[37] Compound this with the onslaught of hormones and the wealth of environmental stimuli available during puberty and it becomes small wonder that adolescent girls are prone to be highly charged emotionally, act on their emotions and unable to explain their actions when their behaviour appears inappropriate.

We must remember that because the prefrontal lobes mediate emotions and the emotional centre of the brain matures earlier than the 'thinking' centre of the brain, girls often lack the tools to deal with everyday feelings of anger, jealousy, betrayal, fear or other forms of emotional upheaval, and consequently vent their frustrations in more covert and hidden ways. Cliques, isolation, body language, popularity, and language itself are powerful mechanisms through which girls deal with emotions and emotional upheaval. Emotionally speaking, the importance of relationships shaping the female brain cannot be overstated, and as such receive greater exploration in the next chapter.

Summary

Human beings are, by their very nature, emotional beings. Regions of the brain associated with survival and emotional processing mature long before the analytical frontal lobes. In truth, if they didn't, we would not have survived as a species! There are a myriad of chemicals and neurotransmitters that play a part in how we 'feel' and behave, and these emotional mechanisms are different, and work differently, in males and females. One of the most interesting and challenging aspects of all of this for parents and teachers is the abundance of research noting how, as they age, females are more prone to negative affect and associated mental health and wellbeing issues. This becomes increasingly evident when girls enter pubescent and start their journey to adulthood via adolescence.

6. 'I hate you': relationships and the female brain

> ... the two sexes have different agendas in relationships. The female agenda seems to be to enjoy an intimate one-to-one relationship. Young girls, on average, are reported to show more pleasure in one-to-one interaction. They are more likely to want reciprocal friendships, and to express intimacy. For example, girls are more likely to say sweet things to one another (things you hardly ever hear between boys), or caress or arrange each other's hair, or sit close to or touch the other person. Girls are more likely to have their arm around the other person, and to make direct eye contact ... Another difference is the concern that girls show about the current status of their friendships, and about what would happen if their friendship broke up. And breaking up is used more as the ultimate threat: 'If you don't do this you won't be my friend.[1]
>
> — *Professor Simon Baron-Cohen*

Relationships are critical in the lives of girls. As the above quote illustrates, relationships are not only formed and expressed differently for girls and boys, but their relative importance is also different. And here, we are not talking exclusively about romantic or sexual relationships but rather, the connections girls make when forging friendships at home and school.[2] These differences, and the different significance of relationships for girls, can be traced back to aspects of a female brain and the processes, chemicals and structures that influence and shape relationships. As we explored in the previous chapter, emotions play an integral role in relationships, and the perception and expression of emotions is heavily influenced by structural and neurochemical differences evident in the female brain.

To remind us of the key differences discussed so far, here is a brief summary of points elaborated in previous chapters:

- Evidence suggests that the 'known' differences between the male and female brain influence how boys and girls, men and women, learn, behave, feel and relate to the people and world around them.
- The female brain appears to have a distinct advantage in language capabilities.
- The limbic system reads and processes emotions with greater detail and expediency in the female brain.
- Different levels of hormones and neurotransmitters impact on cognition and emotion.
- Right from birth, the female brain is on a course for bonding and relationship building.
- Neurological rates of maturation are different between males and females and also between different regions of the brain. For a good part of an adolescent's life, the emotional part of the brain can override the area responsible for many executive functions including responsible decision making, inhibition and mediation of inappropriate emotional responses and the capacity to comprehend the consequences of one's actions.

With these points in mind, we can now turn to the role and significance of relationships in girls' development. It's an important aspect of development to understand, as there is a substantive body of literature across a range of disciplines suggesting that perhaps the greatest challenge for parents and educators in terms of raising and working with girls lies in the relationships they build, nurture, and at times tear down.

There is no shortage of research documenting the highs and lows associated with relationships and girls. Of course, relationships are important for boys as well, but boys' relationships are often less personal, involve different mechanisms for bonding, are competitive and often based on a hierarchy with the main priority being some measure of shared activity.[3] Studies have also found that boys and girls view and act in their friendship networks differently; girls expect greater reciprocity of feelings and intimacy between friends and expect greater demonstrations of empathy, loyalty and commitment.[4] Moreover, for girls, positive relationships appear to be more inclined to centre on communicating and nurturing. That being said, relationships for girls are also often used negatively and as a means of isolating and ostracising others and as such it could be argued that the relationships of girls can be weaponised and by association be more emotionally charged.[5]

Emotions and relationships of course go hand in hand, but the neurological nexus between the two is still an area of great curiosity and research interest. The last chapter identified how the interplay of certain chemicals in the brain impacts behaviour; these same chemicals influence relationships as well. Some have argued that a girl's sense of self is actually centred more around relationships than that of boys and that females 'tend to measure their wellbeing in life in terms of the strength and quality of their close relationships, whether these be with kin, spouse, lover or friends'.[6] Understanding the female brain helps to explain why this is so.

If you recall from chapters 4 and 5, the female brain maintains different chemical and structural characteristics than boys that impact on girls' emotional lives. We notice this immediately from birth and throughout the early years of life. Many of these differences come about due to sex hormones.[7] For females, estrogen appears to be a significant player in how a girl thinks and feels, while progesterone can impact estrogen in numerous ways.[8] Sometimes described as the 'intimacy' hormone, estrogen interacts with other brain chemicals such as oxytocin to reinforce social bonding and influences serotonin (the feel-good neurotransmitter) resulting in girls being more interested in social signals and interactions, feeling good about themselves, being happy in relationships and having a passion for life.[9]

The nature and nurture of relationships

In the early stages of life from birth into childhood, the preservation of harmonious relationships is a priority for girls given the 'non-testosteronised', estrogen influenced female brain. Empathetic and approval seeking behaviour runs parallel to a neurological predisposition to nurture brought on by oxytocin and noted by some as an *'intimacy imperative'*.[10]

During this time in the lives of girls, cooperative behaviour and participation in joint decision-making is easily visible. Girls have been shown to have a greater propensity towards structured activities requiring cooperation and adult-regulated guidelines or rules. This preference is visible as early as age two, up to age seven and is not task determinant.[11] In childhood, estrogen levels are at their lowest and relationships are such that girls are incredibly devoted to their best friends while generally avoiding playing within the competitive confines so appealing to boys.

As already noted, the female brain appears to be especially wired towards forging relationships. Even at two weeks of age girls 'coo' more, look parents in the eye more and hold eye contact longer than boys suggesting an innate predisposition for connecting with others.[12] Girls tend to respond to distressed individuals with greater prosocial behaviour and are more responsive, and perhaps more sensitive, to social cues than boys.[13] Indeed, throughout the lifespan, females appear more adept in fostering, and more concerned with maintaining, relationships. Concurrently, it is safe to assume that when relationships are *positive* and all is well, there is little to be concerned about. However, when relationships sour or are potentially negatively influenced by the female brain's chemical and structural proclivities, problems can arise. This is especially true during adolescence.

When girls enter puberty and begin to move through adolescence, there are myriad factors, both biological and environmental, that can impact on their relationships. Of course, the social and cultural influences are powerful, but we are concerned here with the role of the biology and physiology of the brain. How does the female brain impact relationships, or more accurately, the neuropsychological aspects of relationships and adolescent girls? Perhaps at no other time can relationships have such long-term consequences on the overall wellbeing of girls than at this critical juncture of their lives.

One of the primary reasons why relationships can be problematic for adolescent girls lies at the intersection of the 'thinking' and 'emotional' brain. Adolescent girls are quite vulnerable to negative stressors because their frontal lobes aren't fully mature and as capable of mediating emotions as those of an adult. This situation also occurs during a time when there is a neurologically qualitative shift in the nature of social thinking resulting in adolescents being more self-aware, self-reflective and self-critical.[14] Adolescence is also a time where romantic relationships and sexual behaviour arise due to the physical and biological changes associated with puberty.[15] Indeed, puberty is the first step in the process of reproductive maturation and according to Dr Louann Brizendine, 'a girl's entire *biological* raison d'être is to become sexually desirable'.[16] Needless to say the neurological and biological complexities surrounding relationships, sexual or otherwise, are very profound indeed. However, through understanding the nature of these complexities we are better able to support girls and their relationships.

Sex hormones and relationships

Sex hormones are literally mind-altering substances that can affect moods, behaviour and consequently relationships. It is important to emphasise that a girl's relationships and social skills can be influenced by levels of these important neurochemicals during her monthly cycle. Consider, for example, that many parts of the female brain, especially the hippocampus, hypothalamus and amygdala, all part of the brain's emotional hub, are particularly affected by estrogen and progesterone.[17] Estrogen appears to play an influential role on the amygdala and hippocampus and as noted earlier also impacts on various hormones and the neurotransmitter serotonin, which is important for the regulation of arousal and mood.[18] An abundance of data also suggests that estrogen, or the lack thereof, is strongly implicated in the regulation of mood and behaviour and by association relationships.[19] During the first two weeks of the menstrual cycle, estrogen is elevated resulting in females being more likely to be socially responsive and relaxed with others; the last two weeks may see increased irritability and more negative emotions and thoughts.[20] And as noted above, there is an increasing body of evidence documenting the impact estrogen has on the hippocampus.

As we've seen, the hippocampus plays a key role in processing and storing memories which are important in terms of forming and maintaining relationships. Interestingly, the hippocampi in females appear to grow in volume when estrogen is elevated.[21] It is as if estrogen is expanding the power of the hippocampi to form memories which can certainly play a role in how relationships are viewed. Estrogen and progesterone also influence the female brain's response to stress and thus we must remember that the onset of puberty will often dictate differences in responses to many events in a girl's life, including relationships.

Moreover, and as noted in the previous chapter, the limbic system in girls will also respond differently to anger and stressful situations.

Avoiding conflict and a behaviour characterised as 'tend-and-befriend' are typical responses to confrontation while responses to stress can present themselves as anxiety and depressive disorders.

For adolescent girls, challenges in, and with, relationships are evident in tensions that can occur between their cooperative and collaborative inclinations and their desire for greater independence and autonomy. Adolescence is an important stage of development where both boys and girls are not only going through major neurological changes and maturational processes but are also working to shape their identities and become more independent. This drive for independence and autonomy in girls also occurs at a time when the power of peers has a tremendous influence on the day-to-day realities of life. Moreover, the interplay between a changing neurological and physiological make-up, a psychological drive for self-identity and the complex terrain of peer influence creates many potential challenges, especially with peers and parents.

The formation of peer relationships and friendships are a critical part of a girl's overall socio-emotional development. As noted, girls' friendships tend to differ from boys': girls tend to focus on quality of friendships over quantity, spend more time in relationships with a one or two best friends, are more prepared to disclose more about themselves with those friends and come to rely on their best friends for support and help in solving problems.[22] These types of relationships are very socially demanding. Girls are far more reliant on, and demanding of, a reciprocal give-and-take which is why they generally maintain only one or two close friendships at a time.[23] It is interesting to note that despite the high levels of intimacy and closeness associated with girls' friendships, those relationships appear to be more fragile than those formed by boys.[24]

The closeness of girls' friendship groups, characterised by intimate self-disclosures, expectations of loyalty and empathy along with a significant degree of emotional dependence and support on one another can lead to unrealistic expectations.[25] Arguably, the time and energy required to maintain the intimacy that characterises girls' friendships is more vulnerable to misunderstandings and relationship fatigue. Simply stated, it could be the case that, unlike in boys' friendship groups, girls care too much, and invest too much of themselves, in their relationships. Such large emotional investments in friendships may, therefore, result in greater distress and emotional upheaval, especially when expectations are not met or relationships are threatened.[26] Such intense interest and investment in relationships can be rewarding when all is well, but when things go bad the power of peers can have a tremendously negative influence on the developing brain and a young girl's wellbeing.

Aggression in pink equals 'mean girls'

Chapter 5 offered a cursory look at the differences in how boys and girls perceive and understand aggression. For boys, aggression is something that usually entails some form of direct physical action. Girls, however, tend to be less direct and certainly less physical and as such may appear more passive and 'nicer' to others.[27] However, there is a fairly substantive body of research that has provided important insights into female indirect aggression, which was initially termed by as '*relational aggression*' but has also become known as 'social aggression' and 'female bullying'.[28] In itself, relational aggression appears very sophisticated, often covert and can be more psychologically harmful than other forms of aggression.[29] And while both boys and girls practice relational aggression it appears to be much more prevalent with, and damaging to, girls.[30]

While relational aggression is most often associated with adolescence (the well-known 'mean girls'), it is observed as early as preschool in both girls and boys.[31] It is during adolescence and beyond, however, that it appears to become a far more prevalently employed by females.[32] Of course, relational aggression is not simply punitive: for adolescent girls, relational aggression can build bonds with like-minded peers and facilitate a feeling of inclusion and popularity in a peer group.[33] Bonding premised on relational aggression has long been a trope of books and movies and is a mainstay of any high school drama. However, while arguably a useful tool for fitting in with some peers, relational aggression is extremely problematic and worryingly destructive.

In her in-depth look at female aggression, Rhodes Scholar Rachel Simmons identified many studies in which children cited relational aggression as the most common hurtful behaviour enacted in girls' peer groups, regardless of the target's sex.[34] As noted above, relational aggression has been identified in preschool children but by age three more girls than boys are relationally aggressive; a gulf that only widens as boys and girls mature.[35] Some have suggested relational aggression emerges as a female behaviour in a patriarchal culture that discourages overt physical aggression in women and girls.[36] And while there can be no denying the power of social convention, research has identified this type of aggression across a vast number of cultures, suggesting its roots may be in evolutionary biology.[37] In essence, relational aggression may be the result of a long history of human interaction and as such be part of the hard wiring of the female brain.

Research links the increase in relational aggression in female adolescents with an increased focus on competing with other girls for romantic relationships.[38] Such inclinations appear to be evolutionary in nature: aggression in females has also been associated with mating, reproduction and infant survival.[39] And as noted, relational aggression if often used to establish peer popularity, social visibility and influence.[40] Relational aggression has also been associated with greater dating and sexual behaviour among those who perpetrate the aggression.[41] Taken in its entirety, the evidence suggests a seemingly innate predisposition for females to engage in relational aggression as a mechanism for bonding. Moreover, psychologists, counsellors, parents, teachers and students alike can all testify to being observers of such aggression in various social contexts and there is little denying its pervasiveness.

What exactly constitutes 'relational aggression'? It can take many forms and can be enacted indirectly (the 'silent' treatment) or socially (gossiping and rumour spreading) and often utilises nonverbal gesturing and body language.[42] But whatever the context or mechanism, the end target lies in what girls tend to value most – their friendships, social acceptance and self-esteem. In this sense, relationships are used as a battleground for aggression where exclusion, gossip, rumour, slander and isolation are prominent weapons for the aggressors. Perhaps confirming the well-known sterotype, the most common perpetrators of relational aggression tend to be popular, attractive and socially prominent girls.[43] Multiple studies have also shown a positive link between relational aggression levels and popularity among adolescent girls and that relational aggressiveness has been identified as a predictor of future popularity among girls.[44] This suggests there is a reward for being 'aggressive in pink' and that reward is popularity. Worryingly then, seeking popularity through manipulating relationships can be very pervasive and problematic.

Along with identifying the 'what' of relational aggression, the why of such endeavours has been important in research on gender differences in aggressive behaviour.[45] As noted throughout this chapter, gender differences are evident in a girl's relationship building and nurturance. These differences begin early in life and ultimately play an integral role in identity formation through adolescence. Adolescent friendships are far more intense and important in the lives of girls than they are in boys and as alluded to earlier it can be nearly impossible for a girl to define herself without including her friends within that description. The vulnerability of preadolescent and adolescent girls to relational aggression arises from precisely this centrality of friends and social relationships – again an importance that arguably starts from the female brain's capacity for facial recognition at birth and extends throughout a lifetime. To that end, relational aggression is very effective in its intent – it is used to climb a popularity hierarchy while simultaneously inflicting pain on the recipient; pain that can have long term effects both psychologically and neurologically. Neuroscientists have found that emotional pain arising from social exclusion activates the same regions of the brain that respond to physical pain – sticks and stones may break one's bones but relational aggression can be just as harmful.[46]

Another reason that relational aggression may become the particular province of adolescent girls is their early and superior proficiency in language and communication skills. At the heart of relationships for girls lies the capacity to communicate. Moreover, and as noted earlier, this seemingly innate need to communicate is a profound characteristic of the female brain. Early proficiency in language ability allows girls to develop skills for using language more subtly, manipulatively and indirectly than boys whose use of language for aggression is generally more characteristic of commands, threats, boasts, bragging or as a tool for getting someone to 'shut up.'[47] Concurrently, and as discussed above, a girl's vulnerability to being both a victim and perpetrator of relational aggression is compounded by the changing nature of friendship groups as girls mature.

Maintaining friendships and close relationships seems to be motivated on a molecular and neurological level and this appears especially true from puberty onwards.[48] As girls get older, sharing their innermost secrets and emotional self is paramount in close friendships, which can become ammunition for aggression when relationships turn sour. Therein lies a double edge sword for girls – sharing secrets and the intimate details of one's life feels good both psychologically and neurologically, yet it is also risky business with respect to the fluid nature of adolescent friendships and peer associations. Peers mean a great deal, and when relationships are lost the bottom drops out of some of the female brain's neurochemicals. Recall from the previous chapter that even talking can see increases in levels of serotonin, dopamine and oxytocin but these same chemicals seem to evaporate to make way for stress hormones such as cortisol when relationships sour or 'mean' words are said.

Confronting relational aggression

The challenge for teachers and parents is thus immense. Relational aggression is often hidden, yet of epidemic proportions. It must also be reiterated that it is highly destructive. As Rachel Simmons notes in her discussion of the hidden nature of relational aggression:

… friendship is a weapon, and the sting of a shout pales in comparison to a day of someone's silence. There is no gesture more devastating than the back turning away.

In the hidden culture of aggression, anger is rarely articulated, and every day of school can be a new social minefield that realigns itself without warning.[49]

Relational aggression can lead to serious emotional consequences including anxiety, depression, internalising problems, general social maladjustment, unhealthy parental attachment and by association low academic performance and poor life choices.[50] Girls experience feelings of hurt, blame, anxiety or depression more frequently than boys.[51] Therefore anyone interested in educating and raising girls must be vigilant in identifying any instances of relational aggression, and ensure that relationships are as positive as possible. They must also promote the healthy development of emotions and emotional intelligence as part of a proactive strategy, which becomes especially significant when looking at how girls shape their identity and navigate anxiety and stress when relational problems, or indeed other challenges, occur.

Summary

Relationships are critical in the lives of girls, and as they age, the nature of these relationships – and the ways in which they are nurtured or dismantled – changes too. More so than boys, girls put greater emotional stock into a few close relationships as they grow older and because of this they are more vulnerable to negative affect when things go wrong. When relationships are good, all is well but when relationships sour this can lead to an array of issues associated with mental health and wellbeing. Worryingly, relationships can also become a battlefield, where relational aggression is used to hurt individual girls and their relationships. For parents and educators, it is extremely important to be mindful of the relationships of the girls around them, and to watch for signs when things may not be going well. Changes in demeanour and behaviour often signal problems that need attention, and adult intervention may be required to ensure that girls get the support they need to successfully negotiate relationship troubles.

 'It's a girl thing'

Some girls manifest their depression by starving themselves or carving on their bodies. Some withdraw and go deep within themselves, and some swallow pills. Others drink heavily or use sex as a sedative. Still others refuse to go to school ... Whatever the outward form of the depression, the inward form is the grieving for the lost self, the authentic girl who has disappeared with adolescence. There's been a death in the family.

— Mary & Sara Pipher[1]

As someone who has worked in various educational contexts on four continents, I have had numerous experiences working with both girls and boys of all ages and their teachers and parents across various contexts and within many schools. In a previous volume of work focusing on boys I detailed an experience at a school facing innumerable problems with its male cohort from preschool to Year 7.[2] The boys in this school always seemed to be in trouble and breaking the rules. What I did not discuss in that book at any length was that while the boys created many headaches and were the focus of much attention, the girls also had challenges but they remained largely unseen. In a school of approximately 700 students where just over half were girls, over a third of these girls had experienced bullying and almost half were well below the state average in literacy and numeracy skills. Those girls were, however, compliant – sitting still in class and therefore presumed happy, healthy and scholastically sound. Their troubles went unnoticed.

Compared to boys, girls can present different challenges for parents and teachers at different times in their lives, and particularly in relation to many psychological and socio-emotional disorders.[3] When they are younger, any challenges girls do face can, like in the school noted above, go unnoticed or simply end up labelled as just 'a girl thing'. Unfortunately, and depending on the problem, such problems can manifest into far greater issues as girls mature. The quote opening this chapter offers a prelude into the difficulties many girls must navigate as they get older, and move though pubescence – a time when they are discovering who they are while striving for independence. This chapter explores some of the problems that arise for girls at a time when the body, brain and mind are in a state of biological upheaval and cultural influence.

Changing bodies and minds

Puberty marks a time of major upheaval as girls begin to grapple with mature feelings, expectations and bodily changes. Such changes are evident in body size and shape, hormone levels and brain anatomy and chemistry; changes in the reproductive system also mirror changes in the brain during adolescence.[4] For girls, many of these changes appear to be intimately linked with different facets of the emotional regions of the brain and personality features of the mind.

If you recall from the previous two chapters, a girl's monthly cycle impacts on the brain. Elevations in estrogen and fluctuations in progesterone intertwine with levels of serotonin, oxytocin and dopamine to create changes in mood and behaviour. Additionally, the major hormonal changes that occur after menstruation begins have been linked to a significantly greater risk of major anxiety disorders including depression.[5] Moreover, and until somewhere around her twenty-fourth birthday, a girl's brain is in a state of major reconstruction. During the teenage years in particular, the brain is hot-wired for emotion, while the rational part of the brain is being restructured and refined to be more expeditious and efficient.[6] For girls, adolescence involves a hypersensitivity to negative affect (emotional states), at a time when friendships, relationships and a desire to 'be an adult' become increasingly important and are at the core of her being. In short, the biological, neurological, social and psychological changes that occur during adolescence can become fertile ground for emotional problems.

To what extent the biological changes associated with hormones and neurotransmitters affect the brain as girls move through puberty and into adulthood is still not thoroughly understood. However, we do know that adolescents seem to be hot-wired for emotion, are prone to engage in risk-taking and sensation-seeking behaviours, and to misinterpret emotions and intentions of others and will make poor decisions. This occurs at a time when peers play a more prominent role in the lives of adolescents on a road to adulthood that is fraught with the potholes of identity formation, sexual curiosity and relational upheaval. And while boys face challenges during adolescence, the problems girls face can be quite different and tend to focus on notions of self and relationships.

If you recall from Chapter 6, the importance and influence of relationships on girls is far reaching. At puberty a girl's limbic system becomes highly responsive and sensitive to emotional stimuli, and negative experiences with others can create high levels of anxiety and stress; during adolescence emotions are extreme and changeable – small events can trigger enormous reactions.[7] This may be one reason why anxiety disorders are far more prevalent in adolescent girls than in boys; girls are at least twice as likely as boys to suffer from anxiety, depression and various associated disorders.[8] In fact, it is well documented that levels of neuroticism (the tendency to experience negative feelings such as anxiety, anger or depression) are far higher in females and that neuroticism becomes more pronounced from the onset of puberty.[9] There is some evidence noting sex differences in the neural correlates of neuroticism, but the full extent of such differences is not yet well understood.[10] What is fairly well established, however, is that neuroticism is the polar opposite of emotional stability. Those who score high in measures of emotional stability get upset less easily and are less likely to be emotionally reactive.[11] It is also well established that neuroticism appears to be one of the most powerful predictors of depression.[12] A tendency for experiencing negative feelings can lead to very destructive outcomes, both psychologically and physically.

Everything is *not* awesome: anxiety and depression

Depression and anxiety are common problems affecting the mental health of young people. While they are different conditions, they do commonly occur together.[13] These conditions are evident in a small percentage of children but their prevalence rises markedly from adolescence onward.[14] Approximately half of all mental health disorders in adulthood start by the age of fourteen, and at any given time 20 per cent of adolescents worldwide experience mental disorders, most commonly depression and anxiety.[15] Anxiety disorders in particular are one of the most prevalent mental health disorders and females are more likely than males to develop these types of disorders across the lifespan.[16] Sex differences in such disorders are strongly evident early in life, but by the age of six anxiety levels in girls are about twice as high as in boys.[17] These differences become far more pronounced around thirteen years of age, when most girls are midway through puberty.[18] As with many of the differences we have discussed, whether sex differences in anxiety are the product of nature or nurture is difficult to disentangle. However, there is some evidence that differences in certain neurotransmitters, sex and stress hormones and the limbic system may play a role.[19]

Given the significant changes in the bodies and minds of girls through adolescence, it is not unreasonable to suppose that girls may view the world and act in it differently than boys. For example, what is perceived as a stressor, and the response to stress, is different between boys and girls.[20] For girls, a key trigger for stress and anxiety-related disorders are their interpersonal relationships.

As we have discussed, female friendships are characterised by greater intimacy, caring, relationship repair and self-disclosure. This can not only put girls in a vulnerable position when relationships sour, but can lead to greater co-rumination or the sharing of 'woes', which can have negative consequences.[21] This could conceivably render girls more vulnerable to negative feelings and depression. Moreover, a girl's self-esteem can be especially damaged by relationship problems. This is especially worrisome given that, compared to boys, a girl's sense of self and self-esteem appears to decline in early adolescence.[22]

Technically speaking, self-esteem refers to our subjective beliefs about ourself or our sense of worth as a person.[23] In layperson's terms, self-esteem is how we feel about ourselves. Unlike IQ and various personality traits, self-esteem is not easy to measure using psychological instruments and tests, but it does seem to predict certain outcomes in terms of academic achievement, happiness, satisfaction in relationships and other related behaviours.[24] Aside from these visible outcomes, low self-esteem is a personal stressor that can cause high levels of the stress hormone cortisol, decreased hippocampal volume and associated deficits in working-memory and learning[25]. Perhaps more simply stated, the better we feel about ourselves, the better we are able to function, meet the challenges of the day and perform in most aspects of life.

Interestingly, traits predictive of positive self-esteem include feeling strong, independent and confident, which align more with notions of masculinity and appear to be more prevalent in the behaviour and attitudes of adolescent boys.[26] Moreover, because of the increased importance of peers and relationships for young girls, their self-esteem is also influenced by the perceptions, acceptance and respect from others. This is further exacerbated by an adolescent girl's preoccupation with body image and unfolding issues associated with identity.

Body image plays a major role in self-esteem in both boys and girls. At its most extreme, a preoccupation with appearance, especially perceived flaws or defects not observable to others, can result in body dysmorphic disorder (BDD).[27] The prevalence of BDD in adolescents is not well established, but historically speaking, adolescent girls typically have more negative associations with their body resulting in a plummeting sense of self.[28] Adolescent girls look, feel and move differently than they did as children and many girls spend more time in front of mirrors examining themselves than engaging in homework or other activities.[29] As a result, many girls invest in unrealistic ideals about how they should look, undoubtedly fuelled by a widespread cultural focus on female appearance, the idolising of popular celebrities, a preoccupation with taking 'selfies' and a 24/7 access to social media.[30]

Aspiring to look like someone popular or famous, or to hold unrealistic ideals about how one should look is far more prevalent in adolescent girls than in boys.[31] Such aspirations often lead girls towards investing in a 'thin' ideal, viewing themselves as fatter or less attractive than other girls and developing a sense of dissatisfaction with their bodies.[32] Tragically, such dissatisfaction is a risk factor for a range of anxiety-related disorders beyond BDD including low self-esteem, depression, eating disorders, appearance rumination, self-mutilation and unnecessary cosmetic surgery.[33] It is disturbing and sad to think that some girls become so disillusioned with their appearance that they would consider cosmetic surgery, and worrying to know that social media – which we will discuss in greater detail in Chapter 8 – may be complicit. Equally troubling is a growing array of empirical and anecdotal evidence identifying that changing one's appearance for the sake of popularity or some measure of psychological satisfaction may also be a symptomatic of a range of identity issues linked to adolescent girls.

One of the most consistent characteristics of psycho-social development during adolescence is the journey into becoming an independent individual and shaping one's identity. Such a journey can often lead to feelings of self-doubt and uncertainty and while many adolescents traverse such feelings relatively unscathed, adolescent girls appear more likely to struggle and less likely to cope along the way. Two of the most worrying contemporary manifestations of such struggles are the phenomena of 'peer contagion', and the perhaps related crisis in adolescent girls' sense of gender identity.

Desperately seeking myself!

Identity formation has been described as the core psychological business of adolescence. As originally suggested by the developmental psychologist Erik Erikson, failure to achieve a cohesive sense of self results in a raft of negative psychosocial outcomes.[34] The transition from adolescence to adulthood involves a progressive strengthening of one's sense of self, and adolescents draw on various sources and experiences to shape their identity or 'find themselves'.[35] Erikson also found that role models and peers were the most important social agents in adolescent identity formation.[36] And while parents are, at time, an adolescent's most significant role model, we are aware of the increasingly important role peers play in the lives of adolescents as they journey towards greater autonomy and independence from their parents.

As we have discussed, adolescent girls tend to have a couple of close friendships that are deeply intimate, with high levels of reciprocity of feelings and greater expectations of empathy, loyalty and commitment. Such close relationships require a great deal of nurturing and emotional investment and are founded on communication. The nature of such close relationships appears to be closely linked to a girl's overall sense of self and therefore, by association, her sense of identity.

Peers, therefore, play a large role in the development of identity for girls. There is substantive evidence showing remarkable similarities between adolescent girls and the behaviour and psychological characteristics of their friends.[37] And while this is to be expected, given the both the initial grounds for friendship formation and ongoing mutual influence, sometimes this influence can lead to harmful physical and psychological consequences.

In psychological literature, the process of mutual influence that occurs between an individual and a peer is referred to as 'peer contagion' and can include behaviours and emotions that undermine an individual's own development or cause harm to themselves or others.[38] The social influence of peers increases throughout childhood, peaks during adolescence and becomes of lesser significance in adulthood.[39] In other words, over the course of a lifespan it appears that it is during adolescence where what one girl says and does has the greatest influence on shaping the actions and feelings of her closest friends.

Of concern for parents and teachers alike is the large number of studies noting many forms of maladjustment amongst adolescent girls including externalising problems, depression, body image issues and high levels of social anxiety associated with friendships and peer influence.[40] Moreover, numerous studies have also documented links between anxiety disorders, depression and identity issues and peer contagion.[41] Adolescent girls appear to be especially vulnerable to 'contracting' various social anxiety disorders via co-rumination and peer contagion.[42] Taken in its entirety, emerging evidence suggests that peer contagion impacts negatively on adolescent girls' mental health and is likely exacerbated by social media.

Social media has heightened all of the above factors, and a growing body of research suggesting that social media is responsible for a generational impact on adolescent girls that is largely negative. For example, girls seem more likely than boys to use social media to try to 'fit in' with their online peer group or idols, to deliberately seek out other girls to co-ruminate with (exacerbating issues such as depression and eating disorders), and seem more vulnerable to the impacts of social contagion. The UK's Millenium Cohort study identified a range of concerning outcomes specific to adolescent girls,[43] including girls spending far more time on social media than boys, and a whopping 40 per cent of those spending more than 5 hours per day showing symptoms of depression. Girls tended to feel inferior to those they followed on Instagram and other platforms, leading to self-esteem issues. Research in the UK has documented that mental health problems have soared in the past five years, correlating with the increase in adolescent girls' use of social media, prompting Dr Bernadka Dubicka, the chair of the child and adolescent faculty at the Royal College of Psychiatrists to note that 'emotional problems in young girls have been significantly, and very worryingly, on the rise over the past few years.'[44]

The specific issue of girls' vulnerability to social media forces became prominent in the eating disorder space, where girls tend to 'bandwagon' and copy the efforts of peers and idols to engage in ever-increasing thinning behaviours. The rise of 'thinspiration' websites in defiance of public health messaging compounded health authorities' struggles to curtail unhealthy dieting practices. Adolescent girls' use of social media presents a continued challenge as harmful social fads come and go, taking with them a new cohort of vulnerable casualties.

One of the most recent iterations of social media influence on girls' developing sense of identity has occurred in gender identity. Gender identity encompasses the feelings of belonging to one sex or another – whether you think of yourself as male, female or neither.[45] As established in Chapter 1, in most cases gender identity and physical sex characteristics are congruent: babies born with female genitalia will typically recognise themselves as belonging to the female gender and experience themselves as females.[46] Individual understandings of gender identity appear to emerge between two and three years of age, are a strikingly universal milestone across cultures and are not a problem or struggle for most children.[47] And while the awareness of one's gender appears universal, it can be influenced by the environment until gender *constancy* – the knowledge that gender is fixed and lifelong – appears around the age of six or seven.[48] In other words, young children may, at times, not conform to their gender and proclaim to be something that, biologically, they are not. This is not, uncommon but almost all children will ascribe to their gender via biological identity prior to puberty. For those who do not, as adolescents they will later identify with their biological identity and come out as non-heterosexual.[49] There are cases, however, where an individual's gender identity does not conform to their biological sex during adolescence, and evidence suggests that this experience has a strong genetic, biological and neurological component.[50] This is worthy of repeating: gender nonconformity or transgenderism may be directly linked to genes, biology and the brain, and the influence of environment and culture is highly contentious.

Rates of gender nonconformity are higher in adolescent girls than boys: compared to girls, boys see themselves as more similar to same-sex others, are more content with their gender and are not as fluid in their sexual identity.[51] Previously referred to as 'gender identity disorder' by the American Psychiatric Association, this condition was renamed 'gender dysphoria' in the latest version of the same association's *Diagnostic and Statistical Manual of Mental Disorders*.[52] And while it is important to note that not all transgender or gender nonconforming individuals experience dysphoria around their gender identity, it is worrying that there does appear to be an exponential increase in the rates of gender dysphoria, particularly among adolescent girls, and with even more troubling flow on effects.[53]

Symptoms of gender dysphoria typically occur in early childhood (early-onset GD) or may emerge after puberty (adolescent-onset GD).[54] Healthy children vary considerably in their gender expression and many of those who present with early-onset GD will outgrow this condition and identify with their biological sex once puberty commences.[55] Historically, gender dysphoria was recorded in only 0.01 per cent of the population and was most prevalent in boys.[56] From a biological point of view this makes theoretical sense. The in-utero hormonal influences that are largely thought to result in gender dysphoria should be vastly more likely with a male fetus than a female, given that all brains start out female and male brains are created by testosterone. However, over the last few years there has been a huge increase in the number of adolescent girls presenting with gender dysphoria who never identified as 'feeling in the wrong body' as children.[57] This nascent and expanding condition amongst adolescent girls has been labelled 'rapid-onset gender dysphoria' or ROGD.[58]

The sudden exponential increase in adolescent girls presenting with ROGD and identifying as transgender is concerning, given that ROGD is not nearly as prevalent in male adolescents. Furthermore, the increasing numbers of girls who appear to be experiencing ROGD do not align with the expected rates of gender dysphoria that emerge in childhood, consolidate during adolescence and are representative of the expected numbers of adult transgender individuals.[59] We simply should not see so many girls struggling with gender dysphoria, and the fact that his phenomena is evident primarily in Western countries like Australia, Canada, the United States and U.K. has researchers asking many questions and educators, parents and adults across a number of health-related professions concerned.

For physician and scientist Dr Lisa Littman, who incidentally coined the phrase 'Rapid Onset Gender Dysphoria', one of the most troubling and puzzling aspects of the increasing number of girls dealing with gender dysphoria is that the vast majority never presented as gender dysphoric during their childhood. Historically, adolescents who have presented for care for gender dysphoria experienced childhood or early onset dysphoria that worsened with puberty.[60] This begs the question as to whether the sudden increase of transgender cases in adolescent girls is the result of a social contagion whereby the ordinary teen angst associated with puberty has been influenced by the current, and arguably disproportionate, zeitgeist focusing on transgenderism within identity politics.[61] The inexplicable rise of adolescent girls presenting as gender dysphoric in predominantly Western cultures has been described as an emerging social phenomenon and may prove to be yet another example of a social-media driven intrusion into the insecurities and vulnerabilities of young girls.[62]

Adolescent girls on the edge

Adolescence can be a rocky ride, with the many hormonal and neurobiological changes playing havoc with an adolescent's body, mind and emotions. For girls especially, with their enhanced limbic system, increased awareness of body image and the centrality of relationships to their sense of self leaving them particularly vulnerable to peer approval and influence, the challenges can be immense. They are on a quest to become independent and autonomous individuals, seeking their own identity while juggling feelings of uncertainty and anxiety with a brain that is far from mature. This often leaves girls feeling alone, or co-ruminating with their peers and seeking advice from those they deem to be on a similar journey, which can lead to further anxiety and health-related problems.

For previous generations of adolescents, the major risks related to body dissatisfaction (and most pronounced in girls) included eating disorders such as anorexia and bulimia and self-mutilation in the form of 'cutting'.[63] While these issues are still present, there is a great deal of literature and support available given a substantive history in treatment and research; a simple internet search can provide a pathway for advice and treatment. For the puzzling and new condition of ROGD, no such history exists. A transition from eating and self-harm related disorders to gender dysphoria has garnered much attention and concern from psychiatrists and clinicians.[64] It also appears that a substantive majority of girls who are presenting as individuals with ROGD have done so after intensive and prolonged social media immersion with like-minded individuals and friendship groups.[65] However, ROGD may also a by-product of a number of factors.

There is large body of research indicating that entering puberty earlier than one's peers increases the risks for a range of disorders.[66] On almost all measures, including neurologically and physiologically, girls mature sooner than boys.[67] And while most girls successfully move through adolescence, those who experience maturation earlier are at greater risk of developing a vast array of mental health problems.[68] This accelerated physical maturation, and its associated psychological challenges, may see girls in social contexts they are not socially or cognitively prepared for, thereby exacerbating psychological distress and the risk-taking behaviours linked with a developing adolescent brain.[69] Unfortunately, and like so many of the idiosyncrasies of the developing brain, the full array of neurobiological mechanisms linking pubertal timing to psychopathologies is not yet well understood.[70]

Aside from differences in maturational timelines, the influence of peers, coupled with the ubiquity of technology and social media as mechanisms for co-rumination and self-diagnoses cannot be dismissed or downplayed. As noted earlier, an adolescent girl's mental health can be directly, and negatively, impacted by the mental health of her friends via peer influence.[71] However, unlike previous generations, it is well documented that today's adolescents spend a great deal of time with 'friends' via technology and social media.[72] Social media is too often used to present 'curated' versions of lives, as an instrument for comparisons and relational aggression and as a platform for girls to co-ruminate, self-diagnose and find guidance from 'like-minded' individuals.[73] And of course, online information can be problematic in its scope and accuracy. Moreover, online individuals who purport to be supportive of another individual's challenges around identity or other issues are not likely to be clinicians in the field of adolescent development and as such may not always provide accurate information, or any measure of good advice.

So as adults invested in the wellbeing of the adolescent girls around us, what can parents and teachers do? While mental health issues are not always easy to identify or treat, where issues do become apparent, professional advice may be warranted. Interestingly, and despite the pitfalls of friendship groups discussed above, for young people, positive and rewarding social networks can act as a deterrent against anxiety, depression and psychological distress.[74] A key for parents lies in ensuring that they, as much as possible, are familiar with their daughter's peer groups and the dynamics of those groups, as well as what is being digitally consumed. Challenges associated with online environments and the impact of technology and social media on young girls is explored in more detail in the next chapter. For now, we must remember that adolescence can be a roller-coaster ride for many young girls, and watching for changes in mood and behaviour from the onset of puberty can help to navigate any potential storms ahead.

Summary

The onset of puberty presents many challenges for young people, especially in relation to understanding who they are and who they are becoming. For girls, the changes occurring in mind and body are intimately linked to the limbic system, and in particular negative emotions. Girls tend to spend more time ruminating on how they feel, look and present themselves to the wider world. The downside of this can manifest in issues related to body image, self-esteem and identity such as eating disorders, self-harm and gender dysphoria. The prevalence of online social environments with their focus on image, and easy facilitation of co-rumination, makes the situation that much more complex.

Adolescence can be a difficult time for girls, and just because their schoolwork is fine and their behaviour not an issue in class or at home, doesn't necessarily mean that all is well. Keeping a watchful and compassionate eye on the behaviours and actions of daughters and students is an important way to ensure that girls do not suffer in silence.

8 Experiences matter!

The overall structure and wiring diagram of the brain is determined by genetic programs that work early in life, and these genetic programs also set up the principles by which neurons and synaptic connections grow and change. Experience acts within the framework of these principles.[1]

— *Professor Sam Wang*

From Chapter 2 onwards this book has provided examples and evidence of how the brain shapes, and is shaped by, the interplay between nature and nurture. We have explored how processes, chemicals and activity in the brain shape behaviour and experience, and how experiences can in turn influence the brain and mind. Experiences matter, and this final chapter draws together some of the key issues and challenges we have explored so far, and focuses on four current and key areas for educating and raising girls.

The first two areas of exploration relate to issues around formal education. Specifically, we spend some time looking at the overall learning environment and then examine two subject areas that tend to attract a great deal of attention when it comes to educating girls – maths and science. We then explore the impact of technology on development and learning, and in particular, the challenges associated with social media in the lives of girls of all ages. And finally we look further into relationships and social and emotional well-being in school, before teasing out that same topic beyond the school environment.

Before we explore girls and schooling, a few comments about the bigger picture of education are warranted. Much of what happens in a classroom has not changed all that much since previous generations attended school. To be clear, there are aspects of formal education that have stood the test of time for many reasons, and still maintain efficacy and currency today. There are, however, some things that confound our understandings of education when considering how the brain works, how it learns and how it might work differently depending on gender. A good place to start this conversation is by reflecting on previous arguments and positions on schooling in a new millennium.

Formal education: some broader trends

Not long after the turn of the century I wrote my first two books. Beyond scientific papers and journal articles, these works were my first extended explorations into the differences between boys and girls with a focus on understanding behaviour and modifying educational practice to meet the respective needs of each gender. Looking back, I am struck by a particular quote that I wrote and share here ...

> *When we look at the state of education in the twenty-first century, one of the first things teachers and parents alike must look at is the actual day-to-day routine of 'schooling' and ask themselves if things have changed much since they were students. A traditional model of students passively sitting in rows or groups surrounded by four walls awaiting instruction is one that is still common practice, especially in senior schools where adolescence abounds.*[2]

That quote makes more sense when considering the context of education at the time. At the beginning of the new millennium, the phrases 'twenty-first century education' and 'educating for the twenty-first century' became soundbites for many politicians, were used as headings on glossy education department brochures and were also fodder for conversations by many who were pontificating on the skills and knowledge required for a new generation of young people. And while the turn of the century witnessed many changes in society on the back of rapid technological advancement, schools, arguably, have not evolved with the same fervent change of pace. There have been various initiatives to reinvent curriculum and teaching practice, but by and large, many of the physical structures, procedures and daily routines of schools today are not dissimilar to those of previous generations of learners. However, there are a few things that *have* changed measurably, and are worthy of scrutiny.

First, performance and the collection of data have taken a very strong grip on educational decision making. Today's teachers are now expected to gather and comb through mountains of data in ways that previous generations of teachers never did, under the ostensible purpose of assessing performance and raising standards. This focus on 'standards', and the use of standardised testing to determine student knowledge and school performance, has had a significant impact on schooling. Too much emphasis on standards often becomes the raison d'etre for government policy, forcing schools to favour certain styles of teaching and focus on certain types of tasks in a one-size-fits-all model. This becomes even more problematic when politicians and policy makers use standardised testing to measure performance and enhance 'educational accountability'.

In itself there is very little positive to note about standardised testing. Bear in mind that educators, by virtue of their training, are always considering standards. Teachers have standards for behaviour, for quality of work, for conduct on school outings and innumerable other aspects of daily school routines and expectations. They also apply standards to their own pedagogy and to the work that their students produce and are expected to produce. Standards are part and parcel of being an effective and professional teacher. Standardised tests, on the other hand, have a long and dubious history: their efficacy and utility in actually determining what students know and can do is far from proven, yet they create environments where competition, cheating and accountability detract from any real learning.[3] More worryingly, however, are studies noting that large numbers of students of all ages report experiencing high anxiety and stress related conditions including insomnia, hyperventilation, profuse sweating, headaches, nail biting, stomach aches and migraines when having to participate in standardised testing.[4] Given all that has been presented in previous chapters in relation to girls, negative affect, anxiety, depression and neuroticism, we need to scrutinise and question experiences that may exacerbate such feelings, particularly under the umbrella of education and the guise of improving outcomes.

A second issue with a regime of standardisation is the trend to engage younger children in this type of model under the auspices of some form of preparation for the future. Advances under the pretext of 'early learning' are seeing younger and younger children experiencing 'schooling' at its worst. One of the concerns neuroscientists and researchers in psychology share with regards to 'early learning' is the misappropriation of information about neural stimulation and early development.[5] Such concerns are based on individuals, programs and policies that suggest that if experience and activity are indeed significant factors in neural development then surely the earlier the stimulation (read 'enrichment'), the greater the opportunity for learning and early success to occur. However, while we know that environmental and social stimulation helps to shape the brain, we must also remember that the brain is not primarily an experience-storing device that constantly changes its structure to accommodate new experience: it is a dynamic computing device that is largely rule driven and ***developmentally predictable.***[6] Moreover, the brain does not mature in a similar fashion across all individuals; no two brains are exactly alike. Experience is important, but so too is each individual girl and a one-size-fits-all race to excellence in formal education may not be a good fit for many girls.

And finally, it is important to note that across most measures, and in spite of some of the issues presented above, girls are doing better across all sectors of education. The reasons for this are multifarious and explored in greater detail below. Yet despite this, the education environment for girls is not perfect. In terms of academic outcomes, there are some things that can be done better for the potential benefit of all girls.

Girls, cognition and education

I now want to explore cognition, or the academic side of 'schooling' and the factors that enhance academic outcomes. Cognition generally refers to thinking and the mental processes involved in comprehension and acquiring knowledge.[7] Acquiring knowledge, of course, is a key factor in attaining positive academic outcomes. For some time, research has shown that regardless of socioeconomic background, girls outperform boys across most sectors of schooling, get better grades and go on to post-school qualifications in higher numbers.[8] While academic achievement is frequently linked with intelligence or intellectual ability, there is no significant correlation between gender and intelligence.[9] In other words, there is more than general cognitive ability at play in terms of girls outperforming boys in school.

Exactly what may be contributing to better scholastic outcomes for girls is an area of continued research. A cursory synthesis of the research tells us that the capacity to achieve good academic results depends on aspects of emotion, personality and social wellbeing, all of which vary markedly between girls and boys. Interestingly, gender differences in personality traits may also be a factor in terms of academic outcomes.

Personality can be defined as the unique combinations of qualities, attributes and characteristics that distinguish the thoughts, feelings and behaviours of individual people.[10] Children, adolescents and adults can all be described in terms of personality traits and while such traits are not fixed at any particular age, there is a degree of stability in terms of differences between genders.[11] Furthermore, personality traits account for a great deal of variance in academic achievement, perhaps even more than intelligence, and as noted gender is an important variable in terms of differences in personality.[12]

The study of personality has a long history. From the 1980s onwards, many different models of personality have been developed, with the 'Big Five Personality Traits' model considered the most statistically valid framework for understanding personality traits across cultures.[13] *Openness, conscientiousness, extraversion, agreeableness* and *neuroticism* form the foundation of this model and perhaps, unsurprisingly, conscientiousness (which involves facets such as order, dutifulness, self-discipline, and deliberation) has been systematically linked to achievement at different education levels.[14] Conscientious individuals perform better because they are generally more organised and persevere at tasks longer, and it appears that females are more conscientious across all ages.[15] Interestingly, as we noted in previous chapter, females also display higher levels of neuroticism which could conceivably unbalance any positive personality traits associated with achievement. After all, students who are prone to worrying, anxiety, stress or other negative emotions are likely to disengage from any learning process.[16] As people mature they generally become more agreeable, conscientious and emotionally stable.[17] Taken in its entirety, the effect of sex differences on personality traits as they pertain to academic achievement suggest that parents and educators alike have an important role in supporting girls whenever negative emotions appear to be taking over aspects of their home and school life. Remember, cognition (thinking) and affect (emotion) are intimately linked. We'll now turn to an area where negative affect is often evident when exploring girls' attitudes, approaches and outcomes: maths and science.

Maths and science *for* girls – some perspectives

This chapter is about experiences, and in an educational context, experiences in the guise of subject content are often at the forefront of any conversation related to girls and education. In particular, maths, science and technology garner much discussion and debate. This is not to say that these subject areas present difficulties in terms of achievement for girls, but rather that as girls move through formal educational contexts, they become underrepresented in these disciplines. Indeed, on most measures girls are currently outperforming boys across all subject areas, and moving into post-secondary education at a higher rate than their male counterparts. This trend is evident in many Western countries, including the United States, where more women than men are completing doctoral qualifications, and in Australia, where more women graduate with undergraduate and postgraduate qualifications than men.[18] However, when we examine these figures by discipline, it's clear that despite their overall success, girls remain underrepresented in numbers in STEM (Science, Technology, Engineering and Mathematics) related disciplines at university, and in those professions in general. The million-dollar question is why? The following are some ideas that may help to explain this phenomenon.

First, long-held cultural attitudes and stereotypes can affect participation rates. As noted above, girls appear to be quite capable of attaining good grades in STEM-related subject areas but as they get older they tend to steer away from STEM fields. Some evidence suggests that this is linked to stereotypical viewpoints about STEM fields and careers. Being traditionally male-dominated domains can discourage girls from pursuing such pathways, and their teachers and parents from encouraging them in that direction.[19] The perception of STEM as being something for the boys is further compounded by parental and teacher expectations that boys will do better at STEM-related subjects, in spite of evidence to the contrary.[20] And finally, a teacher's attitude and approach to to their own ability in STEM-related fields can affect student attitudes. A study from the US demonstrated that, unrelated to ability in either student or teacher, the display of 'maths-anxiety' by female teachers in lower primary grades negatively affected girls' beliefs about who is 'good' at maths, and their resultant achievement in maths.[21] Even at such an early stage, negative sterotypes are surprisingly resilient, and despite the significant inroads we have made into recasting STEM-related fields as gender-neutral and encouraging female participation, subconscious biases may persist.

A second reason why girls may not choose STEM as a field of study or future professional endeavour is simply that of interest. As we discussed in Chapter 3 with the stories of Lawrence Summers and James Damore, biological predisposition to an interest in STEM fields on the basis of gender is a controversial topic. Yet statistically speaking, and as discussed in Chapter 3, boys tend to be more interested in things and girls more interested in people, and this appears to have its foundations in early brain development. Pursuing university qualifications or a career in STEM arguably necessitates an interest in things over people. Importantly, there is an abundance of empirical evidence noting that exposure, or lack thereof, to testosterone in utero is associated with male-typical interests and behaviours, regardless of whether that baby is born male or female – a masculinised brain prefers things over people.[22] Furthermore, sex differences in most psychological traits appear larger in cultures with greater egalitarian sex role socialisation and stronger gender equity policies, which lends further credence to the biological explanation for a lack of interest in STEM fields.[23] Scandinavian countries have done more than others to ensure equality opportunity for males and females, yet they still see more males pursuing engineering, for example, and more female than male nurses. It appears that freedom of choice with equality of opportunity exacerbates gender differences rather than diminishes them.[24] Therefore, it could simply be the case that, as they mature and their interests drive their choices, many girls are simply not interested in STEM-related fields. For those who are, however, teachers and parents alike must be supportive of such desires and not assume that girls are less adept at maths and science.

Moving beyond differences in personality traits, researchers and psychologists have also uncovered numerous ways that males and females differ in cognition across most cultures.[25] For example, there is evidence that performance and achievement across certain aspects of maths and science subjects may be related to various cognitive abilities: males tend to do better on mathematical reasoning or problem-solving aptitude tests but females generally outperform males on computation and achievement tests.[26] And while examples such as this may help explain why males, on average, appear to have an affinity for mathematics, the extent to which differences in cognitive abilities can be used in practical ways for parents and teachers is, to date, rather precarious and not easily identifiable.[27] The fact remains that studies in sex differences in the variability of broad cognitive abilities are still very limited, with findings that are often inconsistent and cannot take into account the full range of variables associated with individual differences and context. Nature and nurture remain difficult to disentangle. Consider, for example, that mathematical ability is not easily confined to numbers and often depends on language skills (as in word problems), which gives the advantage to girls. And while girls generally do better in computation in the early grades, things become murkier, and success across many forms of mathematics does seem to diminish, as girls get older.[28] At the same, the fields of mathematics and science become far more diverse and differentiated as students progress: primary school maths and science evolve into algebra, calculus, trigonometry, biology, chemistry and physics in secondary school and beyond. In the end, differences in cognition between males and females are not likely to manifest into workable policies or curriculum initiatives. Alternatively, it would be better for parents and teachers to remember that there aren't any differences in what girls and boys can learn, but there are certainly differences in how, and what, they might like to learn.

Technology, social media and girls

Perhaps some of the most contemporary challenges associated with educating and raising girls are those related to technology usage. The rampant use of technology by children and teens has garnered much research and scrutiny since the turn of the century. There are legitimate questions regarding the efficacy of technology in enhancing academic outcomes across all sectors of education. The OECD recently reported that 'students who frequently use computers at school do a lot worse in most learning outcomes', and that testing results had shown 'no appreciable improvements in student achievement in reading, mathematics and science in the countries that had heavily invested in ICT for education.'[30] A full reading of this report suggests that an overreliance on, or perhaps an overindulgence in, technology and its associated resources is worthy of scrutiny. It is worth noting that this is the same OECD that provides international assessments and rankings of literacy, numeracy and science standards every couple of years that politicians use to cast judgements on teacher efficacy and accountability,[31] and that while Australia has perhaps invested more heavily in technology and internet use in schools than any other country[32], it shows a steady decline in all areas tested since 2003.[33] I am not necessarily suggesting a causal link between the use of technology and poorer academic outcomes, but questioning the idea that *not* using technology will result in poorer scholastic outcomes and students being 'left behind'.

To date, there is scant evidence that technology is the panacea for learning it is often positioned to be. Technology is but a tool for education, and needs to be used in the service of an effective education framework. For educators, the use of technology is most beneficial when it embraces four pillars of learning derived from the psychological sciences which notes that humans learn best when activities and experiences:

1. ***Are engaging and in the service of a learning goal.*** Technology is often inherently engaging but must go beyond engagement and 'edutainment' and have a learning goal as the foundation for engagement.

2. ***Are meaningful.*** Meaningful learning goes beyond simple memorisation and occurs when children find the meaning in what they are learning and are able to not only connect new material to existing knowledge but expand their current knowledge to create new conceptual understanding.

3. ***Are cognitively active.*** Cognitively active learning implies 'minds-on' (executive functioning of the prefrontal cortex) involvement during the learning experience, in addition to any physical activity that may be occurring, such as swiping and tapping.

4. *Are socially interactive.* High-quality interactions (ie. those with knowledgeable social partners or in collaborative learning situations) that are contingent and adaptable to the student.[34]

The importance of teachers employing the learning principles above when using technology must be coupled with effective means of managing 'off-task' behaviours that technology can promote. It is all too easy to meander off task and become distracted when using screen devices – our computers, tablets and smartphones can provide too much information without the means of filtering it appropriately for content and context.

Exactly how much is too much screen time is a vexing issue for parents. Guidelines vary depending on the organisation or bureaucracy, are often more specific for young children with general suggestions to limit time on screens for older children and adolescents.[35] And of course, screen time is an umbrella term that encompasses a huge range of possible social, research, educational and recreational activities. In addition, it is almost impossible to set up any type of experiment to make such determinations; it would be highly unethical and controversial to do a study exposing young people to excessive screen time to see at what point they are harmed. Instead, we must look at a broad range of reports and studies across various research fields to see if there are any correlations that can be drawn. One thing is certain, and that is that time on screen devices is increasing across all age groups.[36] Parents, therefore, can't assume that their daughters live in a world similar to the one they experienced as an adolescent when in fact their daughters live in a media-drenched world flooded with questionable values that can be a girl's source of guidance when they turn away from parents.[37] This is exacerbated by the fact that time on screen devices is taking young people away from the face-to-face social interactions necessary for all aspects of healthy development.

Social media may not be very social or helpful

Human beings are, by their very nature, social creatures. In the 1970s, neuroscientists began to uncover that most aspects of our anatomy, biochemistry and neurology were deeply interwoven with our social relationships, resulting in the conception of the brain as a social organ.[38]

It is the social milieu around us and engagement with people that helps to shape our brain, and positively influences most aspects of healthy development. Conversely, high levels of screen-based activities appear to have detrimental effects on many aspects of children's and adolescent's wellbeing and development.[39] And while a two-hour cap of daily screen usage has been recommended by health and government organisations in Australia and overseas,[40] it has become increasingly apparent across a number of countries that this recommendation is regularly, and increasingly, exceeded.[41] An accurate account of how much time is spent on screen devices is difficult to ascertain. Self-reporting measures are often used to make such determinations and young people and adults alike may not be very forthcoming or detailed in documenting the full extent of time they spend staring into a virtual world, talking on the phone, playing games, organising their lives or any other of the myriad things that can be done using technology. It is a fairly safe assumption, however, that a great deal of time is spent being 'connected', and for girls much of that is via social media platforms.

Before taking a further look at issues and challenges associated with girls and social media, a few important research findings are worth keeping in mind in terms of the use of screen devices. First, prior to the turn of the century, most research showed a consistent increase in psychological wellbeing, including measures of self-esteem, happiness and life satisfaction, among younger populations.[42] Those aspects of wellbeing appear to have declined in tandem with increases in screen usage since the turn of the century,[43] and mirror other health concerns associated with screen usage and eating disorders,[44] weight/body image,[45] sleep disturbance,[46] and a range of behavioural disorders,[47] to name a few. There is a plethora of research suggesting that screen time should be considered a major public health issue, and a reduction in screen time a priority for child and adolescent health.

Second, the use of technology is generally different for boys and girls: boys tend to use technology for gaming while girls tend to engage with social media on a more regular basis.[48] This difference is both intriguing and worrisome given the links between screen usage and negative emotions. Numerous studies have found that individuals who spend less time on social media are less likely to feel sad, angry, anxious, worried or lonely, and that the risk of unhappiness due to social media use is highest in adolescents.[49] Remember also that the emotional lives of girls are fraught with challenges even without the added mix of technology and social media.

Chapters 5 through 7 looked at a range of issues associated with emotions, relationships and identity, and it is a safe assumption that social media, as an experience, plays a role in exacerbating a number of the issues girls struggle with during various times of their lives. For example, social media, by design, promotes a blurring of the line between reality and fantasy. A recent study found that platforms where images can be filtered and girls can compare and despair about their looks might lead to body dysmorphic disorder (BDD),[50] a mental health condition where individuals become fixated on imagined defects in their appearance[51], and in extreme cases can lead to suicide ideation.[52] This is just one example where social media, as a platform for viewing the lives of others, can lead girls down a virtual, and potentially dangerous, rabbit hole. Added to this is the knowledge that the developing adolescent prefrontal cortex may not be the best moderator of virtual content or advice which may be uniformed, naïve, biased or even malicious. There are ample examples of potential links between technology and the challenges girls face with maintaining their emotional and social wellbeing, and the use of technology to facilitate connection raises yet another: adolescent girls who are struggling with anxiety or other types of mental health issues may, in fact, use social media as a mechanism for co-rumination.

Connecting and co-ruminating

Noted earlier in this chapter and others was the proclivity for females to be, comparatively speaking, more neurotic than males. Neuroticism, as a personality trait, describes the tendency toward moodiness and the increased experience of many negative emotions including those associated with anxiety, depression and loneliness. Girls are also more likely to ruminate, or think of those feelings, en route to developing mental health problems.[53] During adolescence, girls, more extensively than boys, will also share those feelings or co-ruminate, with others, especially friends.[54] The trouble with co-ruminating is that while intimacy and support from relationships can be beneficial for emotional wellbeing, there is also the risk of increasing states of anxiety and depression through co-ruminating.[55] And in terms of connecting with friends via technology, it should be rather self-evident that there are many inherent risks with disclosing personal feelings on the internet via social media.

For some, social media can be a mechanism for greater interactions with others and there is some evidence to support social media as a conduit for positive relationship building.[56] It is important to note that many studies exploring the positive aspects of social media occurred not long after social media was available to the wider population and was not as varied or omnipresent as it is now. In other words, the optimistic overtones of earlier studies when people were only beginning to 'trend' and 'influence' may not be indicative of the current issues around social media.

As noted earlier, prior to stepping into the twenty-first century, and before the pervasive influence of technology and 24/7 media on our lives, mental health amongst young people appeared to be on a positive trajectory. Since that time, screen use has increased and so too have numerous mental health concerns. The correlation between the two is interesting, and mirrored in studies showing a decline in many aspects of physical and mental health amongst young people. In their work on young people and cyberbullying, Dr Danfeng Zhang from Penn State's Department of Computer Science and Engineering and colleagues posit that the prevalence of the internet and social media bring various aspects of convenience to adolescents but also afford greater opportunities for an array of problems.[57] For those researchers, the links between neuroticism and depression as predictors of cyberbullying (both perpetration and victimisation) were unequivocal and correlated with other research linking screen use and negative affect. Remember too, that the developing adolescent brain is fueled by emotions, girls are more likely to demonstrate neuroticism and negative affect, and that adolescent girls are more likely to think negative thoughts and co-ruminate with others. Co-rumination may also be a contributing factor in eating disorders, self-harm or other psychological challenges via peer contagion and discussed in the previous chapter. It should, therefore, be apparent that being able to communicate one's thoughts and ideas via social media at any time can present numerous opportunities for things to go wrong. Indeed, increasing volumes of evidence suggests that greater interaction on social media at age ten or earlier is associated with worsening socio-emotional difficulties among girls.[58] The following comments made by adolescent girls and reported by Professor of Psychology Dr Jean Twenge are indicative of these concerns:

> *"Definitely it (social media) makes me depressed. All my friends share the fun details of their glamourous lives and it makes me kinda feel like ****. Kinda hate FB (Facebook) ..."*
>
> *"Scrolling through my feed, seeing my friends being happy, makes me sad. Also, because ... I get no messages ... the sight of the message box with no notifications gives me a really sad, gut wrenching feeling of loneliness. Facebook depresses me ..."*[59]

The comments above mirror comments made by Australian adolescents who took part in an unpublished pilot study I conducted in 2018. As part of a youth mental health symposium, young people across Australia and New Zealand were invited to participate in an online survey focusing on smartphones, screen use and wellbeing. In all, 2150 young people aged 12–17 years old provided a vast amount of data related to screen use and wellbeing and of that full sample, roughly 66 per cent of respondents were girls (n=1414). Within this group, Facebook, Snapchat and Instagram were identified as the most commonly used platforms by adolescents and that overuse, or being on a device too long, was a number one concern. Over 60 per cent of these 'connected' young people noted that smartphone and social media usage was a contributing factor to anxiety and depression, a reduction in social activity and difficulties with maintaining attention. Over 90 per cent identified sleep deprivation as a major problem. Two points of interest come to mind from this data set and further elaborations made by the participants.

First, the prevalence of social media use and the challenges linked to screen devices are issues that adolescents are more than familiar with. And second, while the adolescents in this study were able to identify issues and problems, they were also quick to note that they were not likely to change any habits as a form of preventative measure. However, and this is one of the most fascinating findings arising from the data, while the vast majority of adolescents were not prepared to independently disengage from screens and social media, they were prepared to do so if instructed by their parents. In the world of adolescence, this makes good sense – better to save face and disengage from a virtual world if I am told to do so rather than risk any potential harassment or critique if I do so of my own volition! This is an important message for parents and teachers – the potential issues associated with technology can be mediated by parents and adult caregivers, and despite the desire for complete autonomy, adolescents *need* firm boundaries, particularly around the use of technology.

Girls, emotion and education

Over a quarter of a century ago, in what seems to be a distant past life, I was training to be a teacher and studying education and psychology. During this time my education professors, not too dissimilar to contemporary practice in teacher training, taught me how to design lesson plans. I was taught how to develop and use a template which delineated my planning into three distinct objectives for teaching and learning – cognitive, affective and psycho-motor. In those days, the relative separation of thinking, feeling and doing was commonplace given our limited understanding of the mechanisms of the mind. And while we have much greater insight into how cognition and emotion are linked, I wonder if things have changed all that much in the twenty-first century in terms of recognising the role emotions play in learning and wellbeing.

Current research from the domains of education, psychology and neuroscience tells us that emotion, cognition and academic success are intimately linked.[60] Arguably, teachers have intuitively known that a student's attitudes and beliefs about themselves as learners directly impacts on their capacity to engage positively within the classroom. Such intuitions are supported by psychological research exploring links between emotion and motivation: if a student feels negatively about their own academic competence they will likely disengage or de-emphasise effort in order to protect their overall self-esteem and sense of self.[61] In addition, students who are socially insecure may be unwilling to risk engaging in various classroom activities for fear of being ridiculed.

From a neuroscientific perspective, we know that different areas of the limbic system are directly involved with memory, attention and perception (all important skills and attributes for learning). The amygdala modulates long-term memory and influences how well memories are stored, while the hippocampus is critical for encoding episodic or declarative memory and for long-term storage, or consolidation, of memories.[62] We also know that emotion enhances episodic memory for events – we are more likely to remember and be aware of events that engage our limbic system.[63] Practically speaking, this suggests that educators could enhance their practice by engaging the emotional minds of their students – memory, understanding and learning go hand in hand. In terms of teaching and curriculum, this suggests that content is best absorbed when it is relevant to the lives of young people and where it can be supported with positive emotions. Moreover, and in the context of working with and for girls, an understanding of the emotional and social brain are critical aspects of ensuring that girls succeed.

In chapters 5 through 7 we looked at the importance of emotions and relationships in the minds of girls. We also explored how the very emotional part of the brain often becomes a mechanism for relational aggression or what I like to call *aggression in pink*. This, then, is perhaps the most important aspect of education for girls. If the emotional and social lives of girls can have such an impact on the day-to-day experiences within a school environment, then we need to proactively address emotional processes. Perhaps clinical psychologist and author Dr Roni Cohen-Sandler sums it up best in stating that 'boys are typically unemotional about school ... for girls however, school is all about the process. What happens throughout each and every school day – academically, socially, and emotionally – becomes a yardstick of their success. Every moment really matters.'[64]

Every moment really matters ... a more powerful statement would be hard to find and indeed no greater challenge exists for parents and educators than to always remember that phrase and act on it. Helping girls to understand their emotions and develop their emotional intelligence seems the surest way to enhance their emotional and social wellbeing and resiliency.

Fostering emotional intelligence and wellbeing

In the mid 1990s, Daniel Goleman, psychologist and author, presented a volume of work on emotional intelligence that offers a sound foundation for developing programs associated with emotional and social wellbeing. For Goleman, the foundation for all emotional expression fall into the categories identified in the table below.[65]

Emotion	Related members of the emotional family
Anger	Fury, outrage, resentment, wrath, exasperation, indignation, vexation, acrimony, animosity, annoyance, irritability, hostility; when pathological – hatred and violence.
Sadness	Grief, sorrow, cheerlessness, gloom, melancholy, self-pity, loneliness, dejection, despair; when pathological – severe depression.
Fear	Anxiety, apprehension, nervousness, concern, consternation, misgiving, wariness, qualm, edginess, dread, fright, terror; when pathological – phobia and panic.
Enjoyment	Happiness, joy, relief, contentment, bliss, delight, amusement, pride, sensual pleasure, thrill, rapture, gratification, satisfaction, euphoria, whimsy, ecstasy and at the extreme – mania.
Love	Acceptance, friendliness, trust, kindness, affinity, devotion, adoration, infatuation and agape.
Surprise	Shock, astonishment, amazement and wonder.
Disgust	Contempt, disdain, scorn, abhorrence, aversion, distaste and revulsion.
Shame	Guilt, embarrassment, chagrin, remorse, humiliation, regret, mortification and contrition.

While perhaps not indicative of the full range of emotions available to human beings or cultural variations, Goleman's categories do offer a framework for developing a student's understanding of emotion and some primary emotional catalysts. The key here is that the identification of these emotions and how they impact on our 'feelings', behaviour and/or physiology should form the basis of a strategic curriculum initiative. Indeed, for Goleman, the outcome of being emotionally intelligent via understanding our emotions fosters self-awareness, self-management, social awareness and relationships management; all valuable for a girl's emotional and social wellbeing.[66] The identification of different emotions is the starting point for developing the related skills in coping with those emotions that impact on us negatively. For example, while we all might experience anger differently, our physiological reactions may share similar characteristics – facial expressions, clenched jaw or fists, increased respiration and perspiration and perhaps a shift to other emotional responses including fear or surprise. Education in emotional responses affords us the opportunity to explore this with girls, foster the types of awareness championed by Goleman and develop strategies for coping and resilience. It also fosters opportunities to continually examine the intertwined nature of emotions and relationships.

Developing an awareness of emotions in girls is crucial to helping them understand the power of emotion in the female brain, and how emotions can be used negatively and aggressively. If relational aggression, as explored in Chapter 6, was set out in a framework of understanding emotions and developing emotional intelligence, then perhaps girls would have a greater understanding of its impact. Educators and parents would likewise be more aware of those behaviours often naively attributed to being '*a girl thing*', and could intervene immediately and swiftly to prevent escalation of relational aggression. Back-biting, exclusion, rumours, name calling, manipulation, cliques, isolation, social whispering and popularity are often part of the aggression that exists between and amongst girls, and is often overlooked, leaving the targets of such aggression without an adult to offer assistance.[67] Schools should operate both proactively and reactively to diminish the impact of this kind of behaviour.

One of the ways schools could work to alleviate the many challenges faced by girls in terms of accepting oneself, healthy identity formation and diminishing relational aggression is by revising antibullying policies and handbooks to reflect the newest research on the developing female brain and the interplay between the emotional part of the brain, relationships and social life. This would include information on fostering positive self-identity, heightening understandings of emotional intelligence and fostering recognition of what constitutes aggressive behaviour among **all** students. Existing rules should reflect that specific behaviours such as rumour spreading, alliance building, secret telling and non-verbal aggression warrant the same level of intervention as physical aggression.[68] Moreover, schools must take into account that advances in technology have created another environment for relational aggression to be played out.

As discussed earlier, the use of technology by young people has markedly increased in scope and time over the last two decades, and a consequence of this only briefly noted earlier is the rise of cyberbullying. Cyberbullying is a form of aggression that is intentionally and repeatedly carried out in an electronic context,[69] with some studies showing nearly 75 per cent of school-age children experiencing this form of aggression at least once a year.[70] Cyberbullying is faceless, immediate and transcends physical barriers so that at any given time, and with the right tool in hand, anyone can be a perpetrator of bullying using a screen device. Victims of cyberbullying can experience anxiety, depression, substance abuse, sleep disturbance, truancy, self-harm and even suicide.[71] Schools face the challenge of educating students about the appropriate use of technology while also working to ensure technology is not complicit in bullying; rules and behaviour policies accompanied by clear consequences are important components for mediating and intervening when necessary.

Reactive approaches to inappropriate behaviour and aggression, as detailed above, can of course only go so far. Alternatively, it might be better to revisit the first part of this section with a view to developing proactive arenas for enhancing a girl's understanding of the power of emotions. Given a girl's need for connectedness and relationships, why not take Goleman's work above and ensure that at every level of 'schooling', girls are provided with specific curricular initiatives focusing on the emotional brain? This should also include parents and other community stakeholders as participants. The question for most pragmatists (which is a high percentage of educators) is how do we do this?

There are a number of authors who have studied the nexus between girls, development and education.[72] Each of these has a particular philosophical or theoretical foundation, but the primary motivation of each is providing strategies and ideas for raising healthy and happy girls. Another common denominator of this work is the recognition that the emotional lives of girls are of paramount importance. The following 12 points are a summary of this work, and offer a starting point for individual schools wishing to implement programs for the development of emotional intelligence. As individual contexts will vary, these suggestions are intentionally broad, so that schools can initiate whatever measures necessary for their own unique context. In other words, the points below are not a blanket solution for all schools but a platform for enhancing what is done and what could be done.

12 points for supporting the emotional lives of girls in education

1. Help each girl develop her own sense of self by understanding her emotional self and how she engages with others.

2. Listen carefully to what is said without seeking an immediate solution. Resist the urge to fix anything and everything. Often girls just want to be heard and have their emotions attended to.

3. Always be truthful and provide honest feedback. Remember girls are generally more emotionally mature than boys and open to sincere appraisals.

4. Allow girls the opportunity to express a full range of emotions whenever necessary. Remind them that being angry is a perfectly natural human experience, it is what we do with that anger that requires attention. Provide training in anger management and conflict resolution. This is especially needed during adolescence when the brain's frontal lobes are still developing.

5. Set and maintain consistent and appropriate boundaries. For younger girls, make explanations short. As girls mature, help them to plan goals and negotiate their behaviour around physical and emotional safety. Also remember that while peers are important in the lives of girls we also know that the most influential individual in the life of a child and teenager is a significant adult, especially a parent.

6. Educate girls on the topic of popular culture and offer alternatives where possible. The influence of popular culture on the lives of girls can be quite pervasive or even intrusive. Also, monitor the use of

technology and especially social media sites. There are a number of parental apps that can be downloaded to assist parents in ensuring healthy technology use.

7. Educate girls about developmental inevitabilities and neurological maturation. Teach them about how their brains mature and develop and the differences that exist between male and female brains.

8. Help girls to find balance in life during their school years and as they prepare for their future lives ... girls will often spend too much time stressing about school which can lead to a range of emotional and psychological disorders.

9. Provide positive opportunities for connection. Relationships are integral to the emotional lives of girls. Encourage parental participation in all that the school does and seek parental advice when necessary. Ensure that girls have significant opportunities to use their *own* voice in decision-making regarding their learning and school activities.

10. Always, monitor changes in behaviour, especially those that appear unexpectedly and drastically. Eating and anxiety disorders, depression, self-harm, rapid onset gender dysphoria and other maladies are often the end result of something that started small and manifested itself in an early behavioural change.

11. Teach girls about all types of aggression and inappropriate behaviour. Give girls the information they need and a resource list for seeking help. Each community has plenty of organisations for assisting girls in times of duress or need when a school cannot.

12. Respect a girl's privacy and growing sense of autonomy but remember that until she enters her twenties, her brain is still going through an intense time of development and restructuring. Consistency in approach and rule setting is an adult's way of being a girl's prefrontal lobes.[73]

Summary and some final thoughts on experiences

From the outset of this book, I indicated that writing a work about the female brain and the neuroscientific implications for raising and educating girls was not an easy proposition given my own neurological and social standing. I have attempted to enlighten the reader with the research available and make some suggestions for enhancing formal education. I have also come to embrace the insights of Dr Michael Carr-Gregg, who has identified that a girl's passage through various stages of development are a product of biological growth and change juxtaposed with individual aspects of temperament and personality, adult expectations and social influences.[74]

My own research for this book derived from surveys and interviewing girls, and adolescent girls in particular, across a number of schools, and this process has further entrenched in my mind that the expectations of parents, teachers, administrators and policy makers as well as the social influences that exist in schools warrant far more attention than they currently get. Furthermore, our capacity to engage with the female brain in a manner that suits its unique needs and idiosyncrasies also requires greater consideration. Neuroscientists have only begun to understand the differences that exist between male and female brains, and there may be many further differences as yet undetectable by current technology.[75] What is important to remember, however, is that boys and girls can achieve the same results by using different strategies suited to their needs and abilities. Make no mistake, individual abilities are important but so too are sex differences in the brain. Perhaps the final words and best way to help sum up this chapter can be found in the words of experts in the field who note that:

> *... differences, of course, always harbour the potential to create misunderstanding, even conflict. For now, we must be satisfied that, although we have far to go to understand the detailed neurobiology associated with our own human behaviors, we already have more than enough new information and insight to begin re-evaluating our stereotypes of the sexes, sex differences, and the ever-elusive notion of equality of the sexes.*[76]

It is now time to re-evaluate our understanding of differences in the male and female brain, acknowledge those differences and not confuse equality with a notion that equal means everyone gets the same ... after all, meeting the needs of girls in relation to how their brain grows and develops is truly a matter of experience.

Epilogue

Pink and blue in perspective

More than a decade ago my first book was published. This book focused on boys and the developing male brain. At that time I became anointed as a 'boy' expert, which was certainly not my intent given my interests in most aspects of childhood development. That book was followed by one that focused on girls and now both books have been updated with the girl's version in your hands now. I have learned a great deal since that time and as such am always cautious whenever anyone attempts to label me as a boy and/or girl expert. Expertise is a difficult label to live up to when we continue to learn so much about the developing male and female brain each day. Even as you finish these final pages there are many studies being conducted and concluded that will inform our understanding of the developing brain and offer us even greater insights into how we might best support the young people in our lives. With that in mind, I offer a few final thoughts regarding such matters.

First, it is always important to remember that not all girls, or boys for that matter, are the same. Nature and nurture do not exist in isolation from one another and children do not grow up in environments uninfluenced by the world around them. As a parent and educator, I am buoyed in the knowledge that the environments we create and our own actions can have a positive influence on the neuro-architecture of our children. Relatedly, teachers are in the only profession that focuses on changing the brain each and every day. We know that the experiences that fill a child's first days, months and years have a profound and decisive impact on their neuro-architecture, which will influence the nature and extent of their adult capacities.[1] Moreover, neuroscience provides evidence of the connection between our genetic make-up, our predetermined neural capacities and the role of the environment in shaping our brain and by association our behaviour, intellect, emotions and social wellbeing.

Second, we also know that there is room for improvement in how we educate and raise children. Advances in science and technology have provided us with greater insights into the workings of the mind and as such we can now make better choices for supporting, nurturing and educating the children around us. Paradoxically, technology is also changing the very nature of how students communicate, think and behave, requiring us to continually reflect on what we do as parents and educators. We are going beyond guesswork in understanding how the brain learns, how memory works, how powerful emotions can be and the incredible social nature of the brain. We are also moving past old ideas regarding differences in males and females. Today, simple arguments about 'pink or blue' can longer be identified as defining factors of gender construction and the key elements in understanding girls or boys. Nature and nurture can no longer act as a horse race with one position jockeying over the other for supremacy. Biological sex matters and plays a role in how girls experience the world.

I am not a girl expert, and I don't think the complexity of sex and gender lends itself to such expertise. Instead, I am someone who believes that if we are truly sincere in ensuring that girls succeed in school and in life, then we would do well to better understand how the female brain develops and operates and how this links with the emotional and social lives and cultural contexts of all girls. You may have noticed that the preceding pages embrace a view that greater emphasis on the social and emotional lives of girls is warranted. That is not to say that this has not happened in some contexts, but rather to argue that it should be a compulsory undertaking for parents and teachers alike. This is especially true in a media-rich, technology-driven society where peer and social influence is available 24/7 and where scrutiny and guidance may be lacking.

Finally, like much of what each of us does, this work has been another journey for me. It has been part of an ongoing learning experience that continues to be shaped and influenced by research. As mentioned above, I acknowledge that there is so much more to learn and I welcome the thoughts of those who share the same interests and desires I do to enhance environments for girls. Insights from others will only assist in further developing what we do well, and help us to improve what is problematic. I invite parents and educators to do likewise by continually looking for strategies and ideas that will enhance the lives of the girls around them.

At the beginning of this book I noted that there was a 'boy' crisis. Let's ensure that we are not talking about a girl crisis in the future. Let's do all we can to meet the varying neuro-developmental needs of both boys and girls, or, perhaps more succinctly, let's 'use what we know about gender differences in the brain to enhance learning among all children.'[2]

Chapter Notes

Introduction: Sugar and spice and all things gender specific!
1. Sax 2010, p.5.
2. Committee on Education and Training 2002, p. xviii.
3. Richardson 1997, Shore 1997, Diamond & Hopson 1999 and Shonkoff & Phillips 2000 provide valuable and compelling insights regarding the nature and nurture argument and the role of the environment on shaping our neuro-architecture.
4. Nagel 2006, 2021.
5. Pinker 2002, p. 350–351.

Chapter 1: Sex and gender
1. Yarhouse 2015, p.17.
2. Torgrimson & Minson 2005. See also Hoyenga & Hoyenga 1993, Yarhouse 2015, McGuire 2017.
3. Sax 2002, Soh 2020.
4. Sax 2002, 2017, Yarhouse 2015.
5. Sax 2017.
6. Soh 2020.
7. Savic et al. 2010.
8. Peterson 2018, Soh 2020.
9. Connellan et al. 2000, Pinker 2002, Baron-Cohen 2003, Auyeung et al. 2009, Geary 2010.
10. Sax 2017.
11. de Beauvoir 2011.
12. McGuire 2017.
13. Soh 2020.

14. Yarhouse 2015.
15. Linden 2018a.
16. Ibid.
17. Minton 1997.
18. Ibid.
19. Panksepp & Biven 2012, Yarhouse 2015.
20. Bilodeau 2005. It is noteworthy that the term transgender appears as fluid as its suppositions and continues to evolve as a social construct.
21. The American Psychiatric Association ascribed forms of transgenderism as a form of 'gender identity disorder' in their *Diagnostic and Statistical Manual of Mental Disorders* until 2013 when that label was replaced with 'gender dysphoria' in an effort to limit any stigma associated with the term 'disorder'
22. Gooren 2006, Saraswat et al. 2015, Nota et al. 2017.
23. Panksepp & Biven 2012.
24. Panksepp & Biven 2012, American Psychiatric Association 2013.
25. Littman 2018.
26. Wilson & Shalley 2018.
27. Collin et al. 2016.
28. Ibid.
29. Eliot 2012.
30. Martin et al. 2002.
31. Liben & Bigler 2008.

Chapter 2: The developing brain
1. Carter 2000, p. 8.
2. Goldberg 2001.
3. LeDoux 1998.
4. Hooper & Teresi 1986.
5. Gopnik et al. 1999.
6. Wolfe 2001, Howard 2006.
7. Figure 2.1 is adapted from the work of Diamond & Hopson 1999.
8. Shore 1997.
9. Ibid.
10. Rakic 2002.
11. Nagel 2012.
12. Berninger & Richards 2002, p. 25.
13. Nagel 2006. See also Hardiman 2003, LeDoux 1996, Sylwester 2003.
14. Figure 2.2 is adapted from Balog 2003.
15. Wong & Lichtman 2003.
16. Wang 2018.
17. Chugani et al. 1989.
18. Restak 2001, Howard 2006.
19. Chugani 1996, Shore 1997.
20. LeDoux 2002, Nagel 2014, Nagel & Scholes 2016.
21. Purves et al. 2018.
22. Wiesel 1982. Wiesel & Hubel (1963) and Hubel & Wiesel (1970) provide earlier research examples of sensory deprivation which formed our understanding

of the important links between sensory stimuli and the development of sight in relation to neural connectivity. If you are interested in studies of sensory deprivation with primates or children see Lewis et al. 1990, Beauchamp et al. 1991, Martin et al. 1991, Frank et al. 1996.
23. Johnson 2005, Thomas & Johnson 2008.
24. Nagel & Scholes 2016.
25. Bjorkland 2005, Nagel 2012.
26. Bailey & Kandel 1993, Kandel 2006.
27. Shore 1997.
28. Ibid., Howard 2006.
29. Nagel & Scholes 2016, p. 75.
30. Chugani et al. 1987, 1989, Chugani 1994, 1996, Diamond & Hopson 1999, Eliot 2000, Herschkowitz & Herschkowitz 2004, Hirsch-Pasek & Golinkoff 2004, Nagel 2012.
31. Nagel 2021.
32. Benes 1989.
33. Nagel 2012.
34. Benes et al. 1994, Benes 1989.
35. Brizendine 2006.
36. Giedd et al. 1996, 1999, 2006, Giedd 2004.
37. Nagel 2014.
38. Howard-Jones 2010.
39. Wong & Lichtman 2003, Nelson et al. 2006, Nagel 2014.
40. Kleim & Jones 2008.
41. Diamond & Hopson 1999, p. 239.
42. Nelson et al. 2006, Geier & Luna 2009, Reyna et al. 2011, Nagel 2014.
43. Strauch 2003, Giedd 2010, Geidd et al. 2012, Nagel 2014.
44. MacLean 1990, Carter 2000, Ratey 2001.
45. Ratey 2001, Hardiman 2003.
46. Sylwester 2005.
47. Herschkowitz & Herschkowitz 2004.
48. Carter 2000.
49. Damasio 2001, Nagel 2014.
50. Jensen 1998, Sylwester 2005, Nagel 2012, Nagel & Scholes 2016.
51. Nagel 2014.
52. Carter 2000, Ratey 2001, Hardiman 2003, Sylwester 2005.
53. LeDoux 1998, Berridge 2003.
54. Conlan 1999, Carter 2000, Purves et al. 2018.
55. LeDoux 1998, Hardiman 2003.
56. Carter 2000.
57. Ibid.
58. Wolfe 2001, Sylwester 2005.
59. McEwen & Seeman 2003, Arnsten & Shanskey 2004, Goswami 2004, Lupien et al. 2007, Arnsten 2015, Morgado & Cerqueira 2019.
60. Goldman-Rakic 1993, 1996, Berninger & Richards 2002, Cowan & Morey 2006, Cowan 2008, Li et al. 2014.
61. Hardiman 2003.

62. Carter 2000, Howard 2006.
63. Cowen & Morey 2006, Kandel 2006, Bermudez-Rattoni 2010, Li et al. 2014.
64. Nagel & Scholes 2016.
65. Purves et al. 2018.
66. Carter 2000, Goldberg 2001, 2009, Restak 2001, Howard 2006.
67. Alves et al. 2008.
68. Gazzaniga 1987, Fox 1991, Geary 1998, 2010, Cahill 2005, Howard 2006.
69. Sylwester 2005, Nagel 2014.
70. Hardiman 2003, Sylwester 2005, Nagel 2014.
71. Herschkowitz & Herschkowitz 2004, Sylwester 2005, McDevitt & Ormrod 2020.
72. Wolfe 2001, Hardiman 2003, Purves et al. 2018.
73. Nagel 2012, 2014, Nagel & Scholes 2016.
74. Nagel & Scholes, 2016.
75. Sylwester 2005, Nagel & Scholes 2016.
76. Nagel 2021.
77. Giedd et al. 1999, Casey et al. 2000, Spear 2000a, Goldberg 2001, 2009, Hardiman 2003, Giedd 2004, Sylwester 2005, Nelson et al. 2006, Cole et al. 2012.
78. Bradley 2003, p.6. See also Giedd et al. 1999, Levitt 2003, Strauch 2003, Steinberg 2011, Spear 2013.
79. For research on maturational development of the brain see Giedd et al. 1999, 2006, Giedd 2004 and Sylwester 2003. For information related to gender differences in neurological maturation see Giedd et al. 1996, Blum 1997, Cahill 2005, Brizendine 2006, 2010, Geary 2010).

Chapter 3: Boys and girls are different
1. Kimura 2000, p. 3.
2. These points are adapted from the work of Glucksman 1981. For a further look at the differences presented along with others of note see Legato 2002, Neigh & Mitzelfelt 2016, LoMaura & Aliverti 2018, LaMarca & Alexander 2019.
3. Canadian researchers led by Tomas Paus (Paus et al. 2017) recently documented sex differences in 66 quantitative characteristics of the brain and body measured in a sample of 1,024 adolescents between the ages of 12 and 18.
4. Halpern 2000.
5. Ruigrok et al. 2014.
6. McEwen 2009, p. 144.
7. Hanamsagar & Bilbo 2016, Zagni et al. 2016.
8. Legato, 2002.
9. Ellis 2011a, p. 710.
10. Simon Baron-Cohen researches and teaches at the University of Cambridge where he is a Professor of Developmental Psychopathology and the Director of the Autism Research Centre. As well as being a world-renowned neuroscientist and expert in autistic behaviour, Professor Baron-Cohen is also the author of *The Essential Difference: The Truth About the Male and Female Brain*.
11. Richardson 1997, Diamond & Hopson 1999, Halpern 2000, Strauch 2003, Nagel 2020.
12. Wager & Ochsner, 2005.
13. Legato 2002, p. 19.

14. Soh 2021.
15. Su et al. 2009, De Bolle et al. 2015, Peterson 2018.
16. Peterson 2018. See also Bihagen & Katz-Gerro 2000, Costa et al. 2001, Schmitt et al. 2008, Su et al. 2009, Lippa 2010.
17. Lippa 2005, Scmitt et al. 2008.
18. Baron-Cohen 2003.
19. Ibid.
20. Nagel 2020.
21. See Nadeau 1996 to explore learning difficulties in boys and Alexander 2014 for discussions on social behaviour.
22. Halpern 2000, Legato 2002.
23. Baron-Cohen 2003.
24. Baron-Cohen 2003, Howard 2006, Geary 2010.
25. Halpern 2000, Baron-Cohen 2003, Legato 2002, 2005, Brizendine 2006, Halpern 2000, Howard 2006.
26. Gurian 2011, p.16. See also Moir & Jessel 1998, Cahill 2005, Brizendine 2006, 2010, Howard 2006.
27. Moir & Moir 1999, p. 119.
28. Brizendine 2006, p. 1.
29. Gur et al. 1991, Halpern 2000.
30. Collaer & Hines,1995.
31. Halpern 2000.
32. DeBellis et al. 2001, Koolshijn & Crone 2013.
33. Diamond & Hopson 1999, Eliot 2000, 2012, Legato 2005.
34. Watson et al. 2010, Borgonovi et al. 2018, Mitchell 2018.
35. Watson et al. 2010. For some detailed insights into how the language abilities and capabilities of each sex are orchestrated in the brain see Phillips et al. 2001 and Shaywitz et al. 1995.
36. Kimura 2000, 2004, Brizendine 2006.
37. Howard 2006.
38. Ratey 2001.
39. Shaywitz 1995, Kanasaku et al. 2000, Kimura 2000, Kanasaku & Kitazawa 2001, Howard 2006, Ingalhalikar et al. 2014.
40. Purves et al. 2018.
41. Ibid.
42. Ratey 2001.
43. Dubb et al. 2003, Ardekani et al. 2013.
44. Halpern 2000, Kimura 2000, Legato 2002, Baron-Cohen 2003, Baron-Cohen et al. 2003, Howard 2006, Shin et al. 2005, Mitchell 2018.
45. Ellis 2011a, p709. See also Hausmann 2017.
46. Halpern 2000, Kimura 2000, Miller & Halpern 2014, Asperholm et al. 2019.
47. Brizendine 2006, Geary 2010.
48. Eliot 2000.
49. Kimura 2000, 2004.
50. Kimura 2000.
51. Gur et al. 1999, Howard 2006.
52. Gur et al. 1999, 2002, Canli et al. 2002, Wager & Ochsner 2005, Brizendine 2006,

2010, Gur & Gur 2017, Sax 2017.
53. Eliot 2012.
54. Sylwester 2005, Howard 2006, Purves et al. 2018.
55. Peiper 1925.
56. Connellan et al. 2000.
57. Nadeau 1996, Connellan et al. 2000, Eliot 2000, 2012, Lutchmaya & Baron-Cohen 2002, Gurian & Stevens 2011, Proverbio 2017.
58. Baron-Cohen, 2003.
59. Gur & Gur 1990, 2002, 2017, Gur et al. 1990, 1991, 1995, 1999, 2002.
60. Sax 2005, 2017.
61. Halpern 2000.
62. Mitchell 2018.
63. For an in-depth look at how a larger male brain may be problematic see the work of Dr Emese Nagy and colleagues (2001) who outline how a larger brain and lower metabolic rates possibly contribute to impaired understanding of language, autism and other disorders that occur more frequently in boys than girls.
64. Gur & Gur 1990, Gur et al. 1995, Legato 2005.
65. Giedd et al. 1999, Howard 2006, Strauch 2003, Nagel 2014, Wilbrecht 2018
66. Benes 1989, Diamond & Hopson 1999, Gur et al. 1999, Legato 2005, Brizendine 2006.
67. Adapted from Gurian 2001. See also Baron-Cohen 2003, Brizendine 2006, Eliot 2000, Geary 2010, Goldberg 2001, Gurian & Stevens 2011, Halpern 2000, Koss & Frick 2017, Legato 2002, Moir & Jessel 1989, Reber & Tranel 2017, Sylwester 2005.

Chapter 4: The developing brain and growing up female
1. Gurian 2003, p. 10.
2. Connellan et al. 2000.
3. Lutchmaya & Baron-Cohen 2002, Alexander et al. 2009a, Su et al. 2009, Mitchell 2018.
4. Eliot 2012, Mitchell 2018.
5. Gurian 2003, Baron-Cohen 2003.
6. Howard 2006.
7. Ellis 2011a.
8. Halpern 2000.
9. Baron-Cohen 2003, Brizendine 2006, Howard 2006.
10. Brizendine 2006, p. 15.
11. Both Simon Baron-Cohen (2003) and Louann Brizendine (2006) provide detailed accounts of the impact of testosterone on early language skills and emotion. Other important work in this area includes Geschwind & Galaburda 1985, 1987, Moir & Jessel 1998, Halpern 2000, Sax 2005, 2017, Geary 2010, Mitchell 2018.
12. Lutchmaya & Baron-Cohen 2002, Baron-Cohen 2003.
13. Gurian 2003, Gurian & Stevens 2011.
14. See, for example, Baron-Cohen 2003, Shaffer & Gordon 2005, Brizendine 2006.
15. Del Guidice et al. 2012.

16. Brizendine 2006, 2010, Copeland & Chernausek 2016.
17. Brizendine 2006.
18. Lavelli & Fogel 2002, Leeb & Rejskind 2004, Todd et al. 2018.
19. Pinker 2002, Pankeep 2005, Mitchell 2018.
20. Goleman 1995, Baron-Cohen 2003, Panksepp 2005, Eliot 2012.
21. Baron-Cohen, 2003. For an expansive look at sex differences in early relationships, play and behaviour see Maccoby 1990, McGuiness 1990, Moir & Jessel 1998, Panksepp 2005.
22. Panksepp 2005, Hassett et al. 2008, Geary 2010, Kahlenberg & Wrangham 2010, Mitchell 2018.
23. Maccoby 1990.
24. Sax 2017.
25. Berenbaum et al. 2007.
26. Carlson & Taylor 2005.
27. Nagel 2012.
28. There is a great deal of research evidence and literature identifying chemical, anatomical and functional differences in the male and female limbic systems. A good starting point would be to begin with Brizendine 2006.
29. Cahill 2005.
30. Baron-Cohen 2003.
31. Brizendine 2006.
32. Hoyenga & Hoyenga 1993.
33. Baron-Cohen 2003, Nagel 2021.
34. Simmons 2002, Cohen-Sandler 2005, Brizendine 2006.
35. Gurian 2003, Baron-Cohen 2003, Gurian & Stevens 2010, Sax 2017.
36. Kusche & Greenberg 2006.
37. Brizendine 2006, p. 30.
38. Brizendine 2006.
39. Moir and Jessel 1998, p. 70.
40. Benes 1989, Benes et al. 1994.
41. Oxytocin, dopamine and serotonin receive greater description in later chapters.
42. Mori & Jessel 1998, Gurian 2003, Brizendine 2006, Howard 2006, Sax 2017.

Chapter 5: 'I love you': emotions and the female brain
1. Brizendine 2006, p. 133.
2. Lutchmaya & Baron-Cohen 2002, Baron-Cohen 2003, Brizendine 2006.
3. Geary 2010.
4. The works of Ruben and Raquel Gur and their colleagues are often regarded as the most informative for understanding differences in male and female limbic systems and numerous articles noted in the bibliography provide the foundation of the points made here.
5. Brizendine 2006.
6. Aamodt & Wang 2011.
7. Brizendine 2006.
8. Brody et al. 2016.
9. Tannen 2013.
10. Aamodt & Wang 2011, Ellis 2011a, Lange et al. 2016.

11. Legato 2005, Brizendine 2006.
12. LeDoux 2002, Goleman 2006.
13. Moir & Moir 1999, Panksepp 2005, Legato 2005, Brizendine 2006, Howard 2006, Gao et al. 2016.
14. Taylor et al. 2000, LeDoux 2002, McEwan & Lasley 2005, Goleman 2006, Howard 2006, Preckel et al. 2014, Gao et al. 2016.
15. Taylor et al. 2000, Preckel et al. 2014, Gao et al. 2016.
16. Brizendine, 2006.
17. Chambers et al. 2003, Casey et al. 2008, Galvan 2010, 2012, Purves et al. 2018.
18. Southschek et al. 2017, See also Croson & Gneezy 2009, Rand et al. 2016.
19. Brizendine 2006.
20. Bethea et al. 2002, Legato 2002, Hines 2010, Kret & Gelder 2012, Marrocco & McEwan 2016, McEwan & Milner 2017, Wellman et al. 2018, Hines 2020.
21. Legato 2002, Baron-Cohen 2003, Hamann 2005, Brizendine 2006, Ngun et al. 2011.
22. Canli et al. 2002, Cahill 2005, McEwen & Lasley 2005.
23. Taylor et al. 2000, Brizendine 2006, Sylwester 2007, Wang et al. 2007, Preckel et al. 2014, Gao et al. 2016.
24. Panksepp 2005, Sapolsky 2017, Mitchell 2018.
25. Hoyenga & Hoyenga 1993, Geary 2010, Sapolsky 1997, 2017, Mitchell 2018.
26. Brizendine, 2006.
27. Nagy et al. 2001, Butler et al. 2005, Fields 2016, Ashley et al. 2017.
28. Bradley & Lang 2000, Taylor et al. 2000, Preckel et al. 2014, Gao et al. 2016.
29. Geary 2010, Sapolsky 2017.
30. Bethea et al. 2002, Legato 2002, 2005, Hamann 2005, Brizendine 2006, Howard 2006, Perry & Pauletti 2011.
31. Hoyenga & Hoyenga 1993, Forbes et al. 2004, Young & Altemus 2004, Geary 2010.
32. Legato 2005, Shaffer & Gordon 2005, Geary 2010.
33. Geary, 2010.
34. Strauch 2003, p. 13. See also, Blakemore & Choudhury 2006, Giedd 2004, 2010, Giedd et al. 2006, 2012, Casey et al. 2008, 2011, Galvan et al. 2012, Nagel 2014.
35. Giedd et al. 1996, 1999, Giedd 2004, Nagel 2014.
36. Giedd et al. 1999, Seeman 1999, Spear 2000a, 2000b, Dahl 2003, Giedd 2004, 2010, Sisk & Foster 2004, Legato 2005, Shaffer & Gordon 2005, Nagel 2014, Blakemore 2018.
37. Giedd et al. 1999, Casey et al. 2000, Spear 2000, Nagel 2014, Blakemore 2018.

Chapter 6: 'I hate you': relationships and the female brain
1. Baron-Cohen 2003, pp. 43–44.
2. For an in-depth and insightful look into the intimate side of girls and relationships see Sharon Lamb's 2001 work *The Secret Lives of Girls*.
3. Baron-Cohen 2003. There are a number of different books and articles available that look at boys and relationships. For those who have sons or work with boys, some worth considering include Goleman 1995, Lewis 1997, Gurian 1997, 2000, Biddulph 1998, 2013, Kindlon & Thompson 1999, Stevens 1999, Robinson 2001, Hawkes 2001, 2014, Gurian & Stevens 2005, Shaffer & Gordon 2005a, Nagel 2021.

4. Rys & Bear 1997, Geary 2010.
5. Goleman 1995, Beneson et al. 1997, Baron-Cohen 2003, Legato 2005, Brizendine, 2006.
6. Worrel 1988, p.478, See also Hoyenga & Hoyenga 1993, Baron-Cohen 2003, Brizendine 2006.
7. Gasbarri et al. 2012, Pompili et al. 2016.
8. Brizendine 2006, Bos et al. 2012, Olsson et al. 2016, Toffeletto et al. 2014.
9. Gurian 2003, Hirsh & Brizendine 2007, Derntl et al. 2008, Ngun et al. 2011.
10. Baron-Cohen 2003, Gurian 2003, Brizendine 2006, Gurian & Stevens 2011.
11. For an extensive list of research documenting cooperative and structured play and relationships amongst girls see Hoyenga & Hoyenga 1993. See also Brizendine 2006, Berenbaum et al. 2008.
12. Gurian 2003, Brizendine 2006, Geary 2010.
13. Geary 2010.
14. Blakemore et al. 2007.
15. Moore et al. 2014.
16. Brizendine 2006, p. 31.
17. Brizendine 2006.
18. Wharton et al. 2012, Cservenka et al. 2015.
19. Wharton et al. 2012, see also Halbreich & Kahn 2001.
20. Brizendine 2006.
21. Eberling et al. 2003, Protopescu et al. 2008.
22. Benenson & Christakos 2003, Geary 2010, Sauter et al. 2020.
23. Parker & Seal, Geary 2010.
24. Benenson & Christakos 2003, Rose & Rudolph 2006.
25. Kraft & Mayeaux 2018.
26. Parker et al. 2005.
27. It is noteworthy that within dating relationships, females engage in physical aggression towards their partners as often as males do, but females are more likely to be injured (Frieze 2000, Archer 2000, 2009, Perry & Pauletti 2011, Rode & Rode 2018).
28. The phrase 'relational aggression' was initially coined in the work of psychologists Nick Crick and Jennifer Grotpeter in 1995.
29. Eslea 2010.
30. Crick & Grotpeter 1995, Crick et al. 1996, Paquette & Underwood 1999, Archer 2004, Yoon et al. 2004, Smith et al, 2009, Simmons 2011, Orpinas et al. 2015.
31. Bowie 2010.
32. Orpinas et al. 2015.
33. Putallaz et al. 2004, Bowie 2010.
34. Simmons, 2011.
35. Maccoby 1990, Brizendine, 2006, Bowie 2010.
36. Carr-Gregg 2006.
37. Tomada & Schneider 1997, Owens et al. 2000, Campbell 2004, Kawabata et al. 2010. Of particular significance is the work of Osterman et al. 2000 who note studies of female aggression in 137 societies with descriptions of numerous ways in which females engage in relational or social aggression.
38. Geary 2010.

39. Sapolsky 2017.
40. LaFontana & Cillessen 2002.
41. Vaillancourt 2013.
42. Centifanti et al. 2015.
43. Simmons 2011.
44. Cillessen & Mayeux, 2004, Rose et al. 2004.
45. Card et al. 2008, Marsee et al. 2014, Centifanti et al. 2015.
46. Panksepp 2003.
47. Brizendine 2006, Wiseman 2016.
48. Brizendine 2006.
49. Simmons 2011, p. 3.
50. Orpinas et al. 2015 See also Prinstein et al. 2001, Card et al. 2008, Ellis et al. 2008, Risser 2013, Underwood et al. 2011, Williams & Kennedy 2012.
51. Rode & Rode, 2018.

Chapter 7: 'It's a girl thing'
1. Pipher & Pipher 2019, p. 227.
2. Nagel 2020.
3. Martel 2013.
4. Soto, 2016.
5. Born et al. 2002.
6. Nagel 2014.
7. Pipher & Pipher 2019.
8. Spear 2010, Eliot 2012.
9. Howell et al. 2001, McLean et al. 2011, Eliot 2012, Altemus et al. 2014, Avenevoli et al. 2015, Van Droogenbroeck et al. 2018, Jalnapurkar et al. 2018, Wenjuan et al. 2020. See also Friedman & Schustack 2016.
10. Madsen et al. 2018.
11. Khan 2020.
12. Mu et al. 2020.
13. American Psychiatric Association 2013.
14. Spear 2010.
15. Van Droogenbroeck 2018.
16. Spear 2010, Christiansen 2015, Coplan et al. 2015, Schmitt et al. 2017, Asher & Aderka 2018.
17. Howell et al. 2001.
18. Eliot 2012.
19. Brizendine 2006, Zahn-Waxler et al. 2008, Spear 2010, Eliot 2012, Martel 2013, Altemus et al. 2014.
20. Brizendine 2006, Afifi 2007, Wenjuan et al. 2020.
21. Rose & Rudolph 2006, Perry & Pauletti 2011.
22. Perry & Pauletti 2011.
23. Smith & Mackie 2007, Donnellan et al. 2011, MacDonald & Leary 2012.
24. Baumeister et al. 2003, Orth & Robins 2014.
25. Pruessner et al. 2005.
26. Eliot 2012.
27. Phillips et al. 2006, Schneider et al. 2017, 2018.

28. Perry & Pauletti 2011, Eliot 2012.
29. Pipher & Pipher 2019.
30. Twenge 2017.
31. Perry & Pauletti 2011.
32. Harter 2006, Pipher & Pipher 2019.
33. Ruble et al. 2006, Perry & Pauletti 2011, Kvardova et al. 2020.
34. Erikson 1959, 1963, 1964, 1968.
35. Nagel 2019.
36. Ibid.
37. Prinstein 2007, Brechwald & Prinstein 2011, Schwartz-Mette & Smith 2018.
38. Dishion & Tipsord 2011.
39. Dishion & Tipsord 2011. See also Dishion et al. 2004, Gardner & Steinberg 2005, Steinberg & Monahan 2007.
40. Brechwald & Prinstein 2011, Schwartz-Mette & Smith 2018.
41. Schwartz-Mette & Smith 2018. See also Prinstein et al. 2005, Stevens & Prinstein 2005, Prinstein 2007, Dishion & Tipsord 2011, Schwartz-Mette & Rose 2012, Littman 2018.
42. Prinstein 2007, Starr 2015, Schwartz-Mette & Smith 2018, Littman 2018.
43. Connelly & Platt 2014.
44. Campbell 2017.
45. van Beijsterveldt et al. 2006, Kuyper & Wijsen 2014, Yarhouse 2015.
46. Steensma et al. 2013, Yarhouse 2015, Beek et al. 2016.
47. Eliot 2012.
48. Ibid.
49. Kaltiala-Heino et al. 2018.
50. Coolidge et al. 2002, van Beijsterveldt et al. 2006, Eliot 2012, Saraswat et al. 2015.
51. Diamond 2008, Perry & Pauletti 2011, Zucker 2017.
52. Beek et al. 2016.
53. Pang et al. 2020.
54. Zucker et al. 2016.
55. Ristori & Steensma 2016, Kaltiala-Heino et al. 2018, Laidlaw et al. 2019.
56. Shrier 2020. See also Collin et al. 2016, Pang et al. 2020.
57. Littman 2018. See also Edwards-Leeper & Spack 2012, Cohen-Kettenis & Klink 2015, Zucker 2019.
58. Littman 2018.
59. Soh 2020.
60. Littman 2018. See also Edwards-Leeper & Spack 2012, Steensma et al. 2013.
61. Shrier 2020.
62. de Graaf et al. 2016.
63. Ruble et al. 2006.
64. Littman 2018, Zucker 2019, Hutchinson et al. 2020.
65. Littman 2018, Shrier 2020.
66. Graber 2013, Hamlat et al. 2019.
67. Eliot 2012, Sax 2017.
68. Ullsperger & Nikolas 2017, Hamlet et al. 2019, Colich et al. 2020.
69. Colich et al. 2020.

70. Byrne et al. 2017.
71. Rose et al. 2017, Schwartz-Mette & Smith 2018.
72. Twenge 2017.
73. Keshishian et al. 2016, Lukianoff & Haidt 2018.
74. Van Droogenbroeck 2018.

Chapter 8: Experiences Matter!
1. Wang 2018 p. 34.
2. Nagel 2008 p. 92.
3. Au 2009, Au & Gourd 2013, Watson et al. 2014, Nagel & Scholes 2016, Nagel 2019a.
4. Wyn, Turnbull & Grimshaw 2014.
5. Hirsch-Pasek et al. 2004, 2009, Nagel 2012, Camarata 2015, Hassinger et al. 2019, Schlesinger et al. 2020.
6. Gazzaniga 1998.
7. Santrock 2017.
8. Carvalho 2016. See also Gibb et al. 2008, Matthews et al. 2009, Lane et al. 2012, Voyer & Voyer 2014, Organisation for Economic and Cooperative Development (OECD) 2015a, Peterson 2018.
9. Carvalho 2016.
10. Saucier & Srivastava 2015.
11. Caspi et al. 2005, Soto 2016.
12. Feingold 1994, Bratko et al. 2006, Kappe & van der Flier 2012, Vecchione et al. 2012, Carvalho 2016, Schmitt et al. 2017.
13. Goldberg 1990, Hogan et al. 1996, Costa & McCrae 2008, Schmitt et al. 2008, Poropat 2009, Rothman & Coetzer 2013, Desrochers et al. 2019.
14. Carvalho 2016.
15. Kappe & van der Flier 2012, Soto 2016.
16. Komarraju et al. 2011. It is important to note that stress literally shuts down learning – stressed individuals typically have higher levels of the stress hormone cortisol which has a negative influence on higher order thinking.
17. Soto 2016 See also Roberts & Wood 2006, Roberts, Walton & Viechtbauer 2006.
18. Roberts 2014, OECD 2015a, McCarthy 2018, Australian Bureau of Statistics 2018.
19. Cheryan 2012, Roberts 2014.
20. Varma 2010, Gunderson et al. 2012.
21. Beilock 2008, Beilock et al. 2010.
22. Alexander et al. 2009b, Auyeng et al. 2009, Tapp et al. 2011, Schmitt et al. 2014, Soh 2020.
23. Schmitt 2015, Mitchell 2018, Peterson 2018, Soh 2020.
24. Schmitt et al. 2017.
25. Schmitt 2015. See also Mealey 2000, Ellis 2011b, Archer 2019.
26. Kimura 2000, 2004.
27. Geake 2009.
28. For a detailed discussion on the issues surrounding mathematical aptitude see Halpern 2000, Kimura 2000, 2004 and Howard 2006.
29. Carvalho 2016.

30. OECD 2015b, p. 3.
31. Nagel 2021.
32. OECD 2015b.
33. OECD 2010, 2014, 2019.
34. Adapted from Hirsh-Pasek et al. 2015, pp. 3–34.
35. Twenge & Campbell 2018.
36. Rhodes 2017.
37. Pipher & Pipher 2019.
38. Cozolino 2013.
39. Yu & Baxter 2016. See also Caroli et al. 2004, Martin 2011, Laurson et al. 2014, Lissak 2018, Twenge et al. 2018a, 2018b.
40. Yu & Baxter 2016.
41. Houghton et al. 2015, Rhodes 2017.
42. Twenge et al. 2018a. See also Gentile et al. 2010, Twenge et al. 2016, 2017.
43. Twenge 2017, Twenge et al. 2018a.
44. Kvardova et al. 2020.
45. Costigan et al. 2013.
46. Bruni et al. 2015, Carter et al. 2016.
47. Lissak et al. 2018.
48. Nagel, 2021. See also Kimbrough et al. 2013, Booker et al. 2018, Viner et al. 2019.
49. Twenge 2018.
50. Rajanal et al. 2018.
51. Schneider et al. 2016.
52. Phillips & Menard 2006.
53. Felton et al. 2019.
54. Rose 2002, Stone et al. 2011, Jose et al. 2012, Barstead et al. 2013, Rose et al. 2017.
55. Rose 2002, Rose et al. 2007.
56. See, for example, Brandtzaeg 2012, Grieve et al. 2013.
57. Zhang et al. 2020.
58. Booker et al. 2018.
59. Twenge 2017, p. 83.
60. Nagel & Scholes 2016.
61. Nagel 2019b.
62. McGaugh 2004, Morris 2006, Bermudez-Rattoni 2010, Dudai & Morris 2013.
63. Barrett et al. 2005, Ritchey et al. 2011.
64. Cohen-Sandler 2005, p. 5.
65. Adapted from Goleman 2021.
66. Goleman 2021.
67. Simmons 2011.
68. Ibid.
69. Kowlaski et al. 2014.
70. Juvonen & Gross 2008, Katzer et al. 2009.
71. Kowlaski et al. 2014. See also Beran & Li 2005, Mitchell et al. 2007, Ybarra et al. 2007, Privitera & Campbell 2009, Beran et al. 2012.
72. See, for example, Gurian 2003, Carr-Gregg 2006, Shaffer & Gordon 2005, Sax 2010, Simmons 2011, Wiseman 2016, Pipher & Pipher 2019.

73. The points above are a product of the author's insights and draw on work by Gurian 2003, Carr-Gregg 2006, Shaffer & Gordon 2005, Sax 2010, Simmons 2011, Wiseman 2016, Pipher & Pipher 2019, Shrier 2020.
74. Carr-Gregg 2006.
75. Wager & Ochsner 2005.
76. McEwen & Lasley 2005, p. 15.

Epilogue
1. Shore 1997.
2. Karges-Bone 1998, p. 9.

Bibliography

Aamodt, S & S Wang. (2011). *Welcome to Your Child's Brain: How the Mind Grows From Conception to College.* New York, Bloomsbury.
Adani, S & M Cepenac. (2019). Sex differences in early communication development: Behavioral and neurobiological indicators of more vulnerable communication system development in boys. *Croatian Medical Journal,* 60 (2): 141-49. doi: 10.3325/cmj.2019.60.141
Afifi, M. (2007). Gender differences in mental health. *Singapore Medical Journal,* 48(5): 385-91.
Alexander, GM. (2014). Postnatal testosterone concentrations and male social development. *Frontiers in Endocrinology,* 5: 15. doi:10.3389/fendo.2014.00015
Alexander, GM, T Wilcox & R Woods. (2009a). Sex differences in infants' visual interest in toys. *Archives of Sexual Behavior,* 38(3): 427-33. doi:10.1007/s10508-008-9430-1
Alexander, GM, T Wilcox & MB Farmer. (2009b). Hormone behavior associations in early infancy. *Hormones and Behavior,* 56(5): 498-502. doi:10.1016/j.yhbeh.2009.08.003.
Altemus, M, N Sarvaiya & CN Epperson. (2014). Sex differences in anxiety and depression clinical perspectives. *Frontiers in Neuroendocrinology,* 35(3): 320-30. doi:10.1016/j.yfrne.2014.05.004
Alves, NT, SS Fukusima & JA Aznar-Caqsanova. (2008). Models of brain asymmetry in emotional processing. *Psychology & Neuroscience,* 1(1), 63-66. doi:10.3922/j/psns.2008.1.010.
American Academy of Pediatrics – Council on Communications and Media. (2016). Media and Young Minds. *Pediatrics,* 2016;138(5), 1-6.
American Psychiatric Association. (2013). *Diagnostic and Statistical Manual of Mental Disorders,* 5th ed. Washington, DC: American Psychiatric Association.

Archer, J. (2000). Sex differences in aggression between heterosexual partners: A meta-analytic review. *Psychological Bulletin, 126*(5), 651-80. doi:10.1037/0033-2909.126.5.651

Archer J. (2004). Sex differences in aggression in real-world settings: A meta-analytic review. *Review of General Psychology,* 8(4), 291-322. doi:10.1037/1089-2680.8.4.291

Archer, J. (2009). Does sexual selection explain human sex differences in aggression? *Behavioral and Brain Sciences,* 32(3-4), 249-66. doi:10.1017/S0140525X09990951.

Archer, J. (2019). The reality and evolutionary significance of human psychological sex differences. *Biological Reviews,* 94(4), 1381-1415. doi:10.1111/brv.12507.

Ardekani, BA, K Figarsky, & JJ Sidtis. (2013). Sexual dimorphism in the human corpus callosum: An MRI study using the OASIS brain database. *Cerebral Cortex,* 23(10), 2514-2520. doi:10.1093/cercor/bhs253

Arnsten, AFT. (2015). Stress weakens prefrontal networks: Molecular insults to higher cognition. *Nature Neuroscience,* 18, 1376-85.

Arnsten, AFT & RM Shansky. (2004). Adolescence: Vulnerable period for stress-induced prefrontal cortical function? Introduction to Part IV. *Annals of the New York Academy of Sciences,* 1021, 143-47.

Asher, M. & IM Aderka. (2018). Gender differences in social anxiety disorder. *Journal of Clinical Psychology,* 74(10), 1730-41. doi:10.1002/jclp.22624

Ashley, AA, LM Turnbull, MA Darian, DE Feldman, I Song & NC Tronson. (2017). Sex differences in context fear generalisation and recruitment of hippocampus and amygdala during retrieval. *Neuropsychopharmacology,* 42(2), 397-407. doi:10.1038/npp.2016.174

Asperholm, M, S Nagar, S Dekhtyar & A Herlitz. (2019). The magnitude of sex differences in verbal episodic memory increases with social progress: Data from 54 countries across 40 years. *PLOS ONE* 14(4), e0214945. doi:10.1371/journal.pone.0214945

Au, W. (2009). *Unequal By Design: High Stakes Testing and the Standardisation of Inequality.* New York: Routledge.

Au, W & K Gourd. (2013). Why high-stakes testing is bad for everyone, including English teachers. *The English Journal,* 103(1), 14-19.

Australian Bureau of Statistics. (2018). 4125.0 - Gender Indicators, Australia, Sep 2018. Retrieved from https://www.abs.gov.au/ausstats/abs@.nsf/Lookup/by%20Subject/4125.0~Sep%202018~Main%20Features~Education~5

Australian Human Rights Commission. (2014). *Face the Facts: Lesbian, Gay, Bisexual, Trans and Intersex People.* Sydney: Australian Human Rights Commission.

Auyeung, B, S Baron-Cohen, E Ashwin, R Knickmeyer, K Taylor, G Hackett & M Hines. (2009). Fetal testosterone predicts sexually differentiated childhood behavior in girls and in boys. *Psychological Science,* 20(2), 144-48. doi: 10.1111/j.1467-9280.2009.02279.x.

Avenevoli, S, J Swendsen, JP He, M Burstein & KR Merikangas. (2015). Major depression in the national comorbidity survey-adolescent supplement: Prevalence, correlates, and treatment. *Journal of the American Academy of Child & Adolescent Psychiatry,* 54(1), 37-44.

Bailey, C & ER Kandel. (1993). Structural changes accompanying memory storage. *Annual Review of Physiology*, 55, 397–426. doi:10.1146/annurev.ph.55.030193.002145.

Balog, D, ed. (2003). *The Dana Sourcebook of Brain Science*, 4th ed. New York: Dana Press.

Barbu, S, G Cabanes & G Le Maner-Idrissi. (2011). Boys and girls on the playground: Sex differences in social development are not stable across early childhood. *PLOS ONE*, 6(1), e16047. doi:10.1371/journal.pone.0016407

Baron-Cohen, S. (2003). *The Essential Difference: The Truth About the Male and Female Brain*. New York: Basic Books.

Barrett, LF, PM Niedenthal & P Winkielman. (2005). *Emotion and Consciousness*. New York: The Guilford Press.

Barstead, MG, LC Bopuchard & JS Shih. (2013). Understanding gender differences in co-rumination and confidant choice in young adults. *Journal of Social and Clinical Psychology*, 32(7), 791–808.

Baumeister, RF, JD Campbell, JI Kruegar & KD Vohs. (2003). Does self-esteem cause better performance, interpersonal success, happiness or healthier lifestyles. *Psychological Science in the Public Interest*, 4(1), 1–44. doi:10.1111/1529-1006.01431

Beauchamp, AJ, JP Gluck, HE Fouty & MH Lewis. (1991). Associative processes in differently reared rhesus monkeys (Macaca mulatta): blocking. *Developmental Psychobiology*, 24(3), 175–89.

Beek, TF, T Cohen-Kettenis & BPC Kreukels. (2016). Gender incongruence/gender dysphoria and its classification history. *International Review of Psychiatry*, 28(1), 5–12. doi:10.3109/09540261.2015.1091293

Beilock, SL. (2008). Math performance in stressful situations. *Current Directions in Psychological Science*, 17(5), 339–43. doi:10.1111/j.1467-8721.2008.00602.x

Beilock, SL, EA Gunderson, G Ramirez & SC Levine. (2010). Female teachers' math anxiety affects girls' math achievement. *Proceedings of the National Academy of Sciences*, 107(5), 1860–63. doi:10.1073/pnas.0910967107.

Benenson, JF & A Christakos. (2003). The greater fragility of females' versus males' closest same-sex friendships. *Child Development*, 74(4), 1123–29.

Benes, FM. (1989). Myelination of cortical-hippocampal relays during late adolescence. *Schizophrenia Bulletin*, 15(4), 585–93.

Benes, FM, M Turtle, Y Khan & P Farol. (1994). Myelination of a key relay zone in the hippocampal formation occurs in the human brain during childhood, adolescence and adulthood. *Archives of General Psychiatry*, 51(6), 477–84.

Beran, T & Q Li. (2005). Cyber-harassment: A study of a new method for an old behavior. *Journal of Educational Computing Research*, 32(3), 265–77. doi:10.2190/8YQM-B04H-PG4D-BLLH.

Beran, TN, C Rinaldi, DS Bickham & M Rich. (2012). Evidence for the need to support adolescents dealing with harassment and cyberharassment: Prevalence, progression, and impact. *School Psychology International*, 33(5), 562–76. doi:10.1177/0143034312446976.

Berenbaum, SA, CL Martin, LD Hanish, PT Briggs & RA Fabes. (2008). Sex differences in children's play. In *Sex Differences in the Brain: From Genes to Behavior*, edited by JB Becker, K Berkley, N Geary, E Hampson, JP Herman & EA Young, 275–90. New York: Oxford University Press.

Bermudez-Rattoni, F. (2010). Is memory consolidation a multiple-circuit system? *Proceedings of the National Academy of Sciences*, 107(18), 8051-52.
Berninger, VW & TL Richards. (2002). *Brain Literacy for Educators and Psychologists.* San Diego: Elsevier Science.
Berridge, KC. (2003). Comparing the emotional brains of humans and other animals. In *Handbook of Affective Sciences,* edited by RJ Davidson, KR Scherer & H Hill Goldsmith, 25-52. Oxford: Oxford University Press.
Benenson, JF, NH Apostoleris & J Parnass. (1997). Age and sex differences in dyadic and group interaction. *Developmental Psychology*, 33(3), 538-43.
Bethea, C, NZ Lu, C Gundlah & JM Streicher. (2002). Diverse actions of ovarian steroids in the serotonin neural system. *Frontiers in Neuroendocrinology*, 23(1), 41-100.
Biddulph, S. (1998). *Raising Boys.* Sydney: Finch Publishing.
Biddulph, S. (2013). *The New Manhood.* Sydney: Simon & Schuster Australia.
Bihagen, E & T Katz-Gerro. (2000). Culture consumption in Sweden: The stability of gender differences. *Poetics*, 27(5), 327-49. doi:10.1016/S0304-422X(00)00004-8
Bilodeau, B. (2005). Beyond the gender binary: A case study of two transgender students at a mid-western research university. *Journal of Gay & Lesbian Issues in Education,* 3(1), 29-44.
Bjorklund, DF. (2005). *Children's Thinking: Cognitive Development and Individual Differences,* 4th ed. Belmont, California: Wadsworth/Thomson Learning.
Blakemore, SJ. (2018). *Inventing Ourselves: The Secret Life of the Teenage Brain.* New York: PublicAffairs.
Blakemore, SJ & S Choudhury. (2006). Development of the adolescent brain: Implications for executive function and social cognition. *Journal of Child Psychology and Psychiatry*, 47(3/4), 296-312.
Bloom, FE, MF Beal, & DJ Kupfer, eds. (2006). *The Dana Guide to Brain Health: A Practical Family Reference from Medical Experts.* Washington: Dana Press.
Booker, CL, YJ Kelly & A Sacker. (2018). Gender differences in the associations between age trends of social media interaction and well-being among 10-15 year olds in the UK. *BMC Public Health*, 321, 1-12.
Borgonovi, F, A Ferrara & S Maghnouj. (2018). The gender gap in educational outcomes in Norway. *OECD Education Working Papers*, No. 183. OECD Publishing. doi:10.1787/f8ef1489-en.
Born, L, A Shea & M Steiner. (2002). The roots of depression in adolescent girls: Is menarche the key? *Current Psychiatry Reports*, 4, 449-60. doi:10.1007/s11920-002-0073-y
Bos, PA, J Panksepp, RM Bluthe & J van Honk. (2012). Acute effects of steroid hormones and neuropetides on human social-emotional behaviour: A review of single administration studies. *Frontiers in Neuroendocrinology*, 33, 17-35. doi:10.1016/j.yfrne.2011.01.002
Bowie, B. (2010). Understanding the differences in pathways to social deviancy: Relational aggression and emotion regulation. *Archives of Psychiatric Nursing*, 24(1), 27-37. doi:10.1016/j.apnu.2009.04.007
Bradley, MJ. (2003). *Yes, Your Teen is Crazy: Loving Your Kid Without Losing Your Mind.* Gig Harbor, Washington: Harbor Press.
Bradley, MM & PJ Lang. (2000). Measuring emotion: Behaviour, feeling and physiology. In *Cognitive Neuroscience of Emotion,* edited by R Lane & L Nadel. New York: Oxford University Press.

Brandtzaeg, PB. (2012). Social networking sites: their users and social implications—a longitudinal study. *Journal of Computer-Mediated Communication*, 17(4), 467-88. doi:10.1111/j.1083-6101.2012.01580.x

Bratko, D, T Chamorro-Premuzic & Z Saks. (2006). Personality and school performance: Incremental validity of self- and peer-ratings over intelligence. *Personality and Individual Differences*, 41(1), 131-42. doi:10.1016/j.paid.2005.12.015.

Brechwald, WA & MJ Prinstein. (2011). Beyond homophily: A decade of advances in understanding peer influence processes. *Journal of Research on Adolescence*, 21(1), 166-79. doi:10.1111/j.1532-7795.2010.00721.x

Brizendine, L. (2006). *The Female Brain*. New York: Morgan Road Books.

Brizendine, L. (2010). *The Male Brain: A Breakthrough Understanding of How Men and Boys Think*. New York: Broadway Books.

Brody, LR, JA Hall & LR Stokes. (2016). Gender and Emotion: Theory, Findings, and Content. In *Handbook of Emotions*, 4th edition, edited by LF Barrett, M Lewis & JM Haviland-Jones, 369-92. New York: The Guilford Press.

Bruni, O, S Sette, L Fontanesi, R Baiocco, F Laghi & E Baumgartner. (2015). Technology use and sleep quality in preadolescence and adolescence, *Journal of Clinical Sleep Medicine*, 11(12), 1433-41.

Butler, L, H Pan, J Epstein, X Protopopescu, O Tuescher, M Goldstein, M Cloitre, Y Yang, E Phelps, J Gorman, J Ledoux, E Stern & D Silbersweig. (2005). Fear-regulated activity in subgenual anterior cingulated differs between men and women. *Neuroreport*, 16(11), 1233-36.

Byrne, ML, S Whittle, N Vijayakumar, M Dennison, JG Simmons & NB Allen. (2017). A systematic review of adrenarche as a sensitive period in neurobiological development and mental health. *Developmental Cognitive Neuroscience*, 25, 12-28. doi:10.1016/j.dcn.2016.12.004

Cahill, L. (2005). His brain, her brain. *Scientific American*, May, 40-47.

Camarata, S. (2015). *The Intuitive Parent: Why the Best Thing For Your Child is You*. New York: Portfolio.

Cameron, JL. (2004). Interrelationships between hormones, behavior and affect during adolescence: Understanding hormonal, physical and brain changes occurring in association with pubertal activation of the reproductive axis. *Annals of the New York Academy of Sciences*, 1021, 110-23. doi:10.1196/annals.1308.012

Campbell, A. (2004). Female competition: Causes, constraints, content and contexts. *The Journal of Sex Research*, 41(1), 16-26.

Cambell, D. (2016). Stress and social media fuel mental health crisis among girls. *The Guardian*, September 23. Retrieved from https://www.theguardian.com/society/2017/sep/23/stress-anxiety-fuel-mental-health-crisis-girls-young-women

Canli, T, JE Desmond, Z Zhao & JDE Gabrieli. (2002). Sex differences in the neural basis of emotional memories. *Proceedings of the National Academy of Sciences*, 99(16), 10789-94.

Card, NA, BD Stucky, GM Sawalani & TD Little. (2008). Direct and indirect aggression during childhood and adolescence: A meta-analytic review of gender differences, intercorrelations, and relations to maladjustment. *Child Development*, 79(5), 1185-1229. doi: 10.1111/j.1467-8624.2008.01184.x.

Carlson, M & M Taylor. (2005). Imaginary companions and impersonated characters: Sex differences in children's fantasy play. *Merrill-Palmer Quarterly*, 51(1), 93-118.

Caroli, M, L Argentieri, M Cardone & A Masi. (2004). Role of television in childhood obesity prevention. *International Journal of Obesity*, 28(Suppl 3), 104-8. doi:10.1038/sj.ijo.0802802.

Carr-Gregg, M. (2006). *The Princess Bitchface Syndrome: Surviving Adolescent Girls.* Camberwell, Victoria: Penguin Books.

Carter, R. (2000). *Mapping the Mind.* London: Orion Books Ltd.

Carter, B, P Rees, L Hale, D Bhattacharjee & MS Paradkar. (2016). Association between portable screen-based media device access or use and sleep outcomes: A systematic review and meta-analysis. *JAMA Pediatrics*, 170(12), 1202-8. doi:10.1001/jamapediatrics.2016.2341.

Carvalho, RGG. (2016). Gender differences in academic achievement: the mediating role of personality. *Personality and Individual Differences*, 94, 54-58. doi:10.1016/j.paid.2016.01.011

Casey, BJ, JN Giedd & KM Thomas. (2000). Structural and functional brain development and its relation to cognitive development. *Biological Psychology*, 54, 241-57.

Casey, BJ, S Getz & A Galvan. (2008). The adolescent brain. *Developmental Review*, 28(1), 62-77.

Casey, BJ, RM Jones & LH Somerville. (2011). Braking and accelerating of the adolescent brain. *Journal of Research on Adolescence*, 21(1), 21-33.

Caspi, A, BW Roberts & RL Shiner. (2005). Personality development: Stability and change. *Annual Review of Psychology*, 56, 453-84.

Centifanti, LCM, KA Fanti, ND Thomson, V Demetriou & X Anastassiou-Hadjicharalambous. (2015). Types of relational aggression in girls are differentiated by callous-unemotional traits, peers and parental overcontrol. *Behavioral Sciences*, 5(4), 518-36. doi:10.3390/bs5040518

Chambers, RA, JR Taylor & MN Potenza. (2003). Developmental neurocircuitry of motivation in adolescence: a critical period of addiction vulnerability. *American Journal of Psychiatry*, 160(6), 1041-52.

Cheryan, S. (2012). Understanding the paradox in math-related fields: Why do some gender gaps remain while others do not? *Sex Roles*, 66(3-4), 184-90. doi:10.1007/s11199-011-0060-z.

Christiansen, DM. (2015). Examining sex and gender differences in anxiety disorders. In *A Fresh Look at Anxiety Disorders,* edited by F Durbano, 17-49. Intech Open Publishing: London.

Chugani, HT. (1994). Development of regional brain glucose metabolism in relation to behavior and plasticity. In *Human Behavior and the Developing Brain,* edited by G Dawson & KW Fischer, 153-75. New York: Guilford Press.

Chugani, HT. (1996). Neuroimaging of developmental non-linearity and developmental pathologies. In *Developmental Neuroimaging: Mapping the Development of Brain and Behavior,* edited by RW Thatcher, GR Lyon & J Rumsey, 187-95. Cambridge: Academic Press.

Chugani, HT, ME Behen, O Muzik, C Juhasz, F Nagy & DC Chugani. (2001). Local brain functional activity following early deprivation: A study of post-institutionalised Romanian orphans. *NeuroImage*, 14(6), 1290-1301.

Chugani, HT, ME Phelps & JC Mazziotta. (1989). Metabolic assessment of functional maturation and neuronal plasticity in the human brain. In *Neurobiology of Early Infant Behaviour. Wenner-Gren International Symposium Series. Vol 55*, edited by C von Euler, C Forssberg & H Lagercrantz, 323–30. New York: Stockton Press.

Cillessen, AHN & L Mayeux. (2004). From censure to reinforcement: Developmental changes in the association between aggression and social status. *Child Development*, 75(1), 147–63.

Cohen-Kettenis, PT & D Klink. (2015). Adolescents with gender dysphoria. Best Practice & Research. *Clinical Endocrinology & Metabolism*, 29(3), 485–95. doi:10.1016/j.beem.2015.01.004

Cohen-Sandler, R. (2005). *Stressed-Out Girls: Helping Them Survive in the Age of Pressure*. New York: Viking.

Colich, NL, JM Platt, KM Keyes, JA Sumner, BA Allen & KA McLaughlin. (2020). Earlier age at menarche as a transdiagnostic mechanism linking childhood trauma with multiple forms of psychopathology in adolescent girls. *Psychological Medicine*, 50(7), 1090–98. doi:10.1017/S0033291719000953

Collaer, ML & M Hines. (1995). Human behavioral sex differences: A role for gonadal hormones during early development? *Psychological Bulletin*, 118(1), 55–107.

Cole, M, T Yarkoni, G Repovš, A Anticevic & T Braver. (2012). Global connectivity of prefrontal cortex predicts cognitive control and intelligence. *The Journal of Neuroscience,* 32(26), 8988–99.

Collin, L, SL Reisner, T Tangpricha & M Goodman. (2016). Prevalence of transgender depends on the "case" definition: A systematic review. *The Journal of Sexual Medicine*, 13(4), 613–26.

Committee on Education and Training (2002). *Boys: Getting It Right. Report on the Inquiry into the Education of Boys*. Canberra: Commonwealth of Australia.

Connellan, J, S Baron-Cohen, S Wheelwright, A Batki & J Ahluwalia. (2000). Sex differences in human neonatal social perception. *Infant Behavior & Development*, 23(1), 113–18.

Connelly, R & L Platt. (2014) Cohort profile: UK Millennium Cohort Study (MCS), *International Journal of Epidemiology*, 43(6), 1719–25. doi:10.1093/ije/dyu001.

Coolidge, FL, LL Thede & SE Young. (2002). The heritability of gender identity disorder in a child and adolescent twin sample. *Behavior Genetics,* 32(4), 251–57. doi:10.1023/A:1019724712983

Copeland, KC & S Chernausek. (2016). Mini- puberty and growth. *Pediatrics,* 138(1), e20161301. doi:10.1542/peds.2016-1301

Coplan, JD, CJ Aaronson, V Panthangi & Y Kim. (2015). Treating comorbid anxiety and depression: Psychosocial and pharmacological approaches. *World Journal of Psychiatry*, 5(4), 366–78. doi:10.5498/wjp.v5.i4.366

Costa, PT & RR McCrae. (2008). The revised NEO personality inventory (NEO-PI-R). In *The Sage Handbook of Personality Theory and Assessment—Volume 2: Personality Measurement and Testing,* edited by GJ Boyle, G Matthews & DH Saklofske, 179–198. Thousand Oaks, California: Sage Publications Inc.

Costa, PT, A Terracciano & RR McCrae. (2001). Gender differences in personality traits across cultures: Robust and surprising findings. *Journal of Personality and Social Psychology*, 81(2), 322–31.

Costigan, SA, L Barnett, RC Plotnikoff & DR Lubans. (2013). The health indicators associated with scree-based sedentary behavior among adolescent girls: A systematic review. *Journal of Adolescent Health*, 52(4), 382-92. doi:10.1016/j.jadohealth.2012.07.018.

Cowan, N. (2008). What are the differences between long-term, short-term and working memory? *Progress in Brain Research*, 169, 323-38.

Cowan, N & CC Morey. (2006). Visual working memory depends on attentional filtering. *Trends in Cognitive Sciences*, 10(4), 139-41.

Cozolino, L. (2013). *The Social Neuroscience of Education: Optimizing Attachment and Learning in the Classroom*. New York: WW Norton & Company.

Crick, NR & JK Grotpeter. (1995). Relational aggression, gender and social-psychological adjustment. *Child Development*, 66 (3), 710-22.

Crick, NR, MA Bigbee & C Howes. (1996). Gender differences in children's normative beliefs about aggression: How do I hurt thee? Let me count the ways. *Child Development* 67(2), 1003-14.

Croson, R & U Gneezy. (2009). Gender differences in preferences. *Journal of Economic Literature*, 47(2), 448-74. doi:10.1257/jel.47.2.448

Cservenka, A, ML Stroup, A Etkin & BJ Nagel. (2015). The effects of age, sex and hormones on emotional conflict-related brain response during adolescence. *Brain and Cognition*, 99, 135-50. doi:10.1016/j.bandc.2015.06.002.

Damasio, AR. (2001). Emotion and the human brain. *Annals of the New York Academy of Sciences*, 935(1), 101-106.

De Bellis, MD, MS Keshaven, SR Beers, J Hall, K Frustaci, A Masalehdan, J Noll & AM Boring. (2001). Sex differences in brain maturation during childhood and adolescence. *Cerebral Cortex*, 11(6), 552-57.

De Bolle, M, F De Fruyt, RR McCrae, CE Löckenhoff, PT Jr Costa, ME Aguilar-Vafaie, C-k Ahn, H-n Ahn, L Alcalay, J Allik, TV Avdeyeva, D Bratko, M Brunner-Sciarra, TR Cain, W Chan, N Chittcharat, JT Crawford, R Fehr, E Ficková & A Terracciano. (2015). The emergence of sex differences in personality traits in early adolescence: A cross-sectional, cross-cultural study. *Journal of Personality and Social Psychology*, 108(1), 171-85. doi-org.ezproxy.usc.edu.au/10.1037/a0038497

de Beauvoir, S. (2011). *The Second Sex*. Translated by C Borde & S Malovany-Chevallier. New York: Vintage Books.

de Graaf, NM, G Giovanardi, C Zitz & P Carmichael. (2016). Sex ratio in children and adolescents referred to the gender identity development service in the UK (2009-2016). *Archives of Sexual Behavior*, 47(5), 1301-4. doi:10.1007/s10508-018-1204-9

Del Giudice, M, T Booth & P Irwing. (2012). The distance between Mars and Venus: Measuring global sex differences in personality. *PLOS ONE*, 7(1), e29265. doi:10.1371/journal.pone.0029265

Derntl, B, I Kryspin-Exner, E Fernbach, E Moser & U Habel. (2008). Emotion recognition accuracy in healthy young females is associated with cycle phase. *Hormones and Behavior*, 53(1), 90-95. doi:10.1016/jyhbeh.2007.09.006

Desrochers, JE, G Albert, TL Milfont, B Kelly & S Arnocky. (2019). Does personality mediate the relationship between sex and environmentalism? *Personality and Individual Differences*, 147, 204-13.

Diamond, LM. (2008). Female bisexuality from adolescence to adulthood: Results from a 10-year longitudinal study. *Developmental Psychology*, 44(1), 5-14. doi:10.1037/0012-1649.44.1.5

Diamond, M & J Hopson. (1999). *Magic Trees of the Mind: How to Nurture Your Child's Intelligence, Creativity, and Healthy Emotions from Birth Through Adolescence.* New York: Penguin Putnam Inc.

Dishion, TJ & JM Tipsord. (2011). Peer contagion in child and adolescent social and emotional development. *Annual Review of Psychology*, 62, 189-214. doi:10.1146/annurev.psych.093008.100412

Dishion, TJ, SE Nelson & BM Bullock. (2004). Premature adolescent autonomy: parent disengagement and deviant peer process in the amplification of problem behavior. *Journal of Adolescence*, 27(5), 515-30. doi:10.1016/j.adolescence.2004.06.005.

Donnellan, MB, KH Trzesniewski & RW Robins. (2011). Self-esteem: Enduring issues and controversies. In *The Wiley-Blackwell Handbook of Individual Differences,* edited by T Chamorro-Premuzic, S von Stumm & A Furnham, 718-46. New Jersey: Wiley-Blackwell.

Dubb, A, R Gur, B Avants & J Gee. (2003). Characterization of sexual dimorphism in the human corpus callosum. *Neuroimage*, 20(1), 512-19.

Dudai, Y & RGM Morris. (2013). Memorable trends. *Neuron*, 80(3), 742-50.

Eberling, JL, C Wu, MN Haan, D Mungas, M Buonocore & WJ Jagust. (2003). Preliminary evidence that estrogen protects against age-related hippocampal atrophy. *Neurobiology of Aging*, 24(3), 725-32.

Edwards-Leeper, L & NP Spack. (2012). Psychological evaluation and medical treatment of transgender youth in an interdisciplinary "Gender Management Service" (GeMS) in a major pediatric center. *Journal of Homosexuality*, 59(3), 321-36. doi:10.1080/00918369.2012.653302

Eliot, L. (2000). *What's Going On in There? How the Brain and Mind Develop in the First Five Years of Life.* New York: Bantam Books.

Eliot, L. (2012). *Pink Brain, Blue Brain: How Small Differences Grow Into Troublesome Gaps and What We Can Do About It.* Oxford: Oneworld Publications.

Ellis, L. (2011a). Evolutionary neuroandrogenic theory and universal gender differences in cognition and behaviour. *Sex Roles*, 64(9-10), 707-22.

Ellis, L. (2011b). Identifying and explaining apparent universal sex differences in cognition and behavior. *Personality and Individual Differences*, 51(5), 522-61. doi:10.1016/j.paid.2011.04.004

Ellis, WE, CV Crooks & DA Wolfe. (2008) Relational aggression in peer and dating relationships: Links to psychological and behavioral adjustment. *Social Development*, 18(2), 253-69. doi:10.1111/j.1467-9507.2008.00468.x

Erickson, EH. (1959). Identity and the life cycle: Selected papers. *Psychological Issues*, 1, 1-171.

Erickson, EH. (1963). *Childhood and Society,* 2nd ed. New York: Norton.

Erickson, EH. (1964). *Insight and Responsibility.* New York: Norton.

Erickson, EH. (1968). *Identity, Youth and Crisis.* New York: Norton.

Escudero, P, RA Robbins & SP Johnson. (2013). Sex-related preferences for real and doll faces versus real and toy objects in young infants and adults. *Journal of Experimental Child Psychology*, 116, 367-79.

Eslea, M. (2010) Direct and indirect bullying: Which is more distressing? In *Indirect and Direct Aggression,* edited by K Osterman, 69–84. Frankfurt am Main, Germany: Peter Lang.

Etchell, A, A Adhikari, LS Weinberg, AL Choo, EO Garnett, HM Chow & S Chang. (2018). A systematic literature review of sex differences in childhood language and brain development. *Neuropsychologia*, 114, 19–31. doi: 10.1016/j.neuropsychologia.2018.04.011.

Feingold, A. (1994). Gender differences in personality: A meta-analysis. *Psychological Bulletin*, 116(3), 429–56. doi:10.1037/0033-2909.116.3.429.

Felton, JW, DA Cole, M Havewala, G Kurdziel & V Brown. (2019). Talking together, thinking alone: Relations among co-rumination, peer relationships, and rumination. *Journal of Youth and Adolescence*, 48(5), 731–43. doi:10.1007/s10964-018-0937-z.

Fields, RD. (2016). *Why We Snap: Understanding the Rage Circuit In Your Brain.* New York: Dutton.

Forbes, EE, DE Williamson, ND Ryan & RE Dahl. (2004). Positive and negative affect in depression: Influence of sex and puberty. *Annals of the New York Academy of Sciences*, 1021, 341–47.

Fox, NA. (1991). If it's not left, it's right: Electroencephalograph asymmetry and the development of emotion. *American Psychologist,* 46(8), 863–72.

Frank, DA, PE Klass, F Earls & L Eisenberg. (1996). Infants and young children in orphanages: One view form pediatrics and child psychiatry. *Pediatrics*, 97(4), 569.

Friedman, HS & MW Schustack. (2016). *Personality: Classic Theories and Modern Research.* London: Pearson.

Frieze, IH. (2000). Violence in close relationships – development of a research area: Comment on Archer (2000). *Psychological Bulletin*, 126(5), 681–84. doi:10.1037/0033-2909.126.5.681

Galvan, A. (2010). Adolescent development of the reward system. *Frontiers in Neuroscience*, 4(6), 1–9.

Galvan, A. (2012). Risky behaviour in adolescents: The role of the developing brain. In *The Adolescent Brain: Learning, Reasoning and Decision Making,* edited by VF Reyna, SB Chapman, MR Doughherty & J Confrey, 267–89). Washington, DC: American Psychological Association.

Gao, S, B Becker, L Luo, Y Geng, W Zhao, Y Yin, J Hu, Z Gao, Q Gong, R Hurlemann, D Yao, & KM Kendrick. (2016). Oxytocin, the peptide that bonds the sexes also divides them. *Proceedings of the National Academy of Sciences*, 113(27), 7650–54.

Gardner, M & L Steinberg. (2005). Peer influence on risk taking, risk preference, and risky decision making in adolescence and adulthood: an experimental study. *Developmental Psychology,* 41(4), 625–35. doi:10.1037/0012-1649.41.4.624.

Gasbarri, A, MCH Tavares, RC Rodrigues, C Tomaz & A Pompili. (2012). Estrogen, cognitive functions and emotion: An overview on humans, non-human primates and rodents in reproductive years. *Reviews in the Neurosciences,* 23(5-6), 587–606. doi:10.1515/revneuro-2012-0051

Gazzaniga, MS. (1970). *The Bisected Brain.* New York: Appleton-Century-Crofts.

Gazzaniga, MS. (1987). *The Social Brain.* New York: Basic Books.

Gazzaniga, M. (1998). *The Mind's Past.* Berkeley, California: University of California Press.

Gazzaniga, MS. (2015). *Tales From Both Sides of the Brain: A Life in Neuroscience.* New York: Ecco.

Geake, JG. (2009). *The Brain at School: Educational Neuroscience in the Classroom.* Maidenhead, Berkshire: Open University Press.

Geary, DC. (2002). Sexual selection and sex differences in social cognition. In *The Development of Sex Differences in Cognition,* edited by AV McGillicuddy-De Lisi & RDE Lisi, 23-53). Greenwich, Connecticut: Ablex/Greenwood.

Geary, DC. (2010). *Male, Female: The Evolution of Human Sex Difference,* 2nd ed. Washington DC: American Psychological Association.

Geier, C & B Luna. (2009). The maturation of incentive processing and cognitive control. *Pharmacology, Biochemistry and Behavior,* 93(3), 212-21.

Gentile, B, JM Twenge & WK Campbell. (2010). Birth cohort differences in self-esteem, 1988-2008: A cross-temporal meta-analysis. *Review of General Psychology,* 14(3), 261-68. doi:10.1037/a0019919.

Geschwind, N & AM Galaburda. (1985). Cerebral lateralization, biological mechanisms, associations and pathology: I. A hypothesis and a program for research. *Archives of Neurology,* 42(5), 428-59.

Geschwind, N & AM Galaburda. (1987). *Cerebral Lateralization.* Cambridge Massachusetts: MIT Press.

Gibb, SJ, DM Fergusson & LJ Horwood (2008). Gender differences in educational achievement to age 25. *Australian Journal of Education,* 52(1), 63-80. doi:10.1177/000494410805200105.

Giedd, J. (2004). Structural magnetic resonance imaging of the adolescent brain. *Annals of the New York Academy of Sciences,* 1021, 77-85.

Giedd, J. (2010). The teen brain: Primed to learn, primed to take risks. In *Cerebrum: Emerging Ideas in Brain Science 2010,* edited by D Gordan, 62-70. New York: Dana Press.

Giedd, JN, C Vaituzis, SD Hamburger, N Lange, JC Rajapakse, D Kaysen, YC Vauss & JL Rapoport. (1996). Quantitative MRI of the temporal lobe, amygdala and hippocampus in normal human development: Ages 4-18 years. *Journal of Comparative Neurology,* 366, 223-30.

Giedd, JN, J Blumenthal, NO Jeffries, FX Castellanos, H Liu, A Zijdenbos, T Paus, C Evans & JL Rapoport. (1999). Brain development during childhood and adolescence: A longitudinal MRI study. *Nature Neuroscience,* 2(10), 861-63.

Giedd, JN, LS Clasen, R Lenroot, D Greenstein, GL Wallace, S Ordaz, EA Molloy, JD Blumenthal, JW Tossell, C Stayer, CA Samango-Sprouse, D Shen, C Davatzikos, D Merke & GP Chrousos. (2006). Puberty-related influences on brain development. *Molecular and Cellular Endocrinology,* 254-55, 154-62.

Giedd, JN, M Stockman, C Weddle, M Liverpool, GL Wallace, NR Lee, F Lalonde & RK Lenroot. (2012). Anatomic magnetic resonance imaging of the developing child and adolescent brain. In *The Adolescent Brain: Learning, Reasoning and Decision Making,* edited by VF Reyna, SB Chapman, MR Doughherty & J Confrey, 15-35. Washington, DC: American Psychological Association.

Glidden, D, WP Bouman, BA Jones, J Arcelus. (2016). Gender dysphoria and autism spectrum disorder: A systematic review of the literature. *Sexual Medicine Reviews,* 4(1), 3-14. doi:10.106/j.sxmr.2045.10.003

Glucksman, A. (1981). *Sexual Dimorphism in Human and Mammalian Biology and Pathology.* New York: Academic Press.

Goldberg, E. (2001). *The Executive Brain: Frontal Lobes and the Civilized Mind.* Oxford: Oxford University Press.
Goldberg, E. (2009). *The New Executive Brain: Frontal Lobes in a Complex World.* Oxford, UK: Oxford University Press.
Goldberg, LR. (1990). An alternative "description of personality": The big five factor structure. *Journal of Personality and Social Psychology,* 59, 1216-29.
Goldman-Rakic, PS. (1993). Working memory and the mind. In *Mind and Brain: Readings from Scientific American,* 67-77. New York: WH Freeman & Company.
Goldman-Rakic, PS. (1996). Regional and cellular fractionation of working memory. *Proceedings of the National Academy of Sciences,* 93, 13473-80.
Goleman, D. (2006). *Social Intelligence: Beyond IQ, Beyond Emotional Intelligence.* New York: Bantam Books.
Goleman, D. (2021). *Emotional Intelligence: Why it Can Matter More than IQ,* 25th anniversary edition. London: Bloomsbury.
Gooren, L. (2006). The biology of human psychosexual differentiation. *Hormones and Behavior,* 50(4), 589-601.
Gopnik, A, AN Meltzoff & PK Kuhl. (1999). *The Scientist in the Crib: What Early Learning Tells Us About the Mind.* New York: Harper Collins Publishers Inc.
Goswami, U. (2004). Annual review: Neuroscience and education. *British Journal of Educational Psychology,* 74, 1-14.
Graber, JA. (2013). Pubertal timing and the development of psychopathology in adolescence and beyond. *Hormones and Behavior,* 64(2), 262-69. doi:10.1016/j.yhbeh.2013.04.003.
Grieve, R, M Indian, K Witteveen, GA Tolan & J Marrington. (2013). Face-to-face or Facebook: can social connectedness be derived online? *Computers in Human Behavior,* 29(3), 604-9. doi:10.1016/j.chb.2012.11.017
Gunderson, EA, G Ramirez, SC Levine & SL Beilock. (2012). The role of parents and teachers in the development of gender-related math attitudes. *Sex Roles,* 66(3-4), 153-66. doi:10.1007/s11199-011-9996-2.
Gur, RE & RC Gur. (1990). Gender differences in cerebral blood flow. *Schizophrenia Bulletin,* 16(2), 247-54.
Gur, RE & RC Gur. (2002). Gender differences in aging: Cognition, emotions and neuroimaging studies. *Dialogues in Clinical Neuroscience,* 2002, 4(2), 197-207.
Gur, RC & RE Gur. (2017). Complementarity of sex difference in brain and behavior: From laterality to multi-modal neuroimaging. *Journal of Neuroscience Research,* 95(1-2), 189-99.
Gur, RC, PD Mozley, SM Resnick, GL Gottlieb, M Kohn, R Zimmerman, G Herman, S Atlas, R Grossman, D Berretta, R Erwin & RE Gur. (1991). Gender differences in age effect on brain atrophy measured by magnetic resonance imaging. *Proceedings of the National Academy of Sciences,* April, 88, 2845-49.
Gur, RC, PD Mozley, SM Resnick, JS Karp, A Alavi, SE Arnold & RE Gur. (1995). Sex differences in regional cerebral glucose metabolism during a resting state. *Science,* 267(5197), 228-31.
Gur, RC, BI Turetsky, M Matsui, M Yan, W Bilker, P Hughett & RE Gur. (1999). Sex differences in brain gray matter and white matter in healthy young adults: Correlations with cognitive performance. *The Journal of Neuroscience,* 19(10), 4065-72.

Gur, RC, F Gunning-Dixon, WB Bilker & RE Gur. (2002). Sex differences in temporo-limbic and frontal brain volumes of healthy adults. *Cerebral Cortex*, 12(9), 998-1003.

Gurian, M. (1997). *The Wonder of Boys: What Parents, Mentors and Educators Can Do to Shape Boys Into Exceptional Men*. Los Angeles: Tarcher.

Gurian, M. (2000). *The Good Son: Shaping the Moral Development of Our Boys and Young Men*. Los Angeles: Tarcher.

Gurian, M. (2003). *The Wonder of Girls: Understanding the Hidden Nature of Our Daughters*. New York: Atria Books.

Gurian, M & K Stevens. (2005). *The Minds of Boys: Saving Our Sons From Falling Behind in School and Life*. San Francisco: Jossey-Bass.

Gurian, M & K Stevens. (2011). *Boys and Girls Learn Differently: A Guide for Teachers and Parents*, revised 10th ed. San Francisco: Jossey-Bass.

Halpern, DF. (2000). *Sex Differences in Cognitive Abilities*, 3rd ed. New Jersey: Lawrence Erlbaum Associates, Inc.

Hamann, S. (2005). Sex differences in the responses of the human amygdala. *The Neuroscientist*, 11(4), 288-93.

Hamlat, EJ, HR Snyder, JF Young & BJ Hankin. (2019). Pubertal timing as a transdiagnostic risk for psychopathology in youth. *Clinical Psychological Science*, 7(3), 411-29. doi:10.1177/21677026188110518

Hanamsagar, R & SD Bilbo. (2016). Sex differences in neurodevelopmental and neurodegenerative disorders: Focus on microglial function and neuroinflammation 369 during development. *The Journal of Steroid Biochemistry and Molecular Biology*, 160, 127-33. doi:10.1016/j.jsbmb.2015.09.039

Hardiman, MM. (2003). *Connecting Brain Research with Effective Teaching: The Brain-targeted Teaching Model*. Lanham, Maryland: Scarecrow Press Inc.

Harter, S. (2006). The self. In *Handbook of Child Psychology. Social, Emotional and Personality Development*, 6th ed, edited by W Damon, RM Lerner & N Eisenberg, vol 3, 505-70. New Jersey: John Wiley & Sons.

Hassett, JM, ER Siebert & K Wallen. (2008). Sex differences in rhesus monkey toy preferences parallel those of children. *Hormones and Behavior*, 54(3), 359-64. doi: 10.1016/j.yhbeh.2008.03.008.

Hassinger, B, K Hirsh-Pasek & RM Golinkoff. (2019). Brain science and guided play. In *Serious Fun: How Guided Play Extends Childrens' Learning*, edited by M Masterson & H Bohart, 11-21. Washington, DC: NAEYC Press.

Hausmann, M. (2017). Why sex hormones matter for neuroscience: A very short review on sex, sex hormones, and functional brain asymmetries. *Journal of Neuroscience Research*, 95(1-2), 40-49.

Hawkes, T. (2001). *Boy Oh Boy: How to Raise and Educate Boys*. Frenchs Forest NSW: Pearson Educational Australia.

Hawkes, T. (2014). *Ten Conversations You Must Have With Your Son*. Sydney: Hachette.

Herculano-Houzel, S. (2009). The human brain in numbers: A linearly scaled-up primate brain. *Frontiers in Neuroscience*, 3(31), 1-11.

Herschkowitz, N & E C Herschkowitz. (2004). *A Good Start to Life: Understanding Your Child's Brain and Behavior from Birth to Age 6*. New York: Dana Press.

Himanshu, AK, A Kaur, A Kaur & G Singla. (2020). Rising dysmorphia among adolescents: A cause for concern. *Journal of Family Medicine and Primary Care,* 9(2), 567-70. doi:10.4103/jfmpc.jfmpc_738_19

Hines, M. (2010). Sex-related variation in human behavior and the brain. *Trends in Cognitive Sciences,* 14(10), 448-56. doi:10.1016/j.tocs.2010.07.005

Hines, M. (2020). Neuroscience and sex/gender: looking back and forward. *Journal of Neuroscience,* 40(1), 37-43. doi:10/1523/JNEUROSCI.0750-19.2019

Hirsch, D & L Brizendine. (2007). Teen girl brain: High drama, high risk for depression. *Current Psychiatry,* 6(5), 77-89.

Hirsch-Pasek, K, RM Golinkoff & D Eyer. (2004). *Einstein Never Used Flashcards: How Our Children Really Learn - And Why They Need to Play More and Memorize Less.* New York: Rodale.

Hirsch-Pasek, K, RM Golinkoff, LE Berk & DG Singer. (2009). *A Mandate for Playful Learning in Preschool: Presenting the Evidence.* New York: Oxford University Press.

Hirsh-Pasek, K, JM Zosh, RM Golinkoff, JH Gray, MB Robb & J Kaufman. (2015). Putting education in "educational" apps: Lessons from the science of learning, *Psychological Science in the Public Interest,* 16(1), 3-34.

Hogan, R, J Hogan & BW Roberts. (1996). Personality measurement and employment decisions: Questions and answers. *American Psychologist,* 51, 469-77.

Hooper, J & D Teresi. (1986). *The 3 Pound Universe: Revolutionary Discoveries About the Brain - From Chemistry of the Mind to the New Frontiers of the Soul.* New York: GP Putnam's Sons.

Houghton, S, SC Hunter, M Rosenberg, L Wood, C Zadow, K Martin & T Shilton. (2015). Virtually impossible: Limiting Australian children and adolescents daily screen-based media use. *BMC Public Health,* 15(1), 5. doi:10.1186/1471-2458-15-5.

Howard, PJ. (2006). *The Owner's Manual for the Brain: Everyday Applications from Mind-Brain Research,* 3rd ed. Austin, Texas: Bard Press.

Howard-Jones, P. (2010). *Introducing Neuroeducational Research: Neuroscience, Education and the Brain from Contexts to Practice.* New York: Routledge.

Howell, HB, O Brawman-Mintzer, J Monnier & KA Yonkers. (2001). Generalized anxiety disorder in women. *Psychiatric Clinics of North America,* 24(1), 165-78. doi:10.1016/S0193-953X(05)70212-4

Hoyenga, KB & KT Hoyenga. (1993). *Gender-Related Differences: Origins and Outcomes.* Boston: Allyn and Bacon.

Hubel, DH & TN Wiesel. (1970). The period of susceptibility to the physiological effects of unilateral eye closure in kittens. *Journal of Physiology,* 206, 419-36.

Hutchinson, A, M Midgen & A Spiliadis. (2020). In support of research into rapid-onset gender dysphoria. *Archives of Sexual Behavior,* 49, 79-80. doi:10.1007/s105-8-019-01517-9

Ingalhalikar, M, A Smith, D Parker, TD Satterthwaite, MA Elliott, K Ruparel, H Hakonarson, RE Gur, RC Gur & R Verma. (2014). Sex differences in the structural connectome of the human brain. *Proceedings of the National Academy of Sciences,* 111(2), 823-28

Jalnapurkar, I, M Allen & T Pigott. (2018). Sex differences in anxiety disorders: A Review. *HSOA Journal of Psychiatry, Depression & Anxiety,* 4(012). doi:10.24966/PDA-0150/100012

Jensen, E. (1998). *Teaching with the Brain in Mind*. Alexandria, Virginia: Association for Supervision and Curriculum Development.

Johnson, MH. (2005). Sensitive periods in functional brain development: problems and prospects. *Developmental Psychobiology*, 46(3), 287-92.

Jose, PE, H Wilkins & JS Spendelow. (2012). Does social anxiety predict rumination and co-rumination among adolescents? *Journal of Clinical Child and Adolescent Psychology*, 41, 86-91. doi:10.1080/15374416.2012.632346.

Juvonen, J & EF Gross. (2008). Extending the school grounds? Bullying experiences in cyberspace. *Journal of School Health*, 78(9), 496-505. doi:10.1111/j.1746-1561.2008.00335.x.

Kahlenberg, SM & RW Wrangham. (2010). Sex differences in chimpanzees' use of sticks as play objects resemble those of children. *Current Biology*, 20(24), R1067-R1068. doi:10.1016/j.cub.2010.11.024

Kallitsounaki, A, DM Williams & SE Lind. (2020). Links Between Autistic Traits, Feelings of Gender Dysphoria, and Mentalising Ability: Replication and Extension of Previous Findings from the General Population. *Journal of Autism and Developmental Disorders*. https://doi:10.1007/s10803-020-04626-w

Kaltiala-Heino, R, H Bergman, M Tyolarjarvi & L Frisen. (2018). Gender dysphoria in adolescence: Current perspectives. *Adolescent Health, Medicine and Therapeutics*, 9, 31-41. doi:10.2147/AHMT.S135432

Kandel, ER. (2006). *In Search of Memory: The Emergence of a New Science of Mind*. New York: WW Norton & Company Inc.

Kandel, ER. (2018). *The Disordered Mind: What Unusual Brains Tell Us About Ourselves*. London: Little Brown Book Group.

Kansaku, K & S Kitazawa. (2001). Imaging studies on sex differences in lateralization of language. *Neuroscience Research*, 41(4), 333-37.

Kanasaku, K, AYamamura & S Kitazawa. (2000). Sex differences in lateralization revealed in the posterior language areas. *Cerebral Cortex*, 10(9), 866-72.

Kappe, R & H van der Flier. (2012). Predicting academic success in higher education: What's more important than being smart? *European Journal of Psychology of Education*, 27(4), 605-19. doi:10.1007/s10212-011-0099-9.

Karges-Bone, L. (1998). *More than Pink and Blue: How Gender Can Shape Your Curriculum*. Teaching and Learning Company.

Katzer, C, D Fetchenhauer & F Belschak. (2009). Cyberbullying: Who are the victims? A comparison of victimization in Internet chatrooms and victimization in school. *Journal of Media Psychology*, 21(5), 25-36. doi:10.1027/1864-1105.21.1.25.

Kawabata, Y, NR Crick & Y Hamaguchi. (2010). The role of culture in relational aggression: Associations with social-psychological adjustment problems in Japanese and US school-aged children. *International Journal of Behavioral Development*, 34(4), 352-62. doi:10.1177/0165025409339151

Keshishian, AC, MA Watkins & MW Otto. (2016). Clicking away at co-rumination: Co-rumination correlates across different modalities of communication. *Cognitive Behaviour Therapy*, 45(6), 473-78. doi:10.1080/16506073.2016.1201848

Khan, D. (2020). Gender differences in personality traits in relation to academic performance. *MIER Journal of Educational Studies, Trends & Practices*, 10(1), 124-37.

Kimbrough, AM, RE Guadango, NL Muscanell & J Dill. (2013). Gender differences in mediated communication: Women connect more than men do. *Computers in Human Behavior,* 29(3), 896-900.

Kimura, D. (2000). *Sex and Cognition.* Cambridge, Massachusetts: MIT Press.

Kimura, D. (2004). Human sex differences in cognition: Fact, not predicament. *Sexualities, Evolution and Gender,* 6, 45-53.

Kindlon, D & M Thompson. (1999). *Raising Cain: Protecting the Emotional Life of Boys.* New York: Ballantine Books.

Kleim, JA & TA Jones. (2008). Principles of experience-dependent neural plasticity: Implications for rehabilitation after brain damage. *Journal of Speech, Language and Hearing Research,* 51, S225-S239.

Kommarraju, M, SJ Karau, RR Schmeck & A Avdic. (2011). The Big Five personality trait, learning styles, and academic achievement. *Personality and Individual Differences,* 51, 472-77. doi:10.1016/j.paid.2011.04.019

Koolshijn, PCMP & EA Crone. (2013). Sex differences and structural brain maturation from childhood to early adulthood. *Developmental Cognitive Neuroscience,* 5, 106-18.

Koss, WA & KM Frick. (2017). Sex differences in hippocampal function. *Journal of Neuroscience Research,* 95 (1-2), 539-62.

Kowlaski, RM, GW Giumettin, AN Schroeder & MR Lattanner. (2014). Bullying in the digital age: A critical review and meta-analysis of cyberbullying research among youth. *Psychological Bulletin,* 140(4), 1073-137. doi:10.1037/a0035618.

Kraft, C & L Mayeux. (2018). Associations among friendship jealousy, peer status and relational aggression in early adolescence. *Journal of Early Adolescence,* 38(3), 385-407. doi:10.1177/0272431616670992

Kret, ME & B De Gelder. (2012). A review on sex differences in processing emotional signals. *Neuropsychologia,* 50(7), 1211-21. doi:orr/10.1016/j.neuropsychologia.2011.12.022

Kreukels, BPC & A Guillamon. (2016). Neuroimaging studies in people with gender incongruence. *International Review of Psychiatry,* 28(1), 120-28. doi:/10.3109/09540261.2015.1113163

Kusche, CA & MT Greenberg. (2006). Brain development and social emotional learning. In *The Educator's Guide to Emotional Intelligence and Academic Achievement: Social-Emotional Learning in the Classroom,* edited by MJ Elias & H Arnold, 15-34. Thousand Oaks, California: Corwin Press.

Kuyper, L & C Wijsen. (2014). Gender identities and gender dysphoria in the Netherlands. *Archives of Sexual Behavior,* 43(2), 377-85. doi:10.1007/s10508-013-0140-y

Kvardova, N, H Machackova & D Smahel. (2020). The direct and indirect effects of online social support, neuroticism, and web content internalisation of the drive for thinness among women visiting health-oriented websites. *International Journal of Environmental Research and Public Health,* 17(7), 1-14. doi:10.3390/ijerph17072416

LaFontana, KM & AHN Cillessen. (2002). Children's perceptions of popular and unpopular peers: A multimethod assessment. *Developmental Psychology,* 38(5), 63-47. doi:10.1037//0012-1649.38.5.635

Laidlaw, MK, QL Van Meter, PW Hruz, A Van Mol & WJ Malone. (2019). Letter to the Editor: "Endocrine treatment of gender-dysphoric/gender-incongruent persons: An endocrine society clinical practice guideline." *Journal of Clinical Endocrinology & Metabolism, 104(3),* 686–87. doi:10.1210/jc.2018-01925

Lamb, S. (2001). *The Secret Lives of Girls: What Good Girls Really Do – Sex Play, Aggression and Their Guilt.* New York: The Free Press.

LaMarca, B & BT Alexander, eds. (2019). *Sex Differences in Cardiovascular Physiology and Pathophysiology.* London: Elsevier Inc.

Lane, B. (2020). Judge warns doctors over teen trans hormone consent. *The Australian,* Sep 23. Retrieved from https://www.theaustralian.com.au

Lane, KA, JX Goh & E Driver-Linn. (2012). Implicit science stereotypes mediate the relationship between gender and academic participation. *Sex Roles, 66(3–4).* doi:10.1007/s11199-011-0036z.

Lange, BP, HA Euler & E Zaretsky. (2016). Sex differences in language competence of 3 to 6 year old children. *Applied Psycholinguistics, 37(6),* 1417–38.

Laurson, KR, JA Lee, DA Gentile, DA Walsh & JC Eisenmann. (2014). Concurrent associations between physical activity, screen time, and sleep duration with childhood obesity. *International Scholarly Research Notices,* vol.2014, Article ID 204540. doi:10.1155/2014/204540.

Lavelli, M & A Fogel. (2002). Developmental changes in mother-infant face-to-face communication: Birth to 3 months. *Developmental Psychology, 38(2),* 288–305.

LeDoux, J. (1998). *The Emotional Brain: The Mysterious Underpinnings of Emotional Life.* New York: Simon and Schuster Inc.

LeDoux, J. (2002). *The Synaptic Self: How Our Brains Become Who We Are.* New York: Penguin Books.

Leeb, RT & FG Rejskind. (2004). Here's looking at you, kid! A longitudinal study of perceived gender differences in mutual gaze behavior in young infants. *Sex Roles, 50(1–2),* 1–14.

Legato, M. (2002). *Eve's Rib: The Groundbreaking Guide to Women's Health.* New York: Three Rivers Press.

Legato, MJ. (2005). *Why Men Never Remember and Women Never Forget.* New York: Rodale.

Leibowitz, S & ALC de Vries. (2016). Gender dysphoria in adolescence. *International Review of Psychiatry, 28(1),* 21–35. doi:10.3019/09540261.2015.1124844

Leppanen, JMH. (2001). Emotion, recognition and social adjustment in school-aged girls and boys. *Scandinavian Journal of Psychology, 42(5),* 429–35.

Levitt, P. (2003). Structural and functional maturation of the developing primate brain. *The Journal of Pediatrics, 143(4),* 35–45.

Lewis, R. (1997). *Raising a Modern Day Knight: A Father's Role in Guiding His Son to Authentic Manhood.* Wheaton, Illinois: Tyndale House Publishers.

Lewis, MH, JP Gluck, AJ Beauchamp, MF Keresztury & RB Mailman. (1990). Long-term effects of early social isolation in Macaca mulatta: Changes in dopamine receptor function following apomorphine challenge. *Brain Research, 513(1),* 67–73.

Li, D, SE Christ & N Cowan. (2014). Domain-general and domain-specific functional networks in working memory. *NeuroImage, 102(Part 2),* 646–56.

Liben, LS & RS Bigler. (2008). Developmental gender differentiation. *Journal of Gay & Lesbian Mental Health, 12(1–2),* 95–119.

Linden, DJ. (2018a). Human sexual orientation is strongly influence by biological factors. In *Think Tank: Forty Neuroscientists Explore the Roots of Human Experience,* edited by DJ Linden, 215-24). New Haven, Connecticut: Yale University Press.

Lippa, RA. (2005). *Gender, Nature, and Nurture,* 2nd ed. New York: Routledge.

Lippa, RA. (2010). Sex differences in personality traits and gender-related occupational preferences across 53 nations: Testing evolutionary and social-environmental theories. *Archives of Sexual Behavior,* 39(3), 619-36. doi:10.1007/s10508-008-9380-7

Lissak, G. (2018) Adverse physiological and psychological effects of screen time on children and adolescents: Literature review and case study. *Environmental Research,* 164, 149-57.

Littman, L. (2018). Rapid-onset gender dysphoria in adolescents and young adults: A study of parental reports. *PLOS ONE* 13(8), e0202330. doi:10.1371/journal.ponr.0202330.

LoMaura, A & A Aliverti. (2018). Sex differences in respiratory function. *Breathe,* 14, 131-40. doi:10.1183/20734735.000318

Lukianoff, G & J Haidt. (2018). *The Coddling of the American Mind: How Good Intentions and Bad Ideas Are Setting Up a Generation For Failure.* New York: Penguin Press.

Lupien, SJ, F Maheu, M Tu, A Fiocco & TE Schramek. (2007). The effects of stress and stress hormones on human cognition: Implications for the field of brain and cognition. *Brain and Cognition,* 65(3), 209-37.

Lutchmaya, S & S Baron-Cohen. (2002). Human Sex Differences in social and non-social preferences at 12 months of age. *Infant Behaviour & Development,* 25(3), 319-25. doi:10.1016/S0163-6383(02)00095-4

MacDonald, G & MR Leary. (2012). Individual differences in self-esteem. In *Handbook of Self and Identity,* edited by MR Leary & JP Tangney, 354-77. New York: Guilford Press.

MacLean, PD. (1990). *The Triune Brain in Evolution: Role in Paleocerebral Functions.* New York: Plenum Publishing.

Maccoby, EE. (1998). *The Two Sexes: Growing Up Apart, Coming Together.* Cambridge, Massachusetts: Harvard University Press.

Madsen, KS, TL Jernigan, M Vestergaard, EL Mortensen & WFC Baare. (2018). Neuroticism is linked to microstructural left-right asymmetry of fronto-limbic fibre tracts in adolescents with opposite effects in boys and girls. *Neuropsychologia,* 114, 1-10. doi:10.1016/j.neuropsychologia.2018.04.010

Maki, PM, JB Rich & S Rosenbaum. (2002). Implicit memory varies across the menstrual cycle: Estrogen effects in young women. *Neuropsychologia* 40, 518-29.

Marrocco, J & B McEwan. (2016). Sex in the brain: Hormones and sex differences. *Dialogues in Clinical Neuroscience,* 18(4), 373-83. doi:10.31887/DCNS.2016.18.4/jmarrocco

Marsee, MA, PJ Frick, CT Barry, ER Kimonis, LCM Centifanti & KJ Aucoin. (2014). Profiles of the forms and functions of self-reported aggression in three adolescent samples. *Development and Psychopathology,* 26(3), 705-20. doi:10.1017/S0954579414000339

Martel, M. (2013). Sexual selection and sex differences in the prevalence of childhood externalizing and adolescent internalizing disorders. *Psychological Bulletin*, 139(6), 1221-59. doi:10.1037/a0032247

Martin, K. (2011). *Electronic Overload: The Impact of Excessive Screen Use on Child and Adolescent Health and Wellbeing*. Perth, Western Australia: Department of Sport and Recreation.

Martin, LJ, DM Spicer, MH Lewis, JP Gluck & LC Cook. (1991). Social deprivation of infant rhesus monkeys alters the chemoarchitecture of the brain: subcortical regions. *The Journal of Neuroscience*, 11(11), 3344-58.

Martin, CL, DN Ruble & J Szkrybalo. (2002). Cognitive theories of early gender development. *Psychological Bulletin*, 128(6), 903-33.

Matthews, JS, FJ Morrison & CC Ponitz. (2009). Early gender differences in self-regulation and academic achievement. *Journal of Educational Psychology*, 101(3), 689-704. doi:10.1037/a0014240.

McCarthy, N. (2018). Women are still earning more doctoral degrees than men in the U.S. *Forbes Magazine*, October. Retrieved from https://www.forbes.com/sites/niallmccarthy/2018/10/05/women-are-still-earning-more-doctoral-degrees-than-men-in-the-u-s-infographic/?sh=63e504c745b6

McDevitt, TM & JE Ormrod, JE (2020). *Child Development and Education*, 7th ed. Hoboken, New Jersey: Pearson Education Inc.

McEwen, B. (2009). Introduction: The end of sex as we once knew it. *Physiology and Behavior*, 97(2), 143-45.

McEwen, BS & T Seeman. (2003). Stress and affect: Applicability of the concepts of allostasis and allostatic load. In *Handbook of Affective Sciences*, edited by RJ Davidson, KR Scherer & H Hill Goldsmith, 1117-37. Oxford: Oxford University Press.

McEwen, BS & E Norton Lasley. (2005). The end of sex as we know it. *Cerebrum*, 7(4), 1-15.

McEwan, BS & TA Milner. (2017). Understanding the broad influence of sex hormones and sex differences in the brain. *Journal of Neuroscience Research*, 95, 24-39. doi:10.1002/jnr.23809

McGaugh, JL. (2004). The amygdale modulates the consolidation of memories of emotionally arousing experiences. *Annual Review of Neuroscience*, 27, 1-28.

McGuiness, D. (1990). Behavioral tempo in pre-school boys and girls. *Learning and Individual Difference*, 2(3), 315-25.

McGuire, A. (2017). *Sex Scandal: The Drive To Abolish Male and Female*. Washington DC: Regnery Publishing.

McLean, CP, A Asnaani, BT Litz & SG Hofmann. (2011). Gender differences in anxiety disorders: Prevalence, course of illness, comorbidity and burden of illness. *Journal of Psychiatric Research*, 45(8), 1027-35. doi:10.1016/j.jpsychires.2011.03.006

Mealey, L. (2000). *Sex Differences: Developmental and Evolutionary Strategies*. Cambridge: Academic Press.

Miller, DI & DF Halpern. (2014). The new science of cognitive sex differences. *Trends in Cognitive Sciences*, 18(1), 37-45. doi:10.1016/j.tics.2013.10.011

Mitchell, K.J. (2018). *Innate: How the Wiring of Our Brains Shapes Who We Are*. Princeton, New Jersey: Princeton University Press.

Mitchell, KJ, M Ybarra & D Finkelhor. (2007). The relative importance of online victimization in understanding depression, delinquency, and substance use. *Child Maltreatment*, 12(4), 314-24. doi:10.1177/1077559507305996

Moir, A & D Jessel. (1998). *Brainsex: The Real Difference Between Men and Women*. London: Arrow Books.

Moir, A & B Moir. (1999). *Why Men Don't Iron: The Fascinating and Unalterable Differences Between Men and Women*. New York: Citadel Press.

Moore, SR, KP Harden & J Mendle. (2014). Pubertal timing and adolescent sexual behaviour in girls. *Developmental Psychology*, 50(6), 1734-45. doi:10.1037/a0036027

Morgado, P & JJ Cerqueira, eds. (2019). The Impact of Stress on Cognition and Motivation. *Frontiers in Behavioral Neuroscience*. doi:10.3389/978-2-88945-774-8.

Morris, RGM. (2006). Elements of a neurobiological theory of hippocampal function: The role of synaptic plasticity, synaptic tagging and schemas. *European Journal of Neuroscience*, 23(11), 2829-46.

Mu, W, D Zhu, Y Wang, F Li, L Ye, K Wang & M Zhou. (2020). Three-wave longitudinal survey on the relationship between neuroticism and depressive symptoms of first-year college students: Addictive use of social media as a moderated mediator. *International Journal of Environmental Research and Public Health*, 17(17), 6074. doi:10.3390/ijerph17176074

Mulder, EJH, PG Robles de Medina, AC Huizink, BRH Van den Bergh, JK Buitelaar & GHA Visser. (2002). Prenatal maternal stress: effects on pregnancy and the (unborn) child, *Early Human Development*, 70 (1-2), 3-14.

Nadeau, RL. (1996). *S/He Brain: Science, Sexual Politics, and the Myths of Feminism*. Westport, Connecticut: Praeger Publishers.

Nagel, MC. (2003). Connecting teachers, boys and learning: How understanding the brain can enhance pedagogy in the middle school. *The Australian Journal of Middle Schooling*, 3(2), 20-24.

Nagel, MC. (2004). Boys, brains and behaviour: An emerging perspective. *Perspectives on Educational Leadership*, 14(4), 1-2.

Nagel, MC. (2006). *Boys-Stir-Us: Working WITH the Hidden Nature of Boys*. Melbourne: Hawker-Brownlow Education.

Nagel, MC. (2008). *It's A Girl Thing*. Melbourne: Hawker Brownlow Education.

Nagel, MC. (2012). *In the Beginning: The Brain, Early Development and Learning*. Camberwell, Victoria: Australian Council for Educational Research (ACER).

Nagel, MC. (2014). *In the Middle: The Adolescent Brain, Behaviour and Learning*. Camberwell, Victoria: Australian Council for Educational Research (ACER).

Nagel, MC & L Scholes. (2016). *Understanding Development and Learning: Implications for Teaching*. South Melbourne: Oxford University Press.

Nagel, MC. (2019a). Social development. In *Educational Psychology*, 3rd ed, edited by A O'Donnell, E Dobozy, MC Nagel, S Smala, C Wormald, G Yates, R Spooner-Lane, A Youssef-Shalala, J Reeve, J. Smith & B Bartlett, 155-204). Milton, Queensland: John Wiley & Sons Australia Ltd.

Nagel, MC. (2019b). Understanding and motivating students. In *Teaching: Making a Difference*, 4th ed, edited by R Churchill, S Godinho, NF Johnson, A Keddie, W Letts, K Lowe, J McKay, M McGill, J Moss, MC Nagel, K Shaw & J Rogers, 80-117. Milton, Queensland: John Wiley & Sons Australia Ltd.

Nagel, MC. (2021). *Oh Boy!: Understanding the Neuroscience Behind Educating and Raising Boys.* Melbourne: AMBA Press.

Nagy, E, KA Loveland, H Orvos & P Molnár. (2001). Gender-Related physiological differences in human neonates and the greater vulnerability of males to developmental brain disorders. *Journal of Gender-Specific Medicine*, 4(1):41-49.

Neigh, G & M Mitzelfelt, eds. (2016). *Sex Differences in Physiology.* London: Elsevier Inc.

Nelson, CA, M de Haan, M & KM Thomas. (2006). *Neuroscience and Cognitive Development: The Role of Experience and the Developing Brain.* New York: John Wiley & Sons.

Ngun, TC, N Ghahrami, FJ Sanchez, S Bocklandt & E Vilian. (2011). The genetics of sex differences in brain and behavior. *Frontiers in Neuroendocrinology*, 32(2), 227-46. doi:10.1016/j.yfrne.2010.10.001

Nota, NM, BPC Kreukels, M den Heijer, DJ Veltman, PT Cohen-Kettenis, SM Burke & J Bakker J. (2017). Brain functional connectivity patterns in children and adolescents with gender dysphoria: Sex-atypical or not? *Psychoneuroendocrinology*, 86, 187-95.

Olsson, A, E Kopsida, K Sorjonen & I Savic. (2016). Testosterone and estrogen impact social evaluatins and vicarious emotions: A double-blind placebo-controlled study. *Emotion*, 16(4), 515-23. doi:10.1037/a0039765

Organisation for Economic Cooperation and Development (2010). *PISA 2009 Results: Learning Trends - Changes in Students.* Paris: OECD.

Organisation for Economic Cooperation and Development (2014). *PISA 2012 Results: What Students Know and Can Do - Student Performance in Mathematics, Reading and Science*, vol. 1, rev. ed, February. Paris: OECD Publishing.

Organisation for Economic and Cooperative Development (2015a). *The ABC of Gender Equality in Education: Aptitude, Behaviour, Confidence.* Paris: OECD Publishing.

Organisation For Economic Cooperation and Development (2015b). *Students, Computers and Learning: Making the Connection,* Paris, OECD Publishing.

Organisation For Economic Cooperation and Development (2019). *PISA 2018 Assessment and Analytical Framework.* Paris: OECD Publishing.

Orpinas, P, C McNicholas & L Nahapetyan. (2015). Gender differences in trajectories of relational aggression perpetration and victimization from middle to high school. *Aggressive Behavior*, 41(5), 401-12. doi:10.1002/ab.21563

Orth, U & RW Robins. (2014). The development of self-esteem. *Current Directions in Psychological Science*, 23(5), 381-87. doi:10.1177/0963721414547414

Osterman, K, K Bjorkqvist, KMJ Lagerspetz, A Kaukiainen, SF Landau, A Fraczek & GV Caprara. (1998). Cross-cultural evidence of female indirect aggression. *Aggressive Behavior*, 24, 1-8.

Owens, L, R Shute & P Slee. (2000). Guess what I just heard? Indirect aggression among teenage girls in Australia. *Aggressive Behavior*, 26, 67-83.

Pang, KC, NM de Graaf, D Chew, M Hoq, DR Keith, P Carmichael & TD Steensma. (2020). Association of media coverage of transgender and gender diverse issues with rates of referral of transgender children and adolescents to specialist gender clinics in the UK and Australia. *JAMA Network Open*, 3(7), e2011161. doi:10.1001/jamanetworkopen.2020.11161

Panksepp, J. (2003). Feeling the pain of social loss. *Science*, 302, 237-39.
Panksepp, J. (2005). *Affective Neuroscience: The Foundations of Human and Animal Emotions.* New York: Oxford University Press.
Panksepp, J & L Biven. (2012). *The Archeology of the Mind: Neuroevolutionary Origins of Human Emotions.* New York: WW Norton & Company.
Paquette, JA & MK Underwood. (1999). Gender differences in young adolescents' experiences of peer victimization: Social and Physical Aggression. *Merrill-Palmer Quarterly*, 45(2), 242-66.
Parker, GJ & J Seal. (1996). Forming, losing, renewing, and replacing friendships: Applying temporal parameters to the assessment of children's friendship experiences. *Child Development*, 67(5), 2248-68.
Parker, JG, CM Low, AR Walker & BK Gamm. (2005). Friendship jealousy in young adolescents: Individual differences and links to sex, self-esteem, aggression, and social adjustment. *Developmental Psychology*, 41(1), 235-50. doi:10.1037/0012-1649.41.1.235
Paus, T, A Pui-Yee Wong, C Syme & Z Pausova. (2017). Sex differences in the adolescent brain and body: Findings from the Saguenay Youth Study. *Journal of Neuroscience Research*, 95(1-2), 362-70.
Peiper, A. (1925). Sinnesempfindungen des Kindes vor seiner Geburt. *Monatsschrift fur Kinderheilkunde*, 29, 236-41.
Perry, DG & RE Pauletti. (2011). Gender and adolescent development. *Journal of Research on Adolescence*, 21(1), 61-74. doi:10.111/j.1532-7795.2010.00715.x
Peterson, JB. (2018). *12 Rules for Life: An Antidote to Chaos.* Toronto: Random House Canada.
Phillips, KA & W Menard. (2006). Suicidality in body dysmorphic disorder: A perspective study. *American Journal of Psychiatry*, 163(7), 1280-82.
Phillips, MD, MJ Lowe, JT Lurito, M Dzemidzic & VP Mathews. (2001). Temporal lobe activation demonstrates sex-based differences during passive listening. *Radiology*, 220, 202-7.
Phillips, KA, ER Didie, W Menard, ME Pagano, C Fay & RB Weisberg. (2006). Clinical features of body dysmorphic disorder in adolescents and adults. *Psychiatry Research*, 141(3), 305-14. doi:10.1016/j.psychres.2005.09.014
Pinker, S. (2002). *The Blank Slate: The Modern Denial of Human Nature.* Penguin Books.
Pipher, M & S Pipher. (2019). *Reviving Ophelia: Saving the Selves of Adolescent Girls.* New York: Riverhead Books.
Pompili, A, B Arnone, M D'Amico, P Federico & A Gasbarri. (2016). Evidence of estrogen modulation on memory process for emotional content in healthy young women. *Psychoneuroendocrinology*, 65, 94-101. doi:10.1016/j.psyneuen.2015.12.013
Poropat, AE. (2009). A meta-analysis of the five-factor model of personality and academic performance. *Psychological Bulletin*, 135, 322-38.
Preckel, K, D Scheele, KM Kendrick, W Maier & R Hurlemann. (2014). Oxytocin facilitates social approach behavior in women. *Frontiers in Behavioral Neuroscience*, 8(191). doi: 10.3389/fnbeh.2014.00191
Prinstein, MJ. (2007). Moderators of peer contagion: A longitudinal examination of depression socialization between adolescents and their best friends. *Journal of Clinical Child and Adolescent Psychology*, 36(2), 159-70. doi:10.1080/15374410701274934

Prinstein, MJ, J Boergers & EM Vernberg. (2001) Overt and relational aggression in adolescents: Social-psychological adjustment of aggressors and victims. *Journal of Clinical Child Psychology*, 30(4), 479-91. doi:10.1207/S15374424JCCP3004_05

Prinstein, M.J, JL Borelli, CL Cheah, VA Simon & JW Aikins. (2005). Adolescent girls' interpersonal vulnerability to depressive symptoms: A longitudinal examination of reassurance-seeking and peer relationships. *Journal of Abnormal Psychology*, 114(4), 676-88. doi:10.1037/0021-843X.114.4.676.

Privitera, C & MA Campbell. (2009). Cyberbullying: The new face of workplace bullying? *CyberPsychology & Behavior*, 12(4), 395-400. doi:10.1089/cpb.2009.0025.

Protopopescu, X, T Butler, H Pan, J Root, M Althemus, M Polanecsky, B McEwen, D Silbersweig & E Stern. (2008). Hippocampal structure changes across the menstrual cycle. *Hippocampus*, 18, 985-88.

Proverbio, AM. (2017). Sex differences in social cognition: The case of face processing. *Journal of Neuroscience Research*, 95(1-2), 222-34.

Pruessner, JC, MW Baldwin, K Dedovic, R Renwick, NK Mahini, C Lord, M Meaney & S Lupien. (2005). Self-esteem, locus of control, hippocampal volume, and cortisol regulation in young and old adulthood. *NeuroImage*, 28(4), 815-26. doi:10.1016/j.neuroimage.2005.06.14

Purves, D, GJ Augustine, D Fitzpatrick, WC Hall, AS LaMantia, RD Mooney & LE White, eds. (2018). *Neuroscience*, 6th ed. Oxford: Oxford University Press.

Putallaz, M, JB Kupersmidt, JD Coie, K McKnight & CL Grimes. (2004). A behavioral analysis of girls' aggression and victimization. In *Aggression, Antisocial Behavior, and Violence Among Girls*, edited by M Putallaz & KL Bierman, 110-34. New York: The Guilform Press.

Rajanala, S, MBC Maymone & NA Vashi. (2018) Selfies: living in the era of filtered photographs. *JAMA Facial Plastic Surgery*, 20(6), 443-44. doi:10.1001/jamafacial.2018.0486.

Rakic, P. (2002). Genesis of neocortex in human and nonhuman primates. In *Child and Adolescent Psychiatry: A Comprehensive Textbook*, 3rd ed, edited by M Lewis. Philadelphia, Pennsylvania: Lippincott, Williams & Wilkins.

Rand, DG, VL Brescoll, V Capraro, JM Everett, H Barcelo. (2016). Social heuristics and social roles: Intuition favors altruism for women but not for men. *Journal of Experimental Psychology: General*, 145(4), 389-96. doi:10.1037/xge0000154

Ratey, JJ. (2001). *A User's Guide to the Brain: Perception, Attention and the Four Theatres of the Brain*. New York: Vintage Books.

Reber, J & D Tranel. (2017). Sex differences in the functional lateralization of emotion and decision making in the human brain. *Journal of Neuroscience Research*, 95(1-2), 270-78.

Restak, R. (2001). *Mozart's Brain and the Fighter Pilot: Unleashing Your Brain's Potential*. New York: Three Rivers Press.

Reyna, VF, SM Estrada, JA DeMarinis, RM Myers, JM Stanisz & BA Mills. (2011). Neurobiological and memory models of risky decision making in adolescents versus young adults. *Journal of Experimental Psychology: Learning, Memory and Cognition*, 37(5), 1125-42.

Rhodes, A. (2017). *Screen Time and Kids: What's Happening In Our Homes? - Australian Child Health Poll*. The Royal Children's Hospital Melbourne.

Richardson, JTE. (1997). Conclusions from the study of gender differences in cognition. In *Gender Differences in Human Cognition,* edited by J Caplan, M Crawford, J Shibley-Hyde & JTE Richardson, 131-69. Oxford: Oxford University Press.

Risser, SD. (2013) Relational aggression and academic performance in elementary school. *Psychology in the Schools,* 50(1), 13-26. doi:10.1002/pits.21655

Ristori, J & TD Steensma. (2016). Gender dysphoria in children. *International Review of Psychiatry,* 28(1), 13-20. doi:10.3109/09540261.2015.115754

Ritchey, M, KS LaBar & R Cabeza. (2011). Level of processing modulates the neural correlates of emotional memory formation. *Journal of Cognitive Neurosciences,* 23(4), 757-71.

Roberts, K (2014). *Engaging More Women and Girls in Mathematics and STEM Fields: The International Evidence.* Report prepared for the Australian Mathematical Sciences Institute. Available online, http://amsi.org.au/publications/gender-report-20104/

Roberts, BW & D Wood. (2006). Personality development in the context of the neo-socioanalytic model of personality. In *Handbook of Personality Development,* edited by DK Mroczek & TD Little, 11-39. Mahwah, NJ: Erlbaum.

Roberts, BW, KE Walton & W Viechtbauer. (2006). Patterns of mean-level change in personality traits across the life course: A meta-analysis of longitudinal studies. *Psychological Bulletin,* 132, 1-25.

Robinson, B. (2001). *Fathering From the Fast Lane: Practical Ideas for Busy Dads.* Sydney: Finch Publishing.

Rode, D & M Rode. (2018). Risk factors in committing domestic violence in light of gender psychology. *Current Issues in Personality Psychology,* 6(2), 143-53. doi:10.5114/cipp.2018.72262

Roney, JR & ZL Simmons. (2013). Hormonal predictors of sexual motivation in natural menstrual cycles. *Hormones and Behavior,* 56(4), 636-45.

Rose, AJ. (2002). Co-rumination in the friendships of girls and boys. *Child Development,* 73(6), 1830-43.

Rose, AJ & KD Rudolph. (2006). A review of sex differences in peer relationship processes: Potential trade-offs for the emotional and behavioral development of girls and boys. *Psychological Bulletin,* 132(1), 98-131. doi:10.1037/0033-2909.132.1.98

Rose, AJ, LP Swenson & EM Waller. (2004). Overt and relational aggression and perceived popularity: Developmental differences in concurrent and prospective relationships. *Developmental Psychology,* 40(3), 378-97.

Rose, RJ, GC Glick, RL Smith, RA Schwartz-Mette & SK Borowski. (2017). Co-rumination exacerbates stress generation among adolescents with depressive symptoms. *Journal of Abnormal Child Psychology,* 45(5), 985-95. doi:10.1007/s10802-016-0205-1

Rothmann, S & EP Coetzer. (2003). The Big Five personality dimensions and job performance. *SA Journal of Industrial Psychology,* 29(1). doi:10.4102/sajip.v29i1.88

Ruble, DN, CL Martin & SA Berenbaum. (2006). Gender development. In *Handbook of Child Psychology. Social, Emotional and Personality Development,* 6th ed, edited by W Damon, RM Lerner & N Eisenberg, vol 3, 858-932. New Jersey: John Wiley & Sons.

Ruigrok, ANV, G Salimi-Khorshidi, MC Lai, S Baron-Cohen, MV Lombardo, RJ Tait & J Suckling. (2014). A meta-analysis of sex differences in human brain structure. *Neuroscience and Biobehavioral Reviews*, 39, 34-50.

Rys, GS & GG Bear. (1997). Relational aggression and peer relations: gender and developmental issues. *Merrill-Palmer Quarterly*, 43(1), 87-106.

Santrock, JW. (2017). *Educational Psychology*, 6th ed. New York: McGraw-Hill Education.

Sapolsky, RM. (1997). *The Trouble With Testosterone and Other Essays on the Biology of the Human Predictament*. New York: Scribner.

Sapolsky, RM. (2017). *Behave: The Biology of Humans at Our Best and Worst*. New York: Penguin Press.

Saraswat, A, J Weinand & J Safer. (2015) Evidence supporting the biologic nature of gender identity. *Endocrine Practice*, 21(2), 199-204.

Saucier, G & S Srivastava. (2015). What makes a good structural model of personality? Evaluating the Big Five and alternatives. In *American Psychological Association (APA) Handbook of Personality and Social Psychology: Personality Processes and Individual Differences*, edited by M Mikulincer & PR Shaver, 4, 283-305. Washington Dc: American Psychological Association.

Sauter, SR, LP Kim & KH Jacobsen. (2020). Loneliness and friendlessness among adolescents in 25 countries in Latin America and the Caribbean. *Child and Adolescent Mental Health*, 25(1), 21-27. doi:10.111/camh.12358

Savic, I, A Garcia-Falgueras & DF Swaab. (2010). Sexual differentiation of the human brain in relation to gender identity and sexual orientation. *Progress in Brain Research*, 186(4), 41-62.

Sax, L. (2002). How common is Intersex? A response to Anne Fausto-Sterling. *The Journal of Sex Research*, 39(3), 174-78.

Sax, L. (2005). *Why Gender Matters: What Parents and Teachers Need to Know about the Emerging Science of Sex Differences*. New York: Doubleday.

Sax, L. (2010). *Girls on the Edge: The Four Factors Driving the New Crisis for Girls*. Perseus Books.

Sax, L. (2017). *Why Gender Matters: What Parents and Teachers Need to Know about the Emerging Science of Sex Differences*, 2nd ed. New York: Harmony Books.

Shaffer, SM & LP Gordon. (2005a). *Why Boys Don't Talk and Why It Matters*. New York: McGraw Hill.

Shaffer, SM & LP Gordon. (2005b). *Why Girls Talk and What They Are Really Saying*. New York: McGraw Hill.

Shaywitz, BA, SE Shaywltz, KR Pugh, RT Constable, P Skudlarski, RK Fulbright, RA Bronen, JM Fletcher, DP Shankweiler, L Katz & JC Gore. (1995). Sex differences in the functional organization of the brain for language. *Nature* 373 (6515), 607-9.

Schneider, SC, CM Turner, J Mond & JL Hudson. (2016). Prevalence and correlates of body dysmorphic disorder in a community sample of adolescents. *Australian & New Zealand Journal of Psychiatry*, 51(6), 1-9. doi:10.1177/00048677416665483.

Schlesinger, M.A., Hassinger-Das, B., Zosh, J.M., Sawyer, J., Evans, N. & Hirsh-Pasek, K. (2020). Cognitive behavioral science behind the value of play: Leveraging everyday experiences to promote play, learning, and positive interactions. Journal of Infant, Child, And Adolescent Psychotherapy, 19(2), 202-216. doi:10.1080/15289168.2020.1755084

Schmitt, DP. (2015). The Evolution of Culturally-Variable Sex Differences: Men and Women Are Not Always Different, but When They Are...It Appears Not to Result from Patriarchy or Sex Role Socialization. In *The Evolution of Sexuality*, edited by TK Shackelford & RD Hansen, 221-56. Springer International Publishing.

Schmitt, DP, A Realo, M Voracek & J Alli (2008). Why can't a man be more like a woman? Sex differences in Big Five personality traits across 55 cultures. *Journal of Personality and Social Psychology*, 94(1), 168-82.

Schmitt, DP, AE Long, A McPhearson, K O'Brien, B Remmert & SH Shah. (2017). Personality and gender differences in global perspective. *International Journal of Psychology*, 52(S1), 45-56. doi:10.1002/ijop.12265

Schneider, SC, CM Turner, J Mond & JL Hudson. (2017). Prevalence and correlates of body dysmorphic disorder in a community of sample of adolescents. *Australian & New Zealand Journal of Psychiatry*, 51(6), 595-603. doi:10.1177/0004867416665483

Schneider, SC, AJ Baillie, J Mond, CM Turner & JL Hudson. (2018). The classification of body dysmorphic disorders in male and female adolescents. *Journal of Affective Disorders*, 225, 429-37. doi:10.1016/j.jad.2017.08.062

Schwartz-Mette, RA & AJ Rose. (2012). Co-rumination mediates contagion of internalizing symptoms within youths' friendships. *Developmental Psychology*, 48(5), 1355-65. doi:10.1037/a0027484

Schwartz-Mette, RA & RL Smith. (2018). When does co-rumination facilitate depression contagion in adolescent friendships? Investigating intrapersonal and interpersonal factors, *Journal of Clinical Child & Adolescent Psychology*, 47(6), 912-24. doi:10.1080/15374416.1197837

Seeman, P. (1999). Images in neuroscience. Brain development, X: Pruning during development. *American Journal of Psychiatry*, 156(2), 168.

Shaffer, SM & LP Gordon. (2005). *Why Girls Talk and What They Are Really Saying*. New York: McGraw Hill.

Shaywitz, BA, SE Shaywltz, KR Pugh, RT Constable, P Skudlarski, RK Fulbright, RA Bronen, JM Fletcher, DP Shankweiler, L Katz, & JC Gore. (1995). Sex differences in the functional organization of the brain for language. *Nature*, 373 (6515), 607-9.

Shin, YW, DJ Kim, T Hyon, HJ Park, WJ Moon, EC Chung, JM Lee, IY Kim, SI Kim & JS Kwon. (2005). Sex differences in the human corpus callosum: Diffusion tensor imaging study. *Neuroreport*, 16(8), 795-798.

Shonkoff, JP & DA Phillips, eds. (2000). *From Neurons to Neighborhoods: The Science of Early Childhood Development*. Washington: National Academy Press.

Shore, R. (1997). *Rethinking the Brain: New Insights Into Early Development*. New York: Families and Work Institute.

Shrier, A. (2020). *Irreversible Damage: The Transgender Craze Seducing Our Daughters*. Washington DC: Regnery Publishing.

Simmons, R. (2011). *Odd Girl Out: The Hidden Culture of Aggression in Girls,* 2nd ed. Boston: Mariner Books.

Sisk, CL & DL Foster. (2004). The neural basis of puberty and adolescence. *Nature Neuroscience*, 7(10), 1040-47.

Smith, ER & DM Mackie. (2007). *Social Psychology*, 3rd ed. London: Psychology Press.

Smith, RL, AJ Rose & RA Schwartz-Mette. (2009). Relational and overt aggression in childhood and adolescence: Clarifying mean-level gender differences and associations with peer acceptance. *Social Development*, 19(2):243-69. doi: 10.1111/j.1467-9507.2009.00541.x.

Soh, D. (2020). *The End of Gender: Debunking Myths about Sex and Identity In Our Society*. New York: Threshold Editions.

Soto, CJ. (2016). The Little Six personality dimensions from early childhood to early adulthood: Mean-level age and gender differences in parents' reports. *Journal of Personality*, 84(4), 409-22. doi:10.111/jopy.12168

Southschek, A, CJ Burke, AR BeHarelle, R Schreiber, SC Weber, II Karipidis, J ten Velden, B Weber, H Haker, T Kalenscher & PN Tobler. (2017). The dopaminergic rewardsystem underpins gender differences in social preferences. *Nature Human Behaviour*, 1(11), 819-27. doi:10.1038/s41562-017-0226-y

Spear, LP. (2000a). The adolescent brain and age-related behavioral manifestations. *Neuroscience and Behavioral Reviews*, 24(4), 417-463.

Spear, LP. (2000b). Neurobehavioral changes in adolescence. *Current Directions in Psychological Science*. 9(4), 111-14.

Spear, LP. (2010). *The Behavioral Neuroscience of Adolescence*. New York: WW Norton.

Spear, LP. (2013). Adolescent neurodevelopment. *Journal of Adolescent Health*, 52(2), S7-S13.

Sperry, RW. (1961). Cerebral organisation and behaviour. *Science*, 133(3466), 1749-57. DOI: 10.1126/science.133.3466.1749

Starr, LR. (2015). When support seeking backfires: co-rumination, excessive reassurance seeking and depressed mood in the daily lives of young adults. *Journal of Social and Clinical Psychology*, 34(5), 436-57. doi:10.1521/jscp.2015.34.5.436

Steensma, TD, BPC Kreukels, ALC de Vries & PT Cohen-Kettenis. (2013). Gender identity development in adolescence. *Hormones & Behavior*, 64(2), 288-97. doi:10.1016/j.yhbeh.2013.02.020

Steinberg, L. (2011). *You and Your Adolescent: The Essential Guide for Ages 10-25*. New York: Simon & Shuster.

Steinberg, L & KC Monahan. (2007). Age differences in resistance to peer influence. *Developmental Psychology*, 43(6), 1531-43. doi:10.1037/0012-1649.43.6.1531.

Stevens, P. (1999). *Between Mothers and Sons: Women Writers Talk About Having Sons and Raising Men*. New York: Touchstone Books.

Stevens, EA & MJ Prinstein. (2005). Peer contagion of depressogenic attributional styles among adolescents: A longitudinal study. *Journal of Abnormal Child Psychology*, 33(1), 25-37. doi:10.1007/s10802-005-0931-2

Stone, LB, BL Hankin, BE Gibb & JR Abela. (2011). Corumination predicts the onset of depressive disorders during adolescence. *Journal of Abnormal Psychology*, 120, 752-57. doi:10.1037/a0023384.

Strang, JF, L Kenworthy, A Dominska, J Sokoloff, LE Kenealy, M Berl, K Walsh, E Menvielle, G Slesaransky-Poe, K Kyung-Eun, C Luong-Tran, H Meagher & GL Wallace. (2014). Increased gender variance in autism spectrum disorders and attention deficit hyperactivity disorder. *Archives of Sexual Behavior*, 43(8), 1525-33. doi:10.1007/s10508-014-0285-3

Strauch, B. (2003). *The Primal Teen: What the New Discoveries About the Teenage Brain Tell Us About Our Kids*. New York: Doubleday.

Su, R, J Rounds & PI Armstrong. (2009). Men and things, women and people: A meta-analysis of sex differences in interests. *Psychological Bulletin*, 135(6), 859–84.

Sylwester, R. (2003). *A Biological Brain in a Cultural Classroom*, 2nd ed. Thousand Oaks, California: Corwin Press.

Sylwester, R. (2005). *How to Explain a Brain: An Educator's Handbook of Brain Terms and Cognitive Processes*. Thousand Oaks, California: Corwin Press.

Sylwester, R. (2007). *The Adolescent Brain: Reaching for Autonomy*. Thousand Oaks, California: Corwin Press.

Tannen, D. (2013). *You Just Don't Understand: Women and Men in Conversation*. New York: William Morrow Paperbacks.

Tapp, AL, MT Maybery & AJO Whitehouse. (2011). Evaluating the twin testosterone transfer hypothesis: A review of the empirical evidence. *Hormones and Behavior*, 60(5), 713–22. doi:10.1016/j.yhbeh.2011.08.011

Taylor, SE, LC Klein, BP Lewis, TL Gruenewald, RAR Gurung & TL Updegraff. (2000). Biobehavioral responses to stress in females: Tend-and-befriend, not fight-or-flight. *Psychological Review*, 107(3), 411–29.

Thomas, MSC & MH Johnson. (2008). New advances in understanding sensitive periods in brain development. *Current Directions in Psychological Science*, 17(1), 1–5.

Todd, BK, RA Fischer, S Di Costa, A Roestorf, K Harbour, P Hardiman & JA Barry. (2018). Sex differences in children's toy preferences: A systematic review, meta-regression, and meta-analysis. *Infant and Child Development*, 27: e2064. doi:10.1002/icd.2064.

Toffoletto, S, R Lanzenberger, M Gingnell, I Sundstrom-Poromaa & E Comasco. (2014). Emotional and cognitive functional imaging of estrogen and progesterone effects in the female human brain: A systematic review. *Psychoneuroendocrinology*, 50, 28–52. doi:10.1016/j.psyneuen.2014.07.25

Tomada, G & BH Schneider. (1997). Relational aggression, gender and peer acceptance: Invariance across culture, stability over time and concordance among informants. *Developmental Psychology*, 33(4), 601–9.

Torgrimson, BN & CT Minson. (2005). Sex and gender: What is the difference? *Journal of Applied Physiology*, 99(3), 785–87.

Twenge, JM. (2017). *iGen: Why Today's Super-Connected Kids are Growing Up Less Rebellious, More Tolerant, Less Happy and Completely Unprepared for Adulthood*, New York: Atria Books.

Twenge, JM, RA Sherman & S Lyubomirsky. (2016). More happiness for young people and less for mature adults: Time period differences in subjective well-being in the United States, 1972–2014. *Social Psychological and Personality Science*, 7(2), 131–41. doi:10.1177/1948550615602933.

Twenge, JM, RA Sherman & BE Wells. (2017). Sexual inactivity during young adulthood is more common among US Millennials and iGen: Age, period, and cohort effects on having no sexual partners after age 18. *Archives of Sexual Behavior*, 46(2), 433–40. doi:10.1007/s10508-016-0798-z

Twenge, JM & WK Campbell. (2018). Associations between screen time and lower psychological well-being among children and adolescents: Evidence from a population-based study. *Preventative Medicine Reports*, 12, 271–83. doi:10.1016/j.pmedr.2018.10.003.

Twenge, JM, GN Martin & WK Campbell. (2018a) Decreases in psychological well-being among American adolescents after 2012 and links to screen time during the rise of smartphone technology. *Emotion*, 18(6), 765–80.

Twenge, JM, TE Joiner, ML Rogers & GN Martin. (2018b). Increases in depressive symptoms, suicide-related outcomes, and suicide rates among U.S. adolescents after 2010 and links to increased new media screen time. *Clinical Psychological Science*, 6(1), 3–17. doi:10.1177/2167702617723376.

Ullsperger, JM & MA Nickolas. (2017). A meta-analytic review of the association between pubertal timing and psychopathology in adolescence: Are there sex differences in risk? *Psychological Bulletin*, 143(9), 903–38. doi:or/10.1037/bul0000106

Underwood, MK, KJ Beron & LH Rosen. (2011). Joint trajectories for social and physical aggression as predictors of adolescent maladjustment: Internalizing symptoms, rule-breaking behaviors, and borderline and narcissistic personality features. *Development and Psychopathology*, 23(2), 659–78. doi:10.1017/S095457941100023X

Vaillancourt, T. (2013). Do human females use indirect aggression as an intrasexual competition strategy. *Philosophical Transactions of the Royal Society B*, 368(1631), 20130080. doi:10.1098/rstb.2013.0080

van Beijsterveldt, CEM, JJ Hudziak & DI Boomsma. (2006). Genetic and environmental influences on cross-gender behavior and relation to behavior problems: A study of Dutch twins at ages 7 and 10 years. *Archives of Sexual Behavior*, 35(6), 647–58. doi:10.1007/s10508-006-9072-0.

van der Miesen, AIR, H Hurley & ALC de Vries. (2016). Gender dysphoria and autism spectrum disorder: A narrative review. *International Review of Psychiatry*, 28(1), 70–80. doi:10.3109/09540261.2015.1111199

van der Miesen, AIR, ALC de Vries, TD Steensma & CA Hartman. (2018). Autisitic symptoms in children and adolescents with gender dysphoria. *Journal of Autism and Developmental Disorders*, 48, 1537–48. doi:10.1007/s10803-017-3417-5

Van Droogenbroeck, F, B Spruyt & G Keppens. (2018). Gender differences in mental health problems among adolescents and the role of social support: results from the Belgian health interview surveys 2008 and 2013. *BMC Psychiatry*, 18(6). doi:10.1186/s12888-018-1591-4

Varma, R. (2010). Why so few women enroll in computing? Gender and ethnic differences in students' perception. *Computer Science Education*, 20(4), 301–16. doi:10.1080/08993408.2010.527697.

Vecchione, M, G Alessandri, C Barbaranelli & G Caprara. (2012). Gender differences in the Big Five personality development: A longitudinal investigation from late adolescence to emerging adulthood. *Personality and Individual Differences*, 53, 740–46. doi:10.1016/j.paid.2012.05.033

Viner, RM, G Aswathikutty, N Stiglic, LD Hudson, A Goddings, JL Ward & DE Nicholls. (2019). Roles of cyberbullying, sleep and physical activity in mediating the effects of social media us on mental health and well being among young people in England: A secondary analysis of longitudinal data. *The Lancet: Child and Adolescent Health*, 3(10), 685–96.

Voyer, D & SD Voyer. (2014). Gender differences in scholastic achievement: A meta-analysis. *Psychological Bulletin*, 140(4), 1174–1204. doi:10.1037/a0036620.

Wager, TD & KN Ochsner. (2005). Sex differences in the emotional brain. *NeuroReport,* 16(2), 85–87.
Wang, S. (2018). From birth onward, our experience of the world is dominated by the brain's continual conversation with itself. In *Think Tank: Forty Neuroscientists Explore the Roots of Human Experience,* edited by DJ Linden, 34–39. New Haven, Connecticut: Yale University Press.
Wang, J, M Korczykowski, H Rao, Y Fan, J Pluta, RC Gur, BS McEwen & JA Detre. (2007). Gender differences in neural response to psychological stress. *Social, Cognitive and Affective Neuroscience,* 2(3), 227–39.
Warrier, V, DM Greenberg, E Weir, C Buckingham, P Smith, M Lai, C Allison & S Baron-Cohen. (2020). Elevated rates of autism, other neurodevelopmental and psychiatric diagnoses, and autistic traits in transgender and gender-diverse individuals. *Nature Communications,* 11, 3959. doi:10.1038/s41467-020-17794-1
Watson, A, M Kehler & W Martino. (2010) The problem of boys' literacy underachievement: Raising some questions, *Journal of Adolescent and Adult Literacy,* 53(5), 356–61. doi:10.1598/JAAL.53.5.1
Watson, C, M Johanson, M Loder & J Dankiw. (2014). Effects of high-stakes testing on third through fifth grade students: Student voices and concerns for educational leaders. *Journal of Organizational Learning and Leadership,* 12(1), 1–11.
Wellmam, CL, DA Bangassar, JL Bollinger, L Coutellier, ML Logrip, KM Moench & KR Urban. (2018). Sex differences in risk and resilience: Stress effects on the neural substrates of emotion and motivation. *The Journal of Neuroscience,* 38(44), 9423–32. doi:10.1523/JNEUROSCI.1673-18.2018
Welz, A, S Huffziger, I Reinhard, GW Alpers, U Ebner-Priemer & C Kuehner. (2016). Anxiety and rumination moderate menstrual cycle effects on mood in daily life. *Women & Health,* 56(5), 540–60. doi: 10.1080/03630242.2015.1101739
Wenjuan, G, P Siqing & L Xinqiao. (2020). Gender differences in depression, anxiety, and stress among college students: A longitudinal study from China. *Journal of Affective Disorders,* 263, 292–300. doi:10.1016/j.jad.2019.11.121
Wharton, W, CE Gleason, SRMS Olson, CM Carlsson & S Asthana. (2012). Neurobiological underpinnings of the estrogen-mood relationship. *Current Psychiatry Review,* 8(3), 247–56. doi:10.1274/157340012800792957
Wiesel, T. (1982). Postnatal development of the visual cortex and the influence of environment. *Nature,* 299, 583–92.
Wiesel, TN & DH Hubel. (1963). Single cell response in striate cortex of kittens deprived of vision in one eye. *Journal of Neurophysiology,* 26, 1003–17.
Wilbrecht, L. (2018). Your twelve-year-old isn't just sprouting new hair but is also forming (and being formed by) new neural connections. In *Think Tank: Forty Neuroscientists Explore the Roots of Human Experience,* edited by DJ Linden, 45–51. New Haven, Connecticut: Yale University Press.
Williams, K & JH Kennedy. (2012). Bullying behaviors and attachment styles. *North American Journal of Psychology,* 14(2), 321–38.
Wilson, T & F Shalley. (2018). Estimates of Australia's non-heterosexual population. *Australian Population Studies,* 2(1), 26–38.
Wiseman, R. (2016). *Queen Bees and Wannabes: Helping Your Daughter Survive Cliques, Gossip, Boyfriends and Other Realities of Adolescence,* 3rd ed. New York: Harmony Books.

Wolfe, P. (2001). *Brain Matters: Translating Research into Classroom Practice.* Alexandria, Virginia: Association for Supervision and Curriculum Development.
Wolman, D. (2012). The split brain: A tale of two halves. *Nature*, 483, 260-63.
Wong, RO & JW Lichtman. (2003). Synapse elimination. In *Fundamental neuroscience,* 2nd ed, edited by LR Squire, FE Bloom, SK McConnell, JL Roberts, NC Spitzer & MJ Zigmond, 533-54. New York: Academic Press.
Wyn, J, M Turnbull & L Grimshaw. (2014). *The Experience of Education: The Impacts of High Stakes Testing on School Students and Their Families.* University of Western Sydney: The Whitlam Institute.
Yarhouse, MA. (2015). *Understanding Gender Dysphoria: Navigating Transgender Issues In A Changing Culture.* Westmont, Illinois: InterVarsity Press.
Ybarra, ML, M Diener-West & PJ Leaf. (2007). Examining the overlap in Internet harassment and school bullying: Implications for school intervention. *Journal of Adolescent Health*, 41(6, Suppl 1), S42-S50. doi:10.1016/j.jadohealth.2007.09.004
Yoon, JS, E Barton & J Taiariol. (2004). Relational aggression in middle school: Educational implications of developmental research. *Journal of Early Adolescence,* 24(3), 303-18.
Young, EA & M Altemus. (2004). Puberty, ovarian steroids and stress. *Annals of the New York Academy of Sciences,* 1021, 124-33.
Yu, M & J Baxter. (2016). Australian children's screen time and participation in extracurricular activities. *The Longitudinal Study of Children Annual Statistical Report.* Melbourne: Australian Institute of Family Studies.
Zagni, E, L Simoni & D Colombo. (2016). Sex and gender differences in central-nervous system-related disorders. *Neuroscience Journal,* 2827090. doi:10.1155/2016/2827090
Zahn-Waxler, C, E Shirtcliff & K Marceau. (2008). Disorders of childhood and adolescence: gender and psychopathology. *Annual Review of Clinical Psychology*, 4, 275-303. Doi:10.1146/annurev.clinpsy.3.022806.091358.
Zhang, D, ES Huebner & L Tian. (2020). Longitudinal associations among neuroticism, depression and cyberbullying in early adolescents. *Computers in Human Behavior*, 112, 10675. doi:10.1016/j.chb.2020.106475.
Zucker, KJ. (2017). Epidemiology of gender dysphoria and transgender identity, *Sexual Health* 14(5), 404-11. doi:10.1071/SH17067
Zucker, KJ. (2019). Adolescents with gender dysphoria: Reflections on some contemporary clinical and research issues. *Archives of Sexual Behavior,* 48(7), 1983-1992. doi:10.1007/s10508-019-01518-8
Zucker, KJ, AA Lawrence & BPC Kreukels. (2016). Gender dysphoria in adults. *Annual Review of Clinical Psychology,* 12, 217-47. doi:10.1146/annurev-clinpsy-021815-093034

Index

action potential 21
adolescence 67-70, 79, 84, 101-103
aggression 66-67, 69, 78, 87-91, 119-121
amygdala 28-30, 49-50, 52
anger 66, 77-79, 120, 123
anterior cingulate cortex 52
anxiety 78, 90, 94-97, 115-117
attachment 58, 90
autism 38
axons 17, 24, 45

Baron-Cohen, Simon 38, 49, 81
biology 8-15, 84
bisexuality 11
body dysmorphic disorder 96, 115
brain development 17-18, 20, 23, 42-43, 65
brain structure and function 26-27, 32, 61
Brizendine, Louann 43, 62, 68, 73, 85
Broca's area 32-33, 46
bullying 87, 92, 122
Bush, George 16

Carter, Rita 16
Carr-Gregg, Michael 125
cerebellum 24, 27-28, 32, 52
cerebral cortex 25, 27, 31, 50, 65, 71
cerebrum 30-32
childhood 25-26, 64-67, 84, 100-101
cingulate 25, 52
cisgender individuals 12
cognition 30, 38, 107-109, 111, 118
competition 65-66, 106
Congenital Adrenal Hyperplasia 42
corpus callosum 31, 45-46, 49-50, 53
cortisol 56, 90, 95
co-ruminating 101, 115-118
cyberbullying 116, 122

Damore, James 40, 110
De Beauvoir, Simone 9
Decade of the Brain 16
dendrites 17, 22, 47
depression 38, 77-78, 90, 92-97, 115-117, 122
developmentally predictable 107

diet 19
disgust 120
dopamine 21, 70-71, 75-76, 90, 93

eating disorders 96, 9, 101, 103, 114, 116
education 1, 104-107, 111-112, 118-119, 122-123
emotion 48-49, 71, 73-80, 118-119
emotional intelligence 66, 90, 119-124
empathy 49, 63, 75, 82, 86, 97
enjoyment 120
equal opportunity 37, 110
Erikson, Erik 97
estrogen 42, 56, 63, 68-70, 76-78, 83-85
experiences 104-126

fear 120
fight-or-flight response 27, 29, 77
friendships 81, 86-87, 89-90, 98
frontal lobes 29, 32-34, 48, 53, 66, 84

gaming 114
gender 7-15, 36-38, 64, 66, 75-76
gender dysphoria 13-14, 100-103
gender fluid individuals 12, 14
gender identity 11-12, 99
gender theory 10
gestation 18-19, 41
Goleman, Daniel 119-122
Google 40
Gray, John 48
Gurian, Michael 42, 60, 62

habituation 49
hemispheres 31-32, 45-46, 50-51, 54, 61-62
heterosexuality 11
hippocampus 25, 28-30, 54, 65, 69, 77, 85
homosexuality 11-13, 99

hormones 28-29, 38, 42, 51, 60, 65-69, 76-77, 85-87, 93-94
hypothalamus 28, 48, 55, 69, 76, 85

identity formation 89, 94, 97, 121
impulsivity 21
independence 34, 86, 93, 97
infancy 24, 41, 61-63
infantile puberty 63, 68
intelligence 36, 38, 107-108
intersex individuals 8-12, 14
intimacy imperative 62, 83

Kimura, Doreen 36, 47

language development 44-47, 62, 75-77, 89
lateralisation 46, 61-62
learning difficulties 41
learning environment 5, 104
learning windows 23-25
left hemisphere 31, 45, 61-62
Legato, Marianne 39
LGBTIQ community 11-13
limbic system 27-28, 30, 32, 34, 48-49, 65, 68, 71
literacy development 44-48, 75, 92
Littman, Lisa 101
love 120

maths 47-48, 109-111
maturation 22, 25, 35, 66, 70-71, 75, 85, 102
melatonin 21, 57
memory 30, 33, 65, 77, 118-119
menstruation 69, 93
metabolic rate 36, 57
minipuberty 63
multiple sclerosis 38
myelin 24-25, 44, 69

neurological development 1-2, 22, 38

neurons 17-21, 28, 31, 43, 47, 69, 104
neuroplasticity 22-23
neuroticism 94, 106, 108, 115-116
neurotransmitters 20-23, 57, 65, 75-77, 94-95
numeracy development 44, 47-48, 112

oxytocin 58, 70, 75-76, 83

Parkinson's disease 38
peer contagion 97-98
Peiper, Albrecht 48-49
personality traits 63, 95, 108-110
Pinker, Steven 6
pituitary gland 28, 55
play 42, 63-66
popularity 87-89, 96, 121
prefrontal cortex 29, 33-34, 50, 69, 79
progesterone 68-70, 78, 83, 85
prolactin 58
pruning 25-26
pubescence 67-68

queer individuals 12-13
queer theory 12

rapid-onset gender dysphoria 100-102
rapport-talk 75
reading 44, 112
reading faces 62, 68, 74
relationships 5, 63, 65-66, 76-79, 81-91, 95, 97
reproductive system 41, 93
right hemisphere 31, 45
role models 97

sadness 120
Sax, Leonard 1, 50
schizophrenia 38
science 109-111
screen time 113-114

self-control 66, 79
self-esteem 69, 88, 95-96, 98, 114, 118
serotonin 21, 70-71, 83, 85, 90, 93
sex 4-6, 7-15
sex hormones 85-87
sexual dimorphism 14, 39, 51-52
sexual identity 13, 100
sexual orientation 8-9, 11, 13
shame 120
Simmons, Rachel 87, 90
size 50-51
sleep deprivation 117
social media 96-98, 102-103, 111-116
social relationships 78, 89, 113
standardised testing 106-107
STEM (Science, Technology, Engineering and Mathematics) 109-111
stress 28-30, 69, 76-77, 85-86, 90, 95
Summers, Lawrence 39-40, 47, 110
surprise 120, 121
synapses 19-20, 22, 25-26
synaptic pruning 25-26, 51

technology 103, 109-113, 128
tend and befriend 76-77, 86
testosterone 41-42, 58, 62-63, 76-77, 100, 110
thalamus 27-29, 32, 49, 56
toddlerhood 61-64
transgender individuals 11-14, 100-101

utero 4, 19, 41-42, 48, 110

Wang, Sam 104
wellbeing 117, 119-124
Wernicke's area 33, 46

Yarhouse, Mark 7

www.ingramcontent.com/pod-product-compliance
Lightning Source LLC
Chambersburg PA
CBHW071619080526
44588CB00010B/1191